Surface Collection

Worlds of Archaeology

Series Editors
Heather Burke, Flinders University, Australia
and
Alejandro Haber, Universidad Nacional de Catamarca, Argentina

Sponsored by the World Archaeological Congress

This series of original edited and authored books seeks to access and promote contemporary developments in world archaeology. It will draw upon work conducted in both the northern and southern hemispheres and open a channel for people from non-Western countries to challenge the existing preconceptions about the role of archaeology in contemporary societies. The series editors seek to consciously structure the series to facilitate dialogue and critical exchange both within and between countries. Volume editors and authors will be encouraged to structure their books so that they reflect the global diversity of archaeology, not only in content but also in style and format. The goal is to link a decolonized archaeology to current political issues, as well as to archaeological theory and practice in all parts of the world.

BOOKS IN THE SERIES
Ethnographies of Archaeological Practice: Cultural Encounters, Material Transformations, edited by Matt Edgeworth
Surface Collection: Archaeological Travels in Southeast Asia, by Denis Byrne

Surface Collection

Archaeological Travels in Southeast Asia

Denis Byrne

ALTAMIRA
PRESS

A division of
ROWMAN & LITTLEFIELD PUBLISHERS, INC.
Lanham • New York • Toronto • Plymouth, U.K.

For Daniel Ragani Ng

AltaMira Press
A division of Rowman & Littlefield Publishers, Inc.
A wholly owned subsidiary of The Rowman & Littlefield Publishing Group, Inc.
4501 Forbes Boulevard, Suite 200, Lanham, MD 20706
www.altamirapress.com

Estover Road, Plymouth PL6 7PY, United Kingdom

British Library Cataloguing in Publication Information Available

Library of Congress Cataloging-in-Publication Data
Byrne, Denis (Denis Richard), 1949–
    Surface collection : archaeological travels in Southeast Asia / by Denis Byrne.
        p.   cm. — (Worlds of archaeology series)
    Includes bibliographical references and index.
    ISBN-13: 978-0-7591-1017-5 (cloth : alk. paper)
    ISBN-10: 0-7591-1017-4 (cloth : alk. paper)
    ISBN-13: 978-0-7591-1018-2 (pbk. : alk. paper)
    ISBN-10: 0-7591-1018-2 (pbk. : alk. paper)
    1. Southeast Asia—Description and travel. 2. Cultural property—Protection—
Southeast Asia. 3. Byrne, Denis (Denis Richard), 1949– —Travel—Southeast Asia. I.
Title.
    DS522.6.B97 2007
    363.6'90959—dc22
                                                                    2007011448

Printed in the United States of America

∞™ The paper used in this publication meets the minimum requirements of American National Standard for Information Sciences—Permanence of Paper for Printed Library Materials, ANSI/NISO Z39.48-1992.

Contents

Illustrations

Preface

$\mathcal{N}$otwithstanding the word "surface" in its title, this is a book about the underground, a perfectly appropriate subject for an archaeologist. Like many of my colleagues, I began my career with a much clearer faith in the distinction between the underground and the surface than I have now. What happened to unsettle that distinction was partly an increasing interest in the more recent past, even in what is now termed the "contemporary past."[1] In that sense, having spent the first part of my career focusing on the prehistoric past, I've since ascended, stratigraphically, toward the surface. Relevant to this, no doubt, is that fact that I have worked primarily in the area of archaeological heritage conservation.

As we all know, over the past few decades Indigenous peoples and voices from the non-West in general have been insisting that the past and present are a lived continuum. Cutting across the niceties of absolute dating and stratigraphic sequencing, they seem to regard the past as always-already immanent in the present. Ancient objects are not, for them, inert historical matter, but have agency, efficacy, and personality of various kinds. This idea of a "vital" material past collapses the distinction between the underground and the on-ground. Relative time depth and depth below the surface provide no index of people's intimacy with objects from the past.

More relevant to this book, however, is a notion of the underground as a hidden dimension of the surface. To explain what I mean I will begin with a usage of the word "underground" that became popular in the twentieth century and that refers to those groups of people who, like the French Maquis in the Second World War, work clandestinely to subvert authority. Often operating under the very noses of the authorities, the tactical strength of this kind of movement lies in its ability to mingle or merge with everyday life on the surface. If we now move, rather abruptly, to think of the landscapes on which we live today as containing archaeological traces of the fairly recent past (say the past century or so), and if we acknowledge that governments and elites often work to deny visibility to some of these traces, then we might think of such "suppressed" traces as constituting a kind of underground.

A very brief illustration of this idea can be made by reference to the situation in China in the years immediately following the Cultural Revolution (1966–1976). The state's failure to acknowledge the disastrous nature of the Cultural Revolution and the suffering it caused meant that millions of the victims of that period were fated to live surrounded by traces and reminders of what had happened but constrained to remain silent about it. Incarcerated within the space of their own memories[2] in a world of visible traces that triggered those memories, we might think of the events of 1966–1976 and their physical traces as constituting an "underground" dimension of the post-1976 landscape.

To the extent that all countries have underclasses, or dispossessed Indigenous minorities, or historical episodes written out of their history books, then all contemporary landscapes can be said to have these undergrounds that constitute a kind of "twilight zone" dimension of the earth's surface. For a large proportion of humanity, the experience of everyday life thus includes the silent act of noticing secret traces, of observing the footprints of a past that has been officially forgotten. The terrain in which they dwell can be thought of as vibrating with a tension that derives from the proximity of the hidden and the manifest, the secret and the public.[3]

Archaeologists dwell in all or most of these contemporary landscapes and might be expected to have a particular sensitivity to the "undergrounds" to which I refer (the low-visibility trace is, after all, our specialty). Archaeologists also move through other people's landscapes in the act of travel, and it is this travel experience that is my subject in this book. Archaeology is not a "travel practice"[4] in the sense that anthropology is, but archaeologists do have in common a certain way of looking at terrain, even when that terrain is not the subject of their own research, and this inevitably colors their experience of travel. If this is to claim a specialness for archaeology, it is only so to the extent that the farmer, the real-estate agent, and the botanist presumably also see the world in a certain way as they move through it. It isn't something to celebrate, then; it is simply something one is stuck with.

It may help at this point to introduce the first chapter. In 1989 I was in Manila, attached to the National Museum of the Philippines as a visiting PhD scholar. I was examining the factors that threatened archaeological sites in the archipelago and the local management response to these threats. In my spare time, though, I began to explore the old Spanish walled enclave, Intramuros, which lies between Manila Bay and the mouth of the Pasig River, only a stone's throw from the museum. Almost everything inside the massive walls of Intramuros—the Spanish colonial churches, colleges, houses, administrative buildings—was destroyed in February 1945 by an artillery bombardment as Douglas MacArthur's forces took the citadel from the Japanese who were entrenched there. Strolling through the streets and laneways of Intramuros in 1989, I became interested in the piecemeal attempts being made at restoration. Only later, when I became aware that tens of thousands of civilians had perished in Intramuros in February 1945, did I see that it wasn't just a heritage site, it was the site of a disaster.

I continued researching the history and politics of heritage management in Southeast Asia, but another project had begun for me in Intramuros. It was triggered, I think, by the disjunction between the easily accessible written evidence of the events of February 1945 and the eerie silence about these events in the landscape of present-day Intramuros. The archaeologists and restorationists, for instance, seemed wholly focused on reinstating Intramuros as a Spanish-colonial period piece. Stonemasons were busy restoring damaged sections of the ramparts, and a few of the old Spanish colonial townhouses were being reconstructed to some semblance of their former selves. There were interpretive signboards about life in eighteenth- and nineteenth-century Intramuros but nothing describing or commemorating the disaster of 1945. In Intramuros, the witnessing of past lives was a very selective business.

I read accounts of how, in early March 1945, after the cessation of the bombardment and the surrender of the comparatively few Japanese who were still alive, civilians began emerging from the still smoldering ruins of Intramuros into a now strangely quiet landscape. Walking the streets of Intramuros in 1989 I began to have some consciousness of the tragedy that had engulfed these people and I began to understand how heritage discourse could be as adept at burying the past as it was at revealing it. It buried certain aspects of the past by passing over their traces, traces that sank into the shadow of those other traces that heritage practice foregrounded and illuminated. The aspects of the past that it buried, it buried at the surface: They became an "underground" that shadowed our lives aboveground. So during those months in Manila, in gaining some consciousness of heritage as a surface discourse, one that was all to do with appearances (and disappearances), I'd also begun to see that in choosing heritage as a vocation I'd chosen the surface.

The social turn in archaeology over the past decade or two has meant that our subjects, the people of the past, are real for us now in a way they have not been before.[5] We have a new interest in them as political, spiritual, sensual, and sexual beings. But the people of the past become animated for us as social beings only through intensive analysis of archaeological traces, an option not available to the traveling archaeologist. The people who dwell in the landscapes through which we travel, however, might be thought of as themselves engaging in a kind of archaeology, particularly in relation to those particular events of the recent past that I've suggested constitute an "underground." The commemoration of these events may be forbidden, it may be dangerous to even notice traces of them, but this will not stop people surreptitiously, perhaps even unconsciously, looking for traces and interrogating them.

It may help to introduce, at this point, another of the book's chapters (chapter 3). While living on the south coast of Bali in the early 1990s, I began reading Indonesian modern history. In the course of this reading I learned that in late 1965 and early 1966 Bali had been one of the foci of the violence that had convulsed Indonesia as the new military government of General Soeharto consolidated its grip on power. I already knew a little of this episode but had been under the impression that the mass killing of Communists and other perceived state enemies had been confined to the island of Java. I now discovered that somewhere in the vicinity of one hundred thousand people had been killed at that time in Bali. Given that the Soeharto regime was still firmly in power in the early 1990s, it was no surprise that a public silence still surrounded the bloody circumstances of the regime's origins. The families of those killed in 1965–1966 had been forbidden to publicly mourn or commemorate them. The killings became publicly unmentionable and for the next three decades would have no visibility in the nation's history books.

But none of these measures, I assumed, would stop people who had witnessed the events from remembering them in private. The contemporary landscape would surely contain direct physical traces of the violence but would also be strewn with associative traces and signs that had the potential to trigger memories, many of which would be redolent with sadness or trauma. Reflecting on this, I began to look differently at the idyllic terrain through which I moved during my afternoon walks and motor-scooter rides, becoming conscious that it contained a universe of signs that an outsider could barely begin to decipher.

Ian Hodder cautions that material culture is not a text whose meaning anyone can read.[6] I'm sure this statement applies equally to cultural landscapes: No amount of archaeological skill or "sensibility" will be enough to decode terrain encrypted at this intimate level. And what reason would there be for intruding there anyway? But the fact remains that we do regularly find ourselves in the landscapes of others, landscapes that often harbor traumatic associations of which we are forewarned by our reading or by hearsay. So it is relevant to ask how, as traveling archaeologists, we are to deport ourselves in such places. Do we seek to maintain a scholarly distance or do we allow ourselves to be drawn in subjectively and emotionally? Similar questions are raised by the practice of forensic anthropology, where the excavation and analysis of sites of extreme violence and suffering inevitably "elaborate on the horror" and open the door to voyeurism and the fetishization of violence.[7]

I don't pretend to be able to resolve these questions in the chapters that follow, nor is that my ambition. This is a travel book—what I hope to convey is something of my personal experience of traveling through a universe of traces with insufficient local knowledge to be able, for the most part, to quite see them, or of being conscious of the murmur of traces without, for the most part, ever quite hearing the words.

There are traces suppressed on the surface and then there are those that are simply lost to the surface. In 1976 in Vietnam, only a year after the fall of Saigon, the "body-collecting team" of Vietnamese soldiers in Bao Ninh's novel *The Sorrow of War* return to jungle battlefields that have already been "forgotten by peace."[8] They had spent years of the war, the better part of their youth, in these jungles, and they now watch the traces of that experience evaporating before their eyes. They see "all the tracks disappearing, bit by bit, day by day, into the embrace of the coarse undergrowth and the wild grasses."[9]

Southeast Asia's tropical climate and luxuriant nature hasten away trails that have barely gone cold. It can sometimes seem as if nature is betraying the past. Traveling in the Regency of Karangasem in eastern Bali (chapter 3) in 1994, I had a chance to reflect on the propensity of tropical vegetation to rapidly cover the scars left on the landscape by a volcanic eruption. Later, as I considered its role in covering over the scars left by the 1965–1966 mass killings in Bali, this propensity seemed less benign. The vegetation seemed almost to conspire in the effacement of the traces of what had occurred.

Over the past several decades, Southeast Asia's headlong rush to modernity has created its own trail of ruin and debris. I am drawn to the region's abandoned creeper-laden bungalows and empty, weed-choked swimming pools (chapter 4) as much as to its ruined temples (chapter 8). Such is the rate of change and development that it is in danger of getting ahead of itself, creating, for instance, the instantaneous high-rise ruins of late 1990s Bangkok. These wondrous, unfinished, open-sided skeletons of weather-blackened concrete and rusting steel stood over the city and became canvases for a new generation of graffiti artists as well as camping grounds for squatters who in many cases had lost their jobs in the same financial meltdown that produced the high-rise ruins.

The circumstances that led me to begin writing this book were as follows: I was living in Bali in 1993 and had just submitted my PhD thesis, most of which was written at a desk on the balcony of a thatched-roof bungalow that was a product of vernacular architecture and Orientalist fantasy. The thesis, on the history and politics of archaeological heritage conservation in Thailand and Australia, was based on fieldwork and literature centered on those two places. It excluded the results of an initial four-month period spent in the Philippines in mid-1989 that had prompted me to radically reformulate my topic and approach. By the time I moved on to Bangkok in late 1989, I'd decided to begin the whole project afresh there. This seemed to work. Sitting in Bali three years later, though, I felt I needed to revisit that experience in the Philippines to better understand what had happened there.

At the far end of the balcony in Bali was a freestanding, glass-doored cupboard, an *antik baru* (new antique) made of some kind of cheap wood from Java, the paintwork "distressed" by having been rubbed with soft-drink bottles. Inside it, among other things, were my field journals from the Philippines. The cupboard was home to some kind of wood-boring insect and the paper of the notebooks was undergoing its own form of disintegration due to the dampness of successive monsoons. It was impossible to insulate things from the climate in that open-sided dwelling. Squalls raced in from the sea across the rice fields, and the rain pounding on the thatch sent a mist drifting through the whole house. Among the books on a bamboo shelf downstairs, also fast decaying, were Amitav Ghosh's *In an Antique Land* and the copy of Paul Rabinow's *Reflections on Fieldwork in Morocco*, which I'd had with me in the Philippines.[10]

Over the next few months, using the field journals, I drafted what have become the first two chapters of this book. It was more than a matter of salvaging what the journals contained, more than simply rendering them as a coherent narrative. I was interpreting them and making a new sense out of what I had previously written. If the ordinary act of remembering is always a creative act, then recapitulating through writing is even more so. Chapter 1, concerned with the fate of Intramuros, I have introduced above. Chapter 2 describes a brief trip I made, while still based in Manila, to the spectacular rice terraces of Banaue in the Cordillera of Luzon. Soon to be declared a World Heritage site, the rice terraces were a mainstay of the Philippines' national heritage, but the farmers of Banaue were beginning to resile from the backbreaking work of maintaining these agricultural stairways to heaven. While the farmers seemed keen to embrace modernity, the national elite and the heritage industry wanted to take both them and their terraces out of circulation, anchoring them firmly in an unchanging and, most importantly, visitable past.

Writing about fieldwork and travel in the Philippines had been a way of closing the distance between the intellectual product of research and the spatially situated experience of doing research. But sitting on that balcony writing about the Philippines was distancing me from another experience, that of living in Bali. Wanting to write about Bali and with the 1945 destruction of Intramuros still ringing in my ears, I decided to visit the eastern end of the island and look for traces of the 1963 eruption of the Gunung Agung volcano (chapter 3). The sudden burial of parts of the landscape there under meters of lava and ash literally created an instant "underground." It is a common human experience to walk through life on landscape surfaces that are stratified directly above those walked upon by our predecessors. But in eastern Bali in the years after 1963, as the cultural landscape reinstated itself, people would presumably have had an unusually acute consciousness of the "lost places" sealed off beneath their feet.[11]

If this ramble through eastern Bali represented my first delving into the island's recent past, it was also a precursor to an experience, months later, in which I became aware of a darker chapter of Balinese history, namely the mass killings of 1965–1966 (discussed above). It was darker in the sense that the agents of destruction were human rather than natural. But it was comparable in that it involved radical changes to the cultural landscape (e.g., the destruction of villages) and in that it posed the question of how the survivors of catastrophe live in landscapes that seem at once to remind them of, and to disavow, what has happened.

Chapter 5 is intended as an antidote to, or retreat from, the darkness that precedes it. During the months that I was immersed in the events of 1965–1966, searching for their traces, I stumbled upon and began to follow the trail of a connected but very different kind of trace. This was the delicate trail of a perfume, Shalimar de Guerlain, a bottle of which was discovered among the personal effects of former President Sukarno at the time of his death under house arrest in Jakarta in 1970. It led me across the terrain of Bali, across the floors of department stores, and through the literature. This perfume, which appears to have been part of Sukarno's sensory world, became part of mine also. It constituted a trace that had to be followed with the senses as well as the intellect. Certainly I couldn't claim to be a cool objective observer of Shalimar; I was consuming it in the act of following it. We obviously do come at the past partly through our senses, and it comes at us that way too. Julian Thomas maintains that archaeology's ethical task is to "bear witness to the past other," and this must surely mean bearing witness with our bodies and emotions as well as our intellect.[12] There are reasons why invoking personal experience can be problematic in archaeological writing, but the personal is always nevertheless there at some level.[13]

Chapters 6 and 7 are excursions—literally, in that they are travel narratives—into the archaeology of failed projects. Marguerite Duras, in her 1950 novel *The Sea Wall*, presents a scenario in which a French woman in 1930s Vietnam builds a wall of mangrove logs in an attempt to hold back the spring tides that inundate the low-lying portion of the land concession she has won from the colonial government and upon which she is attempting to grow rice. The eventual collapse of the sea wall leaves her financially ruined and psychologically broken. I travel to Vietnam in an effort to locate the setting of the novel, but, unsurprisingly, this journey begins to blend into a reflection on that other failed project, the 1965–1975 Vietnam War.

Chapter 6 is also concerned with the particular circumstance that arises when people find themselves living on eroding coastlines. Here the lost place is not a buried surface, as was the case in eastern Bali after the Agung eruption, but is like a lost limb whose presence endures in phantom form.

The final chapter relates a journey to the northern Thai town of Fang, following in the footsteps of the Norwegian naturalist Carl Bock. In 1882 Bock was diverted from his quest for butterflies and birds and began collecting ancient bronze Buddha images from Fang's ruined Buddhist temples, bringing himself into direct conflict with the farmers and monks who were recolonizing the long-abandoned town. My problem with Bock's collecting activities begins with the sneaky nature of his thievery but moves on to his refusal to recognize local religious beliefs. As a child of the Protestant Reformation, Carl Bock was immune to the world of the magical-supernatural that, for local people, confers on the Buddha images and the material past in general an immediate influence on the things they cared about—the likelihood, for instance, of tigers attacking their precious livestock.

The discourse of heritage is also a child of the Reformation. It seems unmoved and uninterested in the fact that the majority of the world's population lives in an enchanted world in which old objects and places are animated by a "barely comprehensible virtuosity."[14] The agency these objects and places possess is, of course, one that originates in "causal sequences" that we human agents initiate.[15] But what counts on the ground is that, for local believers, the objects and places have as much capacity to act upon them as they have to act upon the objects and places.[16] In places like Thailand, popular religion is the most powerful and pervasive factor contextualizing the material past within local culture. Our failure to engage with the international heritage conservation movement's claims to be democratic, inclusive, and cosmopolitan. It consigns popular religious belief and practice to the "underground."

NOTES

1. Buchli and Lucas 2001a.
2. Mueggler 1998.

3. See Byrne (1993) for a description of the "nervous landscapes" of racial segregation in eastern Australia.

4. Clifford 1997, 9.

5. For example, Barrett 1994; Dobres 2000; and Meskell and Pruecel 2004.

6. Hodder 2004, 30.

7. Buchli and Lucas 2001b.

8. Ninh 1993, 1.

9. Ibid.

10. Ghosh 1992; Rabinow 1977.

11. Here and elsewhere I have drawn upon Peter Read's (1996) seminal work on the human experience of losing places.

12. Thomas 2004, 238.

13. See Conkey (2005: 26–29) for a discussion of the role of "experience" in archaeological writing.

14. Meskell 2004, 79.

15. Gell 1998, 16.

16. Byrne 2005, 59.

Acknowledgments

$\mathcal{I}$ wish to thank the many people who have helped me during the writing of this book and during the travels on which it is based. In particular, for their comments on drafts of individual chapters I thank Jane Balme, Helen Brayshaw, Paula Hamilton, Steven Muecke, and Graeme Storer. I am grateful for the comments on the manuscript as a whole provided by Heather Burke and three anonymous referees. Thanks also to Robert Cribb, Heather Goodall, and Peggy Read who provided information on materials used. I am grateful to Lynn Meskell for her encouragement and her advice on getting this book published.

I acknowledge the assistance of the following institutions: the Australian National University, the Australian War Memorial, the Intramuros Administration, the National Library of Australia, and the National Museum of the Philippines.

For help and companionship on the road I thank Aniceto Mendez, Le Zuan Nghi, and Aung Aung as well as the many others who generously made visible for me aspects of their landscapes I would otherwise have missed.

An earlier version of chapter 1 was published under the title "Intramuros's Return" in *UTS Review* 1, no. 2 (1995). An earlier version of chapter 4 was published under the title "Traces of '65: Sites and Memories of the Post-Coup Killings in Bali" in *UTS Review* 5, no. 1 (1999). I thank the editors of that journal for permission to republish them here.

Finally, my special thanks to Daniel Ng.

· *1* ·

Intramuros

*T*he fortified town that the Spanish began building on the edge of Manila Bay in the late sixteenth century came to be known as Intramuros, literally, "within the walls." If the name suggests a certain insularity, a certain comfort that was to be taken from being inside rather than outside the walls, then this is hardly surprising. The tiny Spanish colonial enclave was isolated in a sea of non-European people and was so far from home that galleon-delivered mail from the court in Madrid took two years to arrive there. The very idea of holding such a distant possession was, you might think, so preposterous, so presumptuous, that the native population might simply have been unwilling or unable to believe it had been colonized until it was too late to do anything about it. The uneasiness of the Spaniards is intimated by the fact that for hundreds of years they prohibited the native population, together with the Chinese and the mestizos, from dwelling inside the walls or from even being present there after nightfall when the gates were shut and the drawbridges drawn. Perhaps their own daring at having come so far made them nervous; perhaps after dark, lying in their beds, they retraced in their minds the long, tenuous route back home. If, as Susan Sontag says in her novel *The Volcano Lover,* a collection needs an island, then the Spanish, who collected islands, needed Intramuros.

I'd gone to Manila in 1989 to examine issues to do with conserving pre-Hispanic archaeological sites in the Philippines. As a site, Intramuros was therefore outside my brief and I only gradually became conscious of its existence and history. Standing at the window of the second-floor room in the National Museum where I was reading through piles of old reports and archaeological site records, I could see, looking across a stream of traffic and a dusty park, a corner of the Spanish wall and the confusion of rooftops and low

1

facades that lay beyond it. There, in 1571, Miguel Lopez de Legazpi had laid out a gridiron of seventeen streets on the site of what had been the palisaded fort of Rajah Suleiman. The Rajah's small brass cannons, while perfectly adequate under previous conditions, were little more than a joke to the Spanish, and they easily drove him out of his stronghold. Intramuros's defenses were elaborated and modified over time to produce a system of immense stone walls complete with moat, seven gates, several bastions and ravelins, and a large fort in the northwest corner guarding the river mouth.[1]

By the seventeenth century Intramuros housed six monasteries, fifteen churches, two universities, several schools, two palaces, and numerous warehouses for the galleon trade. Fountains played in courtyards and plazas, windows glazed with pearl shell diffused the glare of the sun. This seemingly sleepy town at the edge of Spain's colonial empire seethed with political machinations and intrigues, with commercial rivalries and with ecclesiastical fervors and schemings, to say nothing of the torments and ecstasies of the heart and flesh. The islands never really made any money for Spain. For hundreds of years the colonial government depended upon the annual galleon from Mexico and the cases of silver pieces it brought. The bells of Intramuros rang to greet it when the galleon sailed into the bay, Te Deums were sung, and masses of thanksgiving were said. People slept more soundly at night.

Then into the bay in May 1898 steamed Admiral Dewey's modern armored squadron, which set about sinking the pathetically ill-prepared Spanish fleet. Three months later the Spanish ceded the whole archipelago to the United States in exchange for $20 million. An American army of occupation was landed to scuttle the nationalist revolution that had destabilized the Spanish in the first place. To the American newcomers, the resources of the archipelago were scandalously underdeveloped, crying out for enterprise and modern principles. While in some ways Intramuros stood for everything they rejected in the Philippines, they were not incapable of enjoying its Old World flavor, the exotic nature of the religious fervor concentrated there, and the slightly disreputable air of its back streets, cafés, and bars. However, they located their own business premises and homes outside the walls, across the river and in the bayside suburbs.[2]

The terms "Americanization" and "modernization" were interchangeable and were used with equivalent zeal. The new administration set about providing water and sewage facilities, repairing and widening streets, installing streetcars, and giving the city a "modern cleaning" every day.[3] It planned to demolish the obsolete stone walls around Intramuros in the interests of modernization—it was as if they felt the place needed a good airing—but a report commissioned from an eminent American landscape architect recommended they be retained and the old Spanish city be preserved. In Southern California in the 1890s the Arroyo Set was creating the mock-Mediterranean "mis-

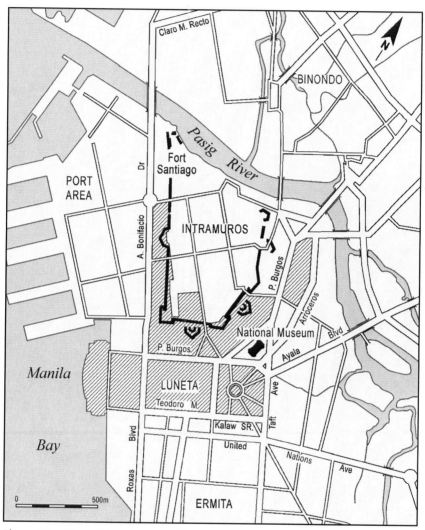

Figure 1.1.   Map of downtown Manila

sion look" from the ground up. In Intramuros the Spanish look was already in place; all that was missing were the palm trees and lawns, and these could easily be arranged. So it was that Intramuros stayed largely unchanged, and modern Manila grew up around it.

I had already been in Manila for two weeks when I first went to Intramuros. The sun beat down out of a clear sky as I made my way purposefully across the Luneta, that strip of public gardens and parched lawns that separated

Intramuros from the once fashionable, now run-down, area to the south. The lawns of the Luneta were where people who came into the city on Sundays lay and slept when the sun slid down into Manila Bay. They slept, whole families of them, and if you strolled through there on a Sunday evening you felt you were intruding.

The gateway in the Spanish wall that I approached from the Luneta was not one of the original portals but a breach punched through it in 1904 to allow vehicle traffic to flow more easily. What must originally have been the jagged edges of this breach had been dressed back and the stone had healed to its old color. The wall was almost as wide at the base as it was high, and I paused for a while in the shade, inside its thirteen-meter thickness. A little further along toward the bay the wall had been breached by British artillery during the Napoleonic Wars in the course of which the Spanish had been temporarily relieved of the archipelago. The Japanese, for their part, had entered Intramuros unopposed in 1941, but three years later the returning Americans blew gaping holes in the wall over on the river side. Through these holes they poured tanks and troops to flush out the Japanese whose fortunes had so dramatically turned. The only people the wall had ever really successfully kept out were Filipinos. And that perhaps was its true significance: a line drawn between colonizer and colonized, white and brown, We and Other. Passing a knot of schoolgirls going in the opposite direction, I passed through to the We side.

I walked slowly along below the three-story facade of a high school, passed by some cheaply built godowns and shop houses, none of which looked more than a few decades old, and then turned into a smaller street. Here the smooth cobbles of the old street were surfacing through the worn bitumen overlay of the present road. On either side, separated by open, weed-grown expanses, there were the roofless shells of what had evidently been large prewar buildings. I stopped in front of one of the stucco-covered shells and peered through a large arched window opening. The remnants of an old tiled floor were just visible through the weeds, its decorative design difficult to make out through the dry leaves, the bits of rusted wire, and the scraps of yellowed newspaper scattered over this space. My eye caught a movement over by the opposite wall: A woman had been sitting on a wooden box, holding a baby, and now she was reaching up to where a towel was hanging on a nail driven into the faded yellow surface of the plastered masonry. She looked to be about my own age but was probably younger and she had her back to me, oblivious to my presence. There was no one but me on the pavement. Back where I'd come from I could see traffic and a few pedestrians passing by the opening of the ruined street, but the sound barely reached me here in what seemed to be a vacuum lodged between the lines of an otherwise overcrowded city.

A bit further along I came to an open area strewn with stone rubble and crossed by a line of telegraph poles festooned with blue-flowering lianas. On the other side of this space, perhaps two hundred meters away, was the inner face of Intramuros's bayside wall, angling up the side of which was a stone stairway. I began to make my way over to it. Where the pavement gave out (the street had simply faded away) I following a walking track worn through the grass. There was still nobody to be seen until I came to the edge of a stone terrace and was about to jump down when I noticed the slight figure of a man asleep on the grass directly below me. I went around him and he didn't wake. A skinny white cat with a bent tail stood in the grass, eyeing me.

Given the general decay in the vicinity I was surprised to find that the brickwork of the stairs, when I reached them, had been recently restored. Up on the rampart, opposite the top of the stairs and projecting several meters out into the former moat, was a roughly semicircular brick-and-stone bastion. Whatever superstructure the masonry may originally have supported, there was nothing there now, just the semicircular wall a couple of meters thick, which you could easily walk out along. The bastion's hollow, well-lit interior was choked with some species of luxuriant and unruly shrub, the long curved arms of which reached up into the still air.

Beyond and below the bastion was the manicured lawn of the golf links that had occupied the moat since early in the century when it had been drained of its brackish water as part of the American sanitation drive. I gazed down at a putting green. Its velvet surface had been mown into broad stripes, and a painted bamboo stick with a flag on the end stood in its neat round hole. Captivated by the disjunction between this vision of smoothness and the scene of ruin I had just walked through, I leaned out and looked directly down to where the smooth green tide of the golf links lapped against the outside of the bastion with an air of intent, an implied threat that the future was recreational.

Turning to look back over Intramuros, the almost complete absence of anything intact dating from the Spanish colonial period came as a surprise even though I'd been warned what to expect. The panorama of broken walls and weed-infested spaces, relieved only by the squared-off concrete shapes of more recent structures, was an artifact not so much of the three hundred years of Spanish rule and the fifty years of American rule that followed, but of the week in February 1945 when Intramuros was caught up in one of the main actions of what we refer to, without irony, as the Pacific War.

What happened in February 1945 had begun with a failure of communication within the Japanese military command. Admiral Iwabuchi Sanji neglected to follow the plan that General Yamashita Tomoyuki had formulated to pull all his forces out of Manila once it became clear that the American advance on the city was unstoppable. After tenaciously defending key installations around the city during the first weeks of February, a substantial part of the Japanese force of some twenty thousand troops withdrew into Intramuros and the major public buildings that stood in the parklike space around it. These buildings had been erected by the American-Philippines Commonwealth administration in the 1920s and 1930s using earthquake-resistant reinforced concrete. The Japanese now fortified them with heavy-caliber guns salvaged from their naval ships, which lay sunk or damaged in Manila Bay. In the ensuing battle the buildings had to be taken by the Americans in "hand-to-hand combat" (which in fact included the use of bazookas, hand grenades, and flame throwers). The fighting proceeded corridor by corridor, room by room, through buildings, including the City Hall, the Executive Building, and the Treasury, whose white-pillared classical forms had been intended to emulate Washington, DC. After the war the Executive Building became home to the National Museum. It took a bit of imagination for me to visualize Japanese machine-gun positions at the corners of those parquet-floored corridors where teenage security guards these days sat quietly at their desks in the torpor of the afternoon heat.

Despite their militarily hopeless position, the Japanese declined either to surrender Intramuros or release the thousands of civilians trapped within it. For a week, commencing 17 February, MacArthur deployed his entire artillery against the Walled City, firing mostly from the other side of the river in a bombardment that destroyed or badly damaged almost every structure inside it, killed most of the civilians, and finally breached the walls in the northeast corner. American assault troops entered there but still had to take Fort Santiago and other heavily defended positions inside. The Japanese fought virtually to the last man. In what is known as the Battle of Manila, they lost 16,665 dead as against 710 American dead. Most estimates put the total of civilian dead at about 100,000, many of them killed by the Japanese in reprisal or sheer anger, but most of them falling victim to the bombardment. The American command was itself shocked at the extent of the devastation when it toured central Manila after fighting ceased on 3 March: "Manila in effect has ceased to exist," commented General Eichelberger.[4] Describing Intramuros, he said, "It is all just graveyard."[5]

A graveyard. Yes, you could imagine that easily enough, even forty-four years later. The vacant lots and the empty shells of buildings that I gazed at from up on the wall were sites where thousands had died under fallen roofs and walls or trapped in raging fires. In the weeks after Intramuros fell, American bulldozers cleared rubble and pulled down parts of structures deemed to be unsafe. The last of the accessible dead were pulled out and taken away to be buried.

I came down from the wall and walked back the way I had come. In Manila now, nobody seemed to speak of the events of that February in 1945.

In the streets of Intramuros there were no monuments commemorating them. If you hadn't known better, you might have concluded that the Spanish churches and convents, the fountains and the rows of pearlshell-windowed townhouses had simply fallen victim to the nonmilitary attrition of earthquakes, termites, and tropical weather.

The heat was draining me. I worked my way over toward the rebuilt cathedral and stood at the counter of a corner store, slowly drinking a cold bottle of Sprite. Across the counter three boys were sitting on boxes, playing a game of cards. They were interrupted by a woman who came to buy matches, sliding her thin silver coins across the scratched lime-green Formica. The radio played an old Pet Shop Boys dance song, the repetitive, disembodied voice from London strangely in harmony with the sweltering, premonsoonal afternoon. A little further up the street were the walls of the cathedral, the neobaroque version that arose in the 1950s from the rubble of its predecessor destroyed in the war. The blocks of gray volcanic stone looked too mean to be left exposed—it looked like a cake waiting to be iced. A few bicycle rickshaws rattled along the street. I lingered over the Sprite, putting off the moment when I would have to make a move, kidding myself that I was blending into the scenery. On the opposite corner, in the yard of a warehouse, two boys without shirts were prancing around in front of a pink radio perched on top of a gas drum. You wouldn't even notice them in a nightclub, but here, in the open air, on their dance floor of oil-stained dirt, poised and ritualistic, they looked significant. One of them left and the other sat down on a stool in front of a mirror nailed to a fence, gazing critically at himself and touching his hair. Along the street there was a woman in a phone booth, her free arm extending out through a broken window, her hand idly tearing strips off a poster pasted onto the outside of the glass. Her hand stopped, motionless, in response to some point in the conversation and then slowly tore another strip off the poster and let it flutter to the ground.

Accounts of March 1945 mention that even after the fighting ceased, it was a few days before haunted-looking survivors began to emerge into the streets from the places they had been hiding or trapped. They emerged into a landscape of ruin that was still smoking and where, with the cessation of the bombardment, the silence must have been extraordinary. Photographs taken at the time of former landmarks like Letran College show them still standing but pockmarked, charred, windowless, and frayed at the edges.

A photograph by Carl Mydans, for *Life* magazine, shows three young women walking down what appears to be a residential street outside Intramuros.[6] The flattened houses and especially the shredded, leafless trees suggest a typhoon has passed through. The women are holding their noses as they pass the corpse of a boy sprawled facedown across a tramline. Another photograph by Mydans seems to have been taken from the hood of an open jeep, looking in over the windshield. There is the young bespectacled soldier driver, a woman with frizzy hair in the passenger seat next to him, and, on a split-bamboo platform laid across the back of the jeep, a woman with a gaping leg wound lying stretched out (her eyes are closed, but she must be alive because her hand is visibly gripping the bamboo). The woman in the front has blood on the hand she is using to hold the front of her dress together and she has a numb, faraway look in her eyes. The driver by contrast is looking straight at the camera and his mouth is open, perhaps in surprise at Mydans's boldness or perhaps in shock at the scale of devastation.

When Douglas MacArthur arrived in Manila back in 1935, clouds of war were gathering over the South China Sea. He was charged with preparing the defense of the Philippines in the eventuality of armed conflict with Japan. MacArthur had been army chief of staff in Washington and came with a reputation, earned in Europe during the First World War, as a brilliant strategist. He was known as an outspoken proponent of right-wing politics and he was notoriously egotistical. Presumably he was unaware that he would barely set foot in mainland America again in the next sixteen years.

The quest for wide open spaces and new resources, or whatever it was that made the frontier a necessary part of the American worldview, had pushed that frontier westward to America's Pacific coast and then further west across the sea to the Philippines (only stopping, you might argue, in 1971 in Vietnam). It was a preoccupation that saw MacArthur's father, Arthur MacArthur Jr., fighting Native Americans on the western frontier in the 1860s and fighting republican Filipinos on Luzon in 1899. One of the ironies of going west was that you eventually and inevitably found yourself in the East.

MacArthur took his task seriously, but the defense of 7,083 islands against a modern naval power was never going to be easy, and it didn't help that Washington was reluctant to provide the necessary money or arms. Still, the feeling in Manila in the mid-1930s was not one of panic. A popular racial chauvinism, shared by MacArthur, derided the notion of the Japanese soldier as a serious opponent for white soldiers. Among his other liabilities, the Japanese soldier was believed to be chronically myopic and unable to shoot straight (cartoon caricatures of the Japanese at this time often showed them with thick-lensed spectacles). When Japan struck the Philippines in 1941, shortly after its attack on Pearl Harbor, MacArthur had a force of 80,000 poorly trained and equipped Filipinos backed by 22,000 US soldiers, 207 military planes, and a small number of torpedo boats. The air force was destroyed on the ground almost instantly, and the ground forces were withdrawn onto the Bataan Peninsula. Manila was declared an open city in order to spare it from attack.

Accompanied by his wife and young son, MacArthur withdrew to Corregidor, the island fortress at the tip of Bataan. Before they took Manila, Japanese planes bombed part of the north side of Intramuros, destroying a church and damaging several other buildings. Even as the hundreds of American civilians still resident in the city were being interned, the majority of the governing elite, their erstwhile "brown brothers," were enlisting in the Japanese collaborationist government.[7] Bataan and Corregidor held out for five months, but before it fell, MacArthur with his wife and son, under orders from Washington, escaped by boat to Mindanao and were flown to Australia. It was in Melbourne in March 1942, standing outside Spencer Street railway station, that MacArthur uttered the famous words, "I came through and I shall return," having scripted them into a speech on the back of an envelope. His office had to run the script past the Office of War Information in Washington, which pleaded for the "I" to be changed to "we."[8] MacArthur stuck with the "I" and the rest, as they say, is history. It is here that the Return appears to have begun its career, but in fact, if fact can be brought to bear at all on so slippery a phenomenon, it traces back to the besieged Corregidor where General Sutherland and the Filipino journalist Carlos Romulo coined the phrase as a slogan to boost morale in the occupied archipelago.[9] They had presented it to MacArthur who assimilated it and, promising he would be back, boarded the PT boat for the hazardous and uncomfortable journey south.

The idea of the Return was so personalized, so mythologized, and so powerful that it is difficult to know how to draw lines around it. Those who still hold to the idea of history as linear narrative might do well to consider the Return of MacArthur because it refracts, it occurs before and after itself, it multiplies, and even, in a sense, it never happens at all. Following its first public appearance, in Melbourne, the idea of the Return began to proliferate. William Manchester, MacArthur's biographer, describes how:

> Throughout the war American submarines provided Filipino guerrillas with cartons of buttons, gum, playing cards, and matchboxes bearing the message, and they were widely circulated. Scraps of paper with "I shall return" written on them were found in Japanese files. There was even a story—which made effective propaganda even if it was apocryphal—that a Japanese artillery battery opening a case of artillery shells in the middle of a battle, found the sentence neatly stencilled on each of them.[10]

The Return had its key symbolic moment on 19 October 1944 at Red Beach on the island of Leyte when MacArthur waded ashore from a landing craft. The US Third Fleet and Seventh Fleet stood off the coast of Leyte near Tacloban and at daybreak they opened an immense bombardment of the beach. Waves of infantry were then sent in, and MacArthur himself headed shoreward in a landing craft with his immediate field staff, journalists, and the president of the Philippine government in exile, Sergio Osmeña. The landing craft ran aground fifty meters from shore, and MacArthur and his party were forced to disembark and wade in through the water, an army photographer taking a picture of them in the process. MacArthur was evidently annoyed. He had long anticipated this moment, and if he had visualized striding up the beach immaculate and heroic—he had a reputation for neatness—he now found himself up to his knees in water. But later he saw a print of the photograph and realized it captured the very essence of the Return. I see him looking at it in the wardroom of his flagship over breakfast the next morning, sipping coffee from a thick china mug, thoughtfully stroking his chin: In a flash of postmodern insight he sees that his botched landing is about to morph into something quite different. The scowl on his face captured by the photograph was actually intended for the person responsible for running him aground, but it would be seen by the world as being addressed at the Japanese.

The following day for the benefit of other cameramen he organized a repeat performance at nearby White Beach, complete with landing craft, wet trousers, and defiant expression. He repeated it during the Luzon landing in Lingayen Gulf, noting in his memoirs that his error in choosing a boat that took too much draft had become a habit with him.[11] There was nothing accidental about it. At Lingayen he refused to alight on the landing pier that had been erected especially for him, insisting that the door of the craft go down in the waves so that he could wade ashore just as he had at Leyte. Mydans's famous picture of this rerun is almost identical to the "original" Leyte enactment. The photographs of the Return—that is to say, one or other of its enactments—spread around the world, a copy of one of the Leyte pictures even reaching the desk of General Yamashita. Yamashita, however, refused to believe MacArthur had really been there at Leyte; the photograph, he suspected, was of a fake landing staged in Australia. Actually, it was probably of the fake landing staged on Leyte the day after the "real" landing.

The replicability of the Return, both by graphic reproduction and live performance, its instantaneous transition into myth, lent it a certain omnipresence. It is always with us now, pulsing away in the space of pure representation.

One Saturday night during the time I was writing this piece in Bali I went to have dinner with some friends at a semi-open-air disco on the edge of the beach a kilometer or so down the coast from where I was living. It was eight o'clock, and the dance floor lay empty beneath its vast thatched roof. We ate at a table on the terrace, directly above the deserted beach. At a certain point during the meal, as clearly as if it were tapping me on the shoulder, I had a vision of MacArthur wading in toward the beach behind me. That's what comes of gazing at certain photographs for too long, I thought. There was the faded cloth general's hat, the Ray-Ban Aviators, the imperious set of the jaw, the accompanying officers beside and behind him, and, fanning out further back, the soldiers in steel helmets and battle dress. I turned and glanced at the empty beach. The conversation at the dinner table continued but so in my imagination did MacArthur: The Seminyak beach dogs stood staring and then ran yapping back along the strand as the moonlit phalanx advanced through the shallows and then up over the dry sand, across the terrace and onto the dance floor, still in formation, where they broke into a 1940s dance step under the dark, lustrous eyes of the waiters whose unmoved, beautiful faces insisted they had already seen everything the West had to show them. There was a thin drift of sand on the dance floor's polished concrete surface.

As one who has chosen to work in a field that is as subject to the play of the human imagination as archaeological heritage conservation, it is not for me to keep my own dream life in some kind of quarantine. My job, I think, is to observe and understand, to unravel or excavate the ways in which heritage is constituted. To undertake an archaeology of Intramuros is to purposefully enter the dreamscape of the Return, not so much in order to sieve out the kernels of fact from the wash of fantasy but rather to attempt to understand how and why it was all put together.

I may seem to have strayed a long way from Intramuros, but I am moving back to it much as MacArthur approached it in late 1944 and early 1945: circuitously but with a certain speed. In his book *Speed and Politics*, Paul Virilio charts the accumulating role of speed in the history of warfare, a sequence that leads from the medieval fortress whose power lay in its immobile, static resistance, through to the "lightning warfare" of the Third Reich in which "stasis is death."[12] MacArthur may not have grasped the full implications of this in 1941 when the Pacific War began. Upon the unexpected arrival of the East in the space of the West, with the Japanese attack on Pearl Harbor (Hawai'i being quasi-West), MacArthur appears to have fallen into a semi-catatonic state of indecision that allowed the Japanese, to their own astonishment, to destroy his air force on the tarmac at Clark Air Field fully nine hours after word of the disaster at Pearl had been radioed to Manila. Other feats of Japanese speed followed, notable among them the extraordinarily fast transit of the Malay Peninsula that led to the fall of Singapore. The West's previous apparent monopoly on rapidity was decisively broken.[13]

Three years later, in the closing months of 1944, MacArthur demonstrated a rejuvenated facility with time and motion, surprising the Japanese by bypassing the Talauds and the island of Mindanao to strike directly at Leyte, and swiftly proceeding from there to the invasion of Luzon. The landing at Lingayen Gulf, some 180 kilometers north of Manila, took place on 10 January. MacArthur was hoping to celebrate his sixty-fifth birthday in Manila on 26 January.[14] He ordered a fast-moving force to make a dash behind Japanese lines to free the American internees at the University of Santo Thomas and Bilibid Prison and meanwhile moved his main force rapidly down the central plain of Luzon, encouraging a situation in which three US divisions competed to be the first to enter the city. On 6 February MacArthur sent out a communique to the effect that US troops were rapidly clearing the Japanese from Manila and that "their complete destruction is imminent." Congratulations poured in from Roosevelt and the Allied leaders, and by 10 February the general was planning a great victory parade through the city. *Newsweek* announced MacArthur's victory in a headline that read: "Prize of the Pacific War: Manila Fell to MacArthur Like Ripened Plum."

The reality as it emerged in the days following was that the Japanese were still firmly entrenched in Manila south of the Pasig River. American tanks and artillery were being brought to bear on Japanese positions and, while US troop losses remained comparatively light, civilian casualties and damage to the city began to escalate. The irony of the Japanese situation was that, after the speed and modernity they had exhibited early in the war, the remnant of their force in Manila was now stationary, entrenched in heavily defended key buildings and holed up in Intramuros, an ancient fortress that was precisely the class of object that gunpowder and speed, Paul Virilio notes, had made obsolete. The original logic of the ancient fortress, that time "was beaten by the static resistance of the construction materials—by duration," no longer applied. In Manila in early 1945 time was already ahead of itself. Or should one say that, victory having already been announced, MacArthur's troops were behind time.

One of MacArthur's lieutenants later stated that the general was shattered by the holocaust in Manila.[15] Be that as it may, he clearly intended to control the way the outside world saw the battle. He censored the heading "Manila Is Dying" from an outgoing press report and regulated against any future use of that particular phrase.[16] Not by this one stroke of the censor's pen, but decisively, methodically, and even as it was happening, the destruction of Manila began to be edited out of history. I came to see the current restoration of Intramuros to its former Spanish-colonial self as a further step in this general line of finesse.

If there was a single main reason for Manila's destruction, it was the perceived necessity of minimizing American combat casualties. In Honolulu in 1944 MacArthur had given Roosevelt an assurance that the Philippines could be taken without a high casualty rate, an understanding crucial to his being allowed to invade the archipelago in the face of opposition from those like Nimitz who argued for a direct strike at Formosa (Taiwan), that island then to serve as a springboard for an invasion of the Japanese mainland. MacArthur refused to sanction aerial bombing of Manila, but it is generally conceded that the massive use of artillery had much the same effect. It is likely that most of the approximately one hundred thousand civilian casualties were the result of artillery fire, and it is difficult not to conclude that the very low American casualty rate was obtained at the expense of the very high civilian one.

The deadliness of the Return was eclipsed for the Allied world at large by the glamour of the idea of poor Filipinos being delivered from the sons of Nippon. The destruction of Manila was lost in the momentum of a myth that had assumed unstoppable proportions even before the liberation hit the city. Thereafter the mythology of the Return rolled on, and the attendant destruction faded away.

Figure 1.2.   American serviceman with field glasses observes the burning city from across Manila Bay, 1945 (William H. Robinson, courtesy of the Australian War Memorial, negative no. P00279.046)

In the library of the Australian War Memorial in Canberra is a photograph, dated February 1945, of a US soldier half sitting, half leaning on a sea wall at the edge of Manila Bay. He is looking through a pair of field glasses across the bay to where, in the distance, an immense plume of smoke rises. He appears to be observing the bombardment of the city. The picture is clearly about distance: the luxury of distance, the closing of distance effected by field glasses, the reduction of space by modern artillery that enables destruction from a safe distance. When I read the daily press coverage of the Pacific War for February 1945 in the *New York Times*, I felt I could understand how distance also affected reporting of the war's impact on civilians. The correspondents were always, obviously, behind the artillery barrage and would not have witnessed its immediate effects. By the time they had the opportunity to move freely around Intramuros and nearby areas and bring the destruction to the attention of the public back home, the center of attention had moved to the assault on Corregidor and then to the battle for Iwo Jima. So the war moved on. Also, though, it seems to have been a matter of policy either not to gather or not to release figures for civilian casualties. Consistently, the press gave casualty figures for Japanese and American soldiers but not for civilians.

One of the last scenes in the drama of the Return was the trip MacArthur made in March 1945 from Manila to Corregidor for a flag-raising ceremony with the troops who had retaken the island fortress from the Japanese. His party traveled in four PT boats, the same number used when he had fled the island in the same month three years before. It was almost as if he were reversing the film, effecting a restoration of things back to the way they had been and, in the process, erasing the loss of face he had suffered when the Japanese invaded and relieved him of the islands he was charged with defending. In his *Reminiscences* MacArthur devoted a page of text to his return visit to Corregidor and was similarly expansive about the visit he made to the ruins of his former penthouse apartment on top of the Manila Hotel and about the emotional scenes that greeted him at the internment and prisoner-of-war camps.[17] But he had nothing at all to say about the bombardment of Manila and the destruction of Intramuros, and he made no mention of the civilian casualties. He had publicly distanced himself from that side of things. Filipinos, for their part, had no choice but to deal with what had happened to Manila and they did so in very different ways. Carlos Romulo blamed it all on the Japanese whom he saw as engaging in a kind of religious war.

> To me, perhaps Manila was more terrible because it was my city that lay black and gutted and reeking, mile on mile, where once had been beauty and modernity and progress, a mingling of the romantic past with the future that was a delight to all who knew Manila.

These were my neighbours and my friends whose tortured bodies I saw pushed into heaps on the Manila streets, their heads shaved, their hands tied behind their backs, and bayonet stabs running them through and through. This girl who looked up at me wordlessly, her breasts crisscrossed with bayonet strokes, had been in school with *my* son.

Beginning with the first week in February, the Japanese Army in retreat had participated in three weeks of unprecedented sadism.

In those twenty-one days they had succeeded, under imperial orders, in blotting out the greatest Christian city in the Orient and wiping out the symbols of Christianity in the Philippines. Only the broken walls of our beautiful, centuries-old churches were left standing in the rubble that had been Manila. . . .

Now in retreat, this February, they tried to wipe out all Christian evidence in our land, for it was this they hated most in the Filipino race. To them our faith was the mark of our trust in the white race to whom we were united in religion and ideology.

To the Japanese Christianity and democracy were twin evils and the Filipinos in Manila paid for holding to both beliefs.[18]

Absent from Romulo's account is any mention of the fact that many or most of those in the class to which he belonged had collaborated with the Japanese. Absent also is any acknowledgment of the toll taken on civilians and churches by MacArthur's bombardment. The "handsome" US Army with which Romulo identified so closely was seen differently through the eyes of the writer Carmen Nakpil:

I spat on the very first American soldier I saw that unspeakable day in February 1945. A few seconds before, he had shouted at me from behind a tree in the Malate street—"Hey you wanna get yourself killed?"

I crossed over from the middle of the street where I had been walking and saw that his features were flushed with fright as he hunched behind a tree, rifle and steel helmet, dusty uniform and large wooden rosary beads which he wore like an amulet round his neck. Damn you: I thought. There's nobody here but us Filipino civilians, and you did your best to kill us.

I spat, but I was dry throated and he was not aware of my scorn. I had not eaten or slept for more than a week. My husband had been tortured by Japanese soldiers in my presence, and then led out to be shot. Our home had been ransacked, put to the torch, its ruins shelled again and again. I had seen the head of the aunt who had taught me to read and write roll under the kitchen stove. . . .

I had seen all the unforgettable, indescribable carnage caused by the detonation of bombs and land mines on the barricaded streets of Ermita and the carpet-shelling by the Americans which went relentlessly on, long after the last Japanese sniper was a carcass on the rubble. I had nothing in all the world except the dress on my back, an unborn child in my belly and in my arms, a little daughter, burning and whimpering with the fever of starvation. . . .

So this was Liberation. I was no longer sure what was worse, the inhumanity of the Japanese or the helpfulness of the Americans. It had turned out to be a macabre sort of friendship.[19]

Nakpil's account is not anti-American, to my mind. Rather, it expresses a common civilian wartime predicament: The distinction between being killed or wounded up close and in a spirit of anger or hatred by the Japanese was not so different from being killed or wounded from a distance, unintentionally (collaterally, as we now say), by the Americans.

In the months after "Liberation," as MacArthur was overseeing the reinstatement of the prewar government prior to his departure for Tokyo, homeless people began to reinhabit the ruins of Intramuros. Some of them may have lived there previously, some gravitated there from other destroyed parts of the city or drifted in from a poverty-stricken countryside looking to try their luck in Manila. They erected shanties out of salvaged bricks and broken beams, sheets of roofing iron and odd blocks of stone: architecture without architects, the genius of necessity. In clearings amid the rubble, in the shadow of the partly destroyed walls, and even in holes gouged out by shellfire in the very body of the walls themselves, the squatters of Intramuros became a familiar aspect of the postwar scene in Manila.

There are accounts that tell of former residents begging the US Army Corps of Engineers in March 1945 not to pull down what remained of their Intramuros houses. They wanted to stay and rebuild, but the bulldozers continued their work. As the Intramuros shanties sprouted out of the ashes, there arose elsewhere, on the edge of town, new elite suburbs like Makati and Forbes Park. A conservation architect I spoke to said he could remember quite substantial portions of some of the Intramuros churches still standing when he was a boy in the late 1950s. But when they began to build Makati these ruins were literally mined for old stone. Now, he said, you could find the fine old granite of Intramuros on the bathroom and living room floors of those suburban mansions.

In a country like the Philippines where the affluent few are proportionately so very few, enclaves like Makati stand not just for luxury, cleanliness, and modernity; they stand for security. This was especially so in the late fifties and early sixties when lawlessness was increasing in Manila and when Intramuros, that former island of Spanish privilege, turned into a slum and a place to be avoided at night. The great walls that had once kept out the rest of the city now served to shield the rest of the city from the sight of the squalor within. What was within was considered by the elite to be a pool of disease and crime; it was "a haven for the underworld" and "a dangerous place to tread."[20]

The elite of Manila looked askance at what had happened to Intramuros, but if they had vacated the place they certainly hadn't relinquished it: Intramuros was simply in extended purgatory awaiting restoration. The waiting lasted through the 1950s. Fort Santiago was declared a Shrine of Freedom in 1950 in honor of the nationalist hero, José Rizal, and of those people tortured and killed in the dungeons there by the Japanese, but it wasn't until 1961 that a program to restore the fort was inaugurated. Five years later Ferdinand Marcos, in his second year of office, established a restoration committee to oversee the reconstruction and maintenance of the walls, gates, and bastions of Intramuros and its surviving "historical edifices."[21] Gradually there developed the idea of a restoration program that would re-create the Walled City as it had been under the Spanish. To achieve this they began moving out the riffraff: Four thousand squatter families were trucked to small settlements forty kilometers north of the city in 1963. The slate was being cleaned.

The restorationists and administrators were installed somewhat to their own embarrassment in a newly built office tower in the heart of Intramuros, on the site of what had been the Spanish governor's palace. The building was the very sort of structure they considered unsympathetic to historic Intramuros, but in it they enjoyed excellent working conditions on the spacious, well-lit, air-conditioned floors they occupied. It was the sort of place you could stay clean in a white shirt, the sort of place that made you feel purposeful and efficient the moment you walked through the glass doors. In the National Museum, by contrast, based in the run-down 1930s Executive Building, where rainwater came in through broken windows during storms and ran down the stairs, my hands were always grimy and sticky from a combination of sweat and the dust that had settled on the old files I was reading. The building's plumbing had failed, and there was nowhere to wash. I could live with the irritation of this, but I enjoyed the few days I spent in the office of the restorationists, asking questions and looking through the archive of pictures that showed Intramuros at various times in its history. My hands didn't stick to the pages of my notebook, but I felt a twinge of disloyalty to my friends sweltering away over in the archaeology department at the museum. The archaeologists resented the disparity between the funding poured into the restoration of Intramuros and the trickle of money they were given to protect and manage the thousands of pre-Hispanic archaeological sites spread across the archipelago. These sites continued to be looted of their ceramics and other artifacts, objects that eventually found their way into the living rooms of the elite (paved, some of them, with Intramuros's granite) and the murky space of the international antiquities market.[22]

The afternoon that I finished with the picture archive in the offices of the Intramuros Administration, I took the elevator down into the pungent reality of the street below and set off walking back to my guesthouse on the other side of the Luneta. Still familiarizing myself with the streets of Intramuros, I followed a meandering course that took me past a restored section of the main wall and then past vacant lots where cars and trucks were being repaired. What littered the ground here were not old potsherds, nineteenth-century roof tiles, broken stone flagging, or anything else that might have suggested colonial Spain, but old tires and rusting springs, engine blocks and chassis. Through the open door of a wooden shack I saw a small girl asleep on a seat taken from an old car and above her, pasted onto the bare wood, were colored pictures cut from magazines. Film stars and volcanoes. I entered a street that had a row of shops and houses that would have been built, I thought, in the 1950s. Weeds grew from ledges on the facades; shirts and a child's Superman suit, complete with cape, were hung out to dry on a balcony. The building was the color of the light-brown concrete blocks it was constructed of, but one of the house fronts on the ground floor was painted pastel yellow, and it had a light blue picket fence outside it, a pink-and-white-striped plastic awning above its doorway, and two plants growing in pink pots on either side of the gate. It stood out like a Samoan postage stamp on a coarse brown envelope. Taped to the inside of the single window was a poster of a singer, a young man with light brown skin and black spiked hair, wearing a faded denim jacket. The hand he held out in front of him looked like it was about to snap its fingers. I'd stopped walking in order to take in this scene, and as I was standing there, savoring it, a youth came out of the door of the colorful house and behind him, her hand on his shoulder, a woman in an apron. She was saying something to him, and he was looking down at the pavement, silently nodding his head. He walked off up the street, and she was about to turn back inside when she saw me looking from the other side of the street. She seemed puzzled for a moment, screwing up her eyes, but then laughed pleasantly. I guess she decided I was just some species of tourist. I moved off, thinking about how nice all this was: uncontrived, not a hint of the mock Spanish about it. Then I thought of the events of 1945, the fire-gutted houses and the people who might have been inside them when the shells hit. Sons and mothers, for instance.

The last thing that caught my attention as I passed out of Intramuros was a black-and-white sign: "You are within a Historical Zone. Vehicular gates and pedestrian gates are open 5.00am to 10.30pm." It was part of the restorationists' effort to stop container trucks and the families of their drivers from using the Walled City as a camping ground, conveniently handy to the docks. Squatters, those opportunists who would insert themselves and their squalor into any available opening, were now thought to number about 2.5 million people in Manila, or about one-third of the city's population. They were not enemies of heritages; it was just that heritage wasn't a priority for them. If they weren't kind to the ruins, perhaps it was because they were too close to ruin themselves, poverty being a form of ruin without the romance.

The National Library building stood on the opposite side of the Luneta to Intramuros. It had the light, optimistic lines of the 1960s, but it had a serious ventilation problem—it was as if it had been designed to be air-conditioned but then, at the last minute, the builders had left the air-conditioning out. On a steamy Saturday morning midway through my time in Manila I went there to work but only lasted an hour or so in the stifling reading room, battling drowsiness, before I shuffled my notes together and left.

The sky had clouded over and a light rain had begun to fall, only to evaporate instantly on the pavement. I bought a drink at a kiosk in the park and then walked along to where a relief model of the Philippines had been constructed in a large shallow blue pool. It was one of Imelda Marcos's more successful ventures in the field of public art and was a personal favorite of mine.[23] I had a weakness for that sort of thing: the fake rocks and boulders of cement grottoes, the blue and white ferro-cement ice caves and cliffs of the polar bear enclosures at the better class of zoo. Imelda's toy archipelago seemed a more innocent, less sinister form of duplicity than that going on in Intramuros. The rain began to fall more heavily. Streams began to flow down the green painted valleys of Luzon's Cordillera, and the miniature islands of Mindoro and Palawan stretched away through the rain-ringed waters of the pool, pointing the way beyond the park to the bars of Ermita.

With my notes dry inside their plastic wallet, there seemed no reason not to get wet. The rain trickled down my face, and the wet shirt felt pleasantly cool where it clung to my skin. Making my way slowly back to the guesthouse, I had gotten as far as the Midtown Hotel when I heard the sound of running feet approaching rapidly from behind. I spun around warily, the way one does, preparing for God knows what, and found myself face to face with Aniceto. I'd met Aniceto during my first week in the city and had gone with him to a beach on Mindoro one weekend shortly afterward. Some years previously his family had been relocated from an inner-city squatter's enclave to a distant shantytown in order to make way for one of Imelda's urban redevelopment projects. He came into the city by bus every couple of days to earn a bit of money here and there; he worked as a waiter and occasionally as a kitchen hand. On the boat over to Mindoro, as we stood at the rail looking at the sea, he told me true stories about mermaids in the Philippines, how they were occasionally caught in fishermen's nets and exhibited at fairgrounds.

That evening on Mindoro, as we were drinking Tanduay rum and enjoying the sound of the waves on the nearby beach, he'd enchanted me with stories from his childhood on the island of Negros. He vividly re-created the family house, built on poles out over the water, and of waking in the mornings to jump out the window straight into the sea. We agreed that I'd retain his services, at a very reasonable fee, as a guide through the madness of Manila's public transport system, but it didn't work out. I could never depend on him to turn up at the right hour or even on the right day.

Now he stood there panting and grinning, hair plastered over his forehead by the rain. I asked him where he'd come from, impressed by his ability to just materialize like that. In the back of my mind stirred the thought that there existed another version of this street, one which was closed to me but which Aniceto walked in and out of at will. The world of local knowledge.

I asked him where he'd come from.

"Up there," he said, gesturing vaguely with his thumb toward an old gray block of apartments that stood behind some dripping broad-leaved trees. "I was visiting my friend and we were standing out on the balcony when I saw you walking past without an umbrella." He said I looked really wet, like a drowned rat.

"Well, yes," I replied absently, looking up at the balconies of the apartment block, looking for a way into Aniceto's version of Manila but seeing only wet concrete and dusty pot plants.

"No," he insisted. "You hardly ever see wet foreigners. They are always in cars or they have umbrellas. They don't get wet." It was as if the white race, in addition to its other advantages, was innately shower-proof.

"You should have been an anthropologist," I said, meaning it.

"Thanks," he replied seriously. "There is still time."

I invited him to come with me to Intramuros, to visit Fort Santiago, after I'd been home to get changed, and an hour or so later we were sitting in the back of a jeepney, the sun now shining fiercely as we edged our way through the heavy traffic along Taft Avenue.

Fort Santiago occupied a wedge of land in that northeastern corner of Intramuros that projected out into the mouth of the Pasig River. Arriving outside the fort's monumental gateway, built by the Spanish in 1741, we paused to admire its stonework and the large wooden relief carving of St. James on horseback that was set into a space above the arch. The gateway had been badly damaged in 1945 when American tanks had blasted their way through it. A plaque informed us that what we were now looking at was the restored version of the gateway, circa 1982. "We are good at fixing things, no?" Aniceto offered, as if some expert comment might be expected from him, but he then took the opportunity to tell me he had never been to Fort Santiago before.

Beyond the gate was a large lawned space that tapered toward the river and was crossed by pathways bordered with low clipped hedges. The only really substantial structure was an old-looking white building of two stories, which housed a museum dedicated to José Rizal. There, in what was now known as the Rizal Shrine, he had been held prisoner by the Spanish for nearly two months before being taken out to be executed by firing squad in Bagumbayan Field, now the Luneta, on 30 December 1896. We stood at the entrance to the cell on the ground floor where Rizal had secretly penned his farewell note to the Philippines, *Me Ultimo Adios*. Like the tens of thousands of schoolchildren and family groups who filed through every year, we cast our eyes over the simple wooden desk in the middle of the small windowless room.

Upstairs was a large gallery housing Rizal memorabilia. Moments of his life were caught in dark oil paintings that lined the walls. He was a fifth-generation Chinese mestizo from a wealthy family. The paintings showed a refined, intelligent young man. We peered into a cabinet containing books owned by his family, one of them open at an engraving of the Spanish Inquisition, showing a man hanging from a ceiling by his hands. A glass case contained some of Rizal's clothes: a white shirt trimmed with fragile lace, a pair of his black pants, a pair of white silk stockings. I was astonished at how small the clothes were, almost like those of a child, and pointed this out to Aniceto in the sort of hushed voice that everyone else in the room was communicating in.

"We *are* small," he murmured back.

As we were going back downstairs Aniceto remarked on how well preserved the building was. He hadn't realized that the present structure was a reconstruction, and I hesitated to tell him this, thinking it might spoil his experience in some way. But not to tell him, I thought, would be cheating him in another way, so I told him the fort had been an absolute ruin by the time the Americans captured it from the Japanese in 1945 and had then been a US Army depot for a while. When the army left, the squatters moved in. It wasn't until the early fifties that some members of the Lions Club visited the place and discovered that the ruins of the building where Rizal, the national hero, had been imprisoned were being used as a toilet.[24] Aniceto was suitably horrified.

At that point in the 1950s all that was left of Fort Santiago were some semicollapsed walls with grass and weeds growing inside them. The Lions Club described the situation as "disgraceful" and persuaded the government to move the squatters out and provide the money to rebuild.

Near the exit there was a big painting of the moment prior to Rizal's execution. Rizal looked out at us from the canvas, his back turned to the line of soldiers. I thought, momentarily, of the clothes upstairs and this small man's body torn by the fusillade of nineteenth-century bullets. Back outside we walked around the compound of the fort for a while before climbing up onto the rampart from where there was a clear view over toward the docks on the edge of Manila Bay. Below us two golfers in Panama hats were walking along the grassed bottom of the broad moat, their heads inclined in conversation, each holding a club and swinging it slowly and decoratively.

I mentioned to Aniceto that there were plans to fill the moat with water again, and we had a chuckle over that, neither of us being what you'd call sportsmen. The golfers were passing directly below. He wanted to know why they were refilling the moat, and I explained that the golf course compromised the heritage values of the moat. It was what people called an unsympathetic use.

He repeated the word "unsympathetic" a few times as we watched one of the golfers shaping up to take his putt. He seemed intrigued that you could speak that way about a building or a moat, and his amusement led me to question the word myself. It implied a way of behaving in which certain delicacies were observed in relation to buildings and places. In the world Aniceto came from perhaps these were delicacies people wouldn't have been able to afford or that they would find amusing even if they were able to afford them.

As we were leaving the fort, Aniceto queried me again about the squatters who'd been living there after the war, but there was nothing more I could tell him. He said he didn't think José Rizal would have objected to them. The place had been his prison, after all. He might have been pleased it was destroyed and that Filipinos later came to shit there.

The previous weekend I'd visited Santa Ana Church and afterward had strolled down a narrow back street where, in the very shadow of the church's back wall, I'd come upon an open-air workshop where plaster statues were being mended. Several were standing together with arms and legs missing, most of them more or less life-sized. They were all of José Rizal. The man working on them told me all the schools had statues of Rizal, and when they were broken they brought them to him. There was a sense, I thought, in which the cult of Rizal had been used to promote a commonality between different social classes, an illusion of common history and common experience to paper over such matters as the upper class's collaboration with the Japanese during the war while ordinary people starved. There was a sense in which heritage conservation stood for amnesia. As when in 1961 President Carlos Garcia made a speech in Fort Santiago to launch the restoration program and said, "[T]hese mute stones shall always be eloquent witnesses that while there has been tyranny in this country, we as a people have never bent our knees before the tyrants."[25] He'd told his audience the place was being restored so that it could be "a shrine to which our people may repair in times of national stress, to draw the inspiration and moral strength needed in solving the serious problems of the nation." In other words, if you were one of the poor whom national independence had only made poorer, don't go to the mountains and join the NPA (New People's Army) guerrillas, go instead to Intramuros and reflect upon your national heritage.[26]

We walked in a circuit that took us past Letran College where boys in white shirts and ties, children of the middle class, looked down into the street from the upstairs windows. You could almost smell the chalk dust and the dog-eared textbooks. No sign of 1945 there: The pockmarked walls had been replastered, the windows had been reglazed. Outside the seventeenth-century church of St. Augustin, one of the only buildings spared by the shelling (miraculously, so it was said), a wedding party had just arrived. The bride stepped gingerly out of a cream-colored Mercedes-Benz and stood like a dried floral arrangement on the old stone flagging while her attendants adjusted the folds of her veil and train. There were video cameras, well-dressed children running about, and a priest talking to a couple of fair-skinned altar boys in the shade of the doorway. I suggested we go in for a few minutes but Aniceto declined, implying that I should know better.

"Look at the way I am dressed," he said. He was dressed the way he was usually dressed, in the best clothes that he had.

Instead, we followed a lane behind the church down toward the bayside wall, quite close to where on my first visit to Intramuros I'd climbed the stone ramp and walked out along the bastion wall. Something I hadn't known at that time and was still unaware of on this visit with Aniceto was that it was upon this structure, the Bastion de San José, that MacArthur's prewar office in Manila (1935–1941) had been located. Known as the House on the Wall, it had windows on all sides and looked a little like a control tower at a mid-twentieth-century airport. In a room furnished with flag standards and a Chinese screen, MacArthur had sat behind a large Chippendale desk, where he struck visitors as immaculate and surprisingly fresh-looking despite the heat (he maintained a wardrobe of thirty-five uniforms and changed three times a day).[27]

Up in his office, MacArthur dominated Spanish Intramuros. The defense of the Philippines against the Japanese was planned there, and during the tense weeks of December 1941, following Pearl Harbor and the destruction of his air force at Clark Field, MacArthur continued to work in the office as Japanese Mitsubishi Zeros flew freely overhead. The humiliation must have been difficult to bear. He ostentatiously insisted the Stars and Stripes continue to be flown over the office, disregarding warnings that this made it an obvious target.

So there we stood, Aniceto and I, at that time of the afternoon when the air was so still, looking across at the House on the Wall but not seeing it. Aniceto had his hands in the back pockets of his jeans and his feet well apart; squinting in the sunlight, he looked both sensitive and tough. He looked composed. In his way, he was every bit as immaculate as the general. I suppose he had other things to think about. For my part, I probably looked a little perplexed and tired. My research project seemed to be going nowhere, and I wasn't sleeping well. It was stiflingly hot, and for the moment we'd run out of things to say to each other. We looked across at the absent office as if it had never existed, as if certain decisions hadn't been made there in 1941, and as if our lives were untouched by them. As if the chain of events that ended by producing the state of ruin around our feet had not begun up on that wall. Unaware of any of this, we turned around and walked off to find somewhere to eat.

On the side of the river opposite Intramuros sprawls Binondo, Manila's Chinatown, the congested heart of the old commercial district where dim sum vendors and noodle bars rub shoulders with cinemas and Catholic churches. Attached to the side of a building near the Binondo end of the MacArthur Bridge at the time I was in Manila stood a giant hand-painted billboard of Bruce Lee, "The Legend," in cutout style. Naked to the waist and a few shades browner than he might have been on the equivalent poster in Hong Kong, he surveyed the streets of Binondo with his disciplined gaze, his pumped-up preparedness contrasting with the disorder in the streets below.

In 1945 this district had been badly damaged by demolition charges set by the retreating Japanese and by the ensuing fires. But even while the American shelling of the south side of the river was still in progress, the Binondo area came to life in a frenzy of haphazard Liberation commerce. Manuel Buenafe, in *Wartime Philippines*, describes how, as southbound shells whispered and roared overhead, people set up tables on the footpaths selling fountain pens, wooden shoes, cigarettes, and shellfish. Barbershops and shoeshine boys appeared.

> And there were cafes—the Victory, the American, the Mabuhay, Uncle Sam's, Sloppy Joe's, all hole-in-the-wall places selling coffee at 15 centavos (20 with sugar), egg sandwiches at a peso-fifty, and liquor at a peso a shot. While GIs surged through their doors, the owners hammered and pounded and sawed enlarging their establishments.[28]

Life has a way of going on. It went on again, too, in Intramuros when the tanks moved out and the squatters moved in. But whereas in Binondo people opportunistically hammered and sawed their way to a new future, in

Figure 1.3.   American Jeeps enter the city across a pontoon bridge as refugees leave, Manila, 1945 (William H. Robinson, courtesy of the Australian War Memorial, negative no. P00279.058)

Intramuros this was only permitted to happen until the authorities had marshaled their resources to stop it. And when they did stop it, they did so in the interests of restoring the place to its colonial Spanishness.[29] In addition to the lean-to huts of the squatters, a whole raft of other urban facilities and activities were outlawed as unsympathetic. They included gasoline stations, bus terminals, mortuaries, lumberyards, junkyards, cock pits, racetracks, massage and sauna parlors, burlesque theaters, jukeboxes, overly loud transistor radios and fun machines, bullrings, and neon signs.[30] Not just a class of people but a part of the city's ordinary life was to be declared inappropriate and sanctioned against. It went without saying that Aniceto and most of the things he might have cared to do would have no place in this environment of rarefied, historical wholesomeness.

This litany of exclusion apparently included an embargo on any mention of the one hundred thousand dead civilians. MacArthur's Return would be commemorated not where it ended, in the smoking ruins of Intramuros, but at the site of its finest moment, on the beach at Leyte. A larger-than-life sculpture of the general's unscheduled wading now stands in a pool at Red

Beach. An almost perfect realization in bronze of the photographic image of the event, the formation of metal men in uniform now wades forever toward the shore. Also in Leyte, in 1974, Imelda Marcos spent several million dollars constructing what purported to be her ancestral home as a venue for a party celebrating the thirtieth anniversary of MacArthur's landing.[31] One drama queen, you might say, deserves another.

"Stratigraphic inversion" refers to the reversal of a standard archaeological rule of thumb. Usually, the lower a layer is in the stratigraphic sequence, the older it is, but in cases of stratigaphic inversion, that order is reversed. This can happen when, for instance, the later occupants of a site have dug a pit down through the deposit, discarding the archaeologically older "spoil" from the pit over the younger surrounding ground surface. Over subsequent time more deposit builds up on the site, sealing this inversion into the sequence where it will bide its time, waiting to test the interpretive skill of some future archaeologist.

In the restoration of Intramuros the veneer of a mock-Spanish heritage townscape was being laid down over the place, effectively burying the traces of more recent phases of the site's history that comprised the American colonial period, the Japanese occupation, the American liberation, and also the eyesore phase of postwar squatter occupation. While archaeologists puzzle out the stratigraphic inversions perpetrated in the past, we heritage practitioners, their colleagues, perpetrate other stratigraphic inversions in the present.[32]

I was sitting at a café in Bali one morning in 1994 reading the *International Herald Tribune* when I came upon a mention that, on that day fifty years previously, American carrier-based planes had destroyed Japanese airfields in the vicinity of New Guinea. I guessed this meant that, leading up to the fiftieth anniversary of the landing at Leyte, there would now be a succession of newspaper stories and references recapitulating MacArthur's progress through the southwest Pacific on his way back to the Philippines. I looked across the empty beach to where the waves were breaking. Three thousand kilometers away to the east of Bali, MacArthur was on the move again, island by island, battle by battle. It almost made me nervous.

A few weeks later, while looking at some photocopied photographs of war damage in Manila, I came upon a picture of one of the 1930s neoclassical administration buildings that looked strangely familiar. The front portion of this four-story building, with its row of columns and its sculpted pediment, had evidently been so heavily shelled that most of it had collapsed into a hill slope of rubble. It looked like the Legislative Building, now the National Museum. But it couldn't have been, I told myself, as I knelt on the plywood floor of the bungalow holding the picture up to the light. I had been based at the museum during my time in Manila, had sat in its rooms and walked its corridors confident in the belief that I was in a prewar building. Which, of course, I had been. It was just that the building had been largely destroyed in the war and had subsequently been rebuilt. It was just that nobody there had thought it worth telling me this. I spent a confused half-hour carefully comparing the 1945 photo with recent photos of the building before finally accepting the truth of this. The room where I'd spent weeks working on the dusty old files simply didn't exist in the 1945 picture. It had disintegrated and fallen into the tangled mass of rubble and twisted steel reinforcing. My confusion was gradually replaced by an odd sense of lightness.

NOTES

1. De la Costa 1975.
2. Wright 1990.
3. See the *Fourth Annual Report of the Philippine Commission* (Washington, DC: Government Printing Office, 1903), 88.
4. James 1975, 644.
5. Schaller 1989, 97.
6. The photographs of Carl Mydans I have looked at are in *Carl Mydans, Photo-journalist* (New York: Harry N. Abrams, 1985).
7. The term "little brown brothers" was coined by William Howard Taft, the first American governor general of the Philippines.
8. Manchester 1978, 271.
9. Ibid., 271.
10. Ibid., 272.
11. Ibid., 409.
12. Virilio 1986, 10, 67–68.
13. "Western man has appeared superior and dominant, despite inferior demographics, because he appeared *more rapid*" (Virilio 1986, 47).
14. Petillo 1981, 223.
15. Rogers 1991, 263.
16. Ibid., 263.
17. MacArthur 1964.
18. Romulo 1946, 223–24.
19. Nakpil 1967.
20. Juanico 1983, 115. See also editorial, *Evening Express*, 17 June 1980.
21. Lucero 1975.
22. Byrne 1999.
23. As the wife of Ferdinand Marcos, Imelda was first lady of the Philippines from 1965 to 1986, during which time she oversaw the construction of a number of major public buildings, including the Cultural Center of the Philippines.

24. Da Silva 1961.

25. Ibid., 224–25.

26. See Da Silva (1961) for a review of the postwar restoration work in Fort Santiago.

27. Manchester 1978, 165. Imelda Marcos was also known to have multiple copies of the same outfit and maintained a mysterious freshness in the hot, humid climate by quick behind-the-scenes changes from one to another (Bonner 1987, 159).

28. Buenafe 1950, 256.

29. Because of the adoption of Catholicism by the majority of Filipinos and the growth of a large Spanish mestizo population, the architectural and other manifestations of colonial Spanish heritage have been absorbed into the national heritage far more readily than has been the case, for instance, of French colonial traces in Vietnam or Dutch traces in Indonesia.

30. *Rules and Regulations Governing the Development of Intramuros* (Manila: Intramuros Administration, 1981), sections 3 and 7.

31. Bonner 1987, 159.

32. See Byrne (2003) for a discussion of how a poorly studied postcontact (post-1788) Aboriginal heritage in Australia has been discursively buried below a precontact "classic" Aboriginal heritage that is less threatening to settler society and has attracted a great deal more archaeological interest.

Rice Growing and Heritage

$\mathcal{I}$n 1887 a steamer left Manila with forty-four representatives of various of the Philippines' ethnic "tribal" minorities on board, their destination the Madrid Exposition. The eight Igorots in this party, three of them battle-scarred and tattooed chiefs from Bontoc, had traveled from their homes in the valleys of the Luzon Cordillera. Arriving at the exposition site they built and then inhabited a model village, the Ranchería de los Igorrotes. Whether or not they felt at home in this simulacrum, it was a display that infuriated the young nationalist, José Rizal, who happened to be in Europe at the time. "I have worked hard," he wrote, "against this degradation of my fellow Filipinos that they should not be exhibited among the animals and plants!"[1] Fellow nationalist Antonio Luna, who was also in Spain at the time, complained that "on the streets of Madrid passing young ladies would turn around to stare and murmur audibly, "Jesus, how horrible . . . an 'Igorot!'"[2]

But it was precisely the horrible that the Igorots were intended to represent to the people of Madrid. It was for this they had been brought so far from their mountain homes. Had a drawing room full of urbane young mestizos from Manila been installed at the exposition, the metropolitan audience wouldn't have been impressed at all. The public wanted to see the real thing, the primitive Other. And Rizal could not have been more right to worry about the plants and animals: That the Igorots were exhibited in the way they were both reflected and reinforced the view that they belonged to the natural as distinct from the civil order. The Igorots were known, classified, and collected within the same European episteme as the world's plants and animals.[3]

These great nineteenth-century expositions were an occasion for the metropolitan population to savor the sense of being at the center to which all roads led, of being at the pinnacle to which history had climbed. The technology and logistics required to get the Igorots down from the mountains and over to Madrid was itself eloquent of Europe's progress (the Romans, of course, had done this sort of thing, but not over such vast distances). And the real excitement at these expositions, the star acts that left people gasping, were the new machines and the products of these machines. As industrialization progressed through the nineteenth century, Westerners came to see technology, more than anything else, as the measure of their civilization's superiority.[4] It put them, quite simply, in a different class from the rest of the world.

But what better way to emphasize industrial advancement than to juxtapose industrial products with the handmade artifacts of the nonindustrialized world? Displayed at world expositions, those "venues . . . that reduced cultures to their objects," in proximity to the machines and gadgetry of the industrialized nations, the Igorots with their spears and their grass huts spoke of the inevitability of the West's global dominance.[5]

Seven years later it was another steamer, another venue, another imperial power. Forty Igorots from Bontoc were among the contingent of 215 representatives from the Philippine non-Christian minority groups who traveled as exhibits to the 1904 St. Louis Exposition, accompanied by a collection of eighteen thousand ethnographic artifacts. They built and occupied one of a total of six villages set among the rolling hills of the forty-seven-acre lot that housed the Philippine exhibit.[6] This seems a generous allocation of space and indicates the sheer size of the St. Louis event. But for the different "tribal" contingents at St. Louis who, when they weren't giving displays of dancing and the making of handicrafts, were expected to live "just as they did at home," it might have seemed as though they were inhabiting a strangely collapsed archipelago.[7]

Otley Beyer, who would become the grandfather of archaeology in the Philippines, had seen the St. Louis Exposition the year before he left for Manila, and shortly after arriving in the islands he found himself in the Cordillera collecting ethnographic artifacts. William Scott was not born in time to see the exposition, but when he was a small boy he played with spears in "Cousin Stille's attic," spears his mother later told him had been made by the Igorots she had seen in 1905. A village of them had been set up in that year in a park in Bethlehem, Pennsylvania, where she lived. "They wore their native G-strings and lived in their own little houses, and you could watch them do their work and buy the things they made. That's where those spears came from."[8] In the period after the Second World War, Scott became a missionary in the Cordillera and soon began writing books on its history.

The near-naked Igorots had been such a hit in St. Louis that it became "a profitable business to gather groups of these people for exhibition in other places," including London and, apparently, Bethlehem, Pennsylvania.[9] Then in 1914 the American colonial administration in Manila set a fine of 10,000 pesos or five years in jail for anyone caught "taking tribal peoples out of the country for purposes of exploitation or exhibition."[10]

One begins to think of colonialism and its aftermath in terms of traffic, of the Spanish and the Americans crossing the oceans to reach these islands

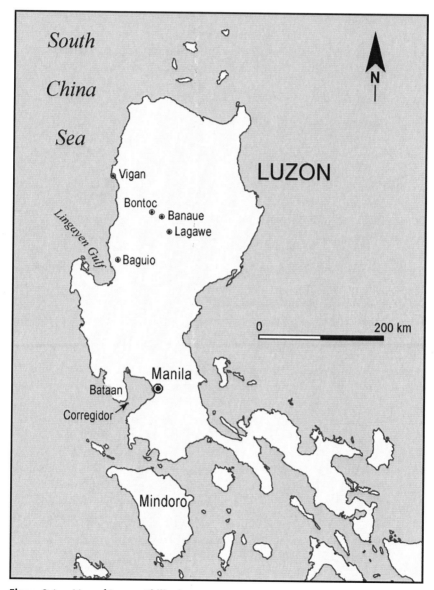

Figure 2.1.   Map of Luzon, Philippines

and then finding ways to transport themselves up into the most remote of their valleys, then shipping parties of the people they find there back home to the West, where in various ways, directly and indirectly, they touch the lives and imaginations of people there, like the young Americans who are themselves soon on the road to the mountains of Luzon. The traffic in people-as-exhibits finally ceases to flow, but this only marks the turning of a tide: Soon a reverse flow of well-heeled early twentieth-century adventurers begins arriving in Luzon to see the mountain people in their own habitat. Not much has changed, really. The crowds who had flocked to see the peoples of the Cordillera in Madrid, St. Louis, Bethlehem, and at other stops on their travels through the West now take to the road themselves as backpackers or adventure tourists.

This review of the traffic that has moved up and down the Luzon Cordillera over the past few centuries provides a genealogy into which I can place myself. One morning in 1989 I found myself riding in an old bus driving out of Bontoc, a town in the central Cordillera that was hardly bigger than a village. From Bontoc the bus climbed through the thick mist up the winding road toward the village of Banaue. About halfway into its slow ascent the bus stopped, still in the clouds, and let on two youths who were carrying baskets and sickles and who, I thought, must be on their way to work in some distant rice field. They stood in the front stairwell near the driver, their faces and hair beaded with mist and their eyes darting around the bus's interior. Most of the passengers were also local people and many of them, I guessed, were farmers. The two new passengers wore old denim jackets and jeans that were torn virtually to shreds. Initially I'd thought this must be the result of some incredibly arduous labor they were engaged in, but then on closer and more careful consideration I decided that most of the rents and tears had been deliberately contrived. That was interesting. It wasn't something you'd have expected up there in the Cordillera of Luzon, three hundred kilometers and a sixteen-hour bus ride north of Manila.

We passed in and out of the clouds. At one point I saw a village on a hillside about a kilometer away, surrounded by rice terraces. The small wooden houses with their rusting red iron roofs and the crops in the terraced fields were lit by brilliant rays of sunlight streaming through a gap in the clouds. Watched by the people around me, I self-consciously took out my camera, slid back the window, and took a photo. I was acting like a tourist. I was a tourist. Then the bus swerved into another of the road's zigzag curves and the cloud closed in again.

In the seat next to me was an old man in shorts who held a gnarled walking stick. He was chain-smoking coarse mountain tobacco wrapped in leaves, surrounding us both in a cloud of smoke that was like a continuation of the cloud on the other side of the windows. The two in the torn clothing were now sitting on the top step of the stairwell. When I thought about the fascination we Westerners have had with the naked flesh of people like the Ifugao, I could almost be led to wonder whether they hadn't arranged these rents in their clothing specifically to tantalize us. The forebears of these two had made a big impression on the first colonial Americans in these parts. In the early American accounts they are described as going about in a near-naked state, meaning that apart from tattoos, earrings, armlets, shell-work girdles, strings of beads, and various other accessories, the men wore only G-strings. This was the term the writers used for the lengths of bright hand-woven cloth Ifugao men wore like a loincloth whose ends could be left to hang down at the front and back or could be wound around their hips when they were working in the spectacular rice terraces. The women wore a length of woven cloth wrapped around the lower waist. After lavish descriptions of the depravity of their customs and the squalor of their houses, the early twentieth-century writer's eye would come to rest admiringly upon their bodies, conceding that while they mightn't be all that clean, they were well-proportioned, muscular, and devastatingly fit. Albert Jenks, writing in 1905, believed "the perfection of muscular development of two-thirds of the men of Bontoc between the ages of 25 and 30 would be the envy of the average college athlete in the States."[11] A year later, in the pages of *National Geographic*, Dean Worcester wrote that "for their strong, muscular bodies they doubtless have to thank the pure air and water of the rugged country which they inhabit, no less than the tremendous exercise involved in going up and down its steep mountain sides."[12]

There was always an ambivalence, though, about the nakedness of the native: It was seen as entirely natural to their savage condition but scandalous at the same time. We urged them to cover themselves up, even to the extent of sending them our own cast-off clothes, but a part of us still longed for their nakedness. Under Western eyes, David Spurr tells us, "the body is that which is most proper to the primitive, the sign by which the primitive is represented. The body, rather than speech, law, or history, is the essential defining characteristic of primitive peoples. They live, according to this view, in their bodies and in natural space, but not in a body politic worthy of the name."[13]

The two youths in the stairwell were gathering up their things. One of them called to the driver who immediately slowed down to let them out. They jumped onto the wet road and vanished into the cloud, taking their baskets and sickles and their strangely torn clothing with them.

It was the famous rice terraces, not the celebrated bodies of their creators, that had drawn me to the Cordillera. I saw pictures of the terraces out of the corner of my eye a number of times as I walked the streets of Manila during my first week there. There were postcards of them for sale on the footpaths of Ermita, and they appeared on sun-bleached posters on the walls of travel offices. These were not the gentle rice terraces of the lowlands of Asia where each field is poised a few feet above or below its neighbor, where the fields themselves are large and, walking through them, you barely register the changing elevation. The pictures I saw in Manila showed plunging hillsides lined with hundreds of narrow terraces, each separated from the other by a dramatic drop down a steep embankment. The effect was extraordinary, almost to the point of being laughable. Several weeks later I came upon files of newspaper clippings and other material about the terraces in the office of the National Historical Commission and spent half an afternoon writing notes and copying verbatim the most colorful descriptive passages. The newspapers proclaimed the terraces to be the Eighth Wonder of the World, the Philippines' answer to Angkor Wat. And now there was a move afoot to have them put on the World Heritage List. I felt I had to see them.

The mist had cleared, and the sun was shining when the bus arrived at Banaue. It was warm by now, but the air was crisp and the oppressiveness of Manila seemed a world away. The village was made up of a strip of houses and small shops along either side of a steep narrow road running down the spur of a hill. There were rickety guesthouses with floral curtains and colorful signs with names like Half Way House (apparently indicating that it was halfway down the street), Green View Lodge, and Stairway Lodge. It wasn't easy to avoid the stairway metaphor with all these terraced hillsides around.

The place I chose was on the downhill side of the street. It had two floors above street level, each with three or four small rooms that smelled sweetly of untreated wood, and more floors below street level. Most of the rooms looked out from the back of the building across the valley to the terraced slopes opposite. Standing at the open window of my room, gazing at the panorama, I thought the rice terraces here were actually less than spectacular. They weren't quite up to the postcard terraces I'd seen in Manila, but then I cautioned myself not to expect the best of them to be on my doorstep. This train of thought, though, was just my rational self trying to impose itself on a situation in which the rest of me was fast dissolving into the beauty of the surroundings. The smell of sun-warmed rice fields wafted through the window along with the sound of insects, and I was conscious that all the woodwork in the room around me, and on the stairs I'd just climbed, had been crafted with hand tools. My fingers were moving unbidden across the surface of the windowsill, registering the tiny bumps and irregularities there, as if rediscovering a language long forgotten in a world of prefabricated, power-tooled joinery.

In the café downstairs I had an omelette made with eggs laid by the village hens. There were a few backpackers here, mainly Europeans and Japanese, some of them wearing embroidered waistcoats they might have picked up in India, some with Ifugao bone pendants around their necks. You hardly noticed backpackers in Manila, a place that held few attractions for them and where even the budget hotels were surprisingly expensive. These travelers moved around the archipelago following a map of their own whose key points were places like Boracay, Puerto Galera, Baguio, Sagada, and Banaue. Beaches and mountains. In the Cordillera there was a similar itinerary for rice-terrace viewing that included the Kiangan, Bontoc, and Malicong areas, along with Banaue. These were road maps of what was thought to be authentic and unspoiled in the archipelago, maps that few Filipinos followed, and those who did—mainly the children of the middle class—seemed to do so partly out of curiosity as to how their country appeared from the outside.

Before heading off for a walk down the valley, I asked the woman who ran the café where I could get a good view of the rice terraces. She suggested I walk back up the main road till I came to a car park where there was a lookout. She traced the route with her finger on a map under the glass countertop. "We call it the Eighth Wonder," she added softly. I looked up at her for a moment, caught off guard, not expecting the term to be parlayed so casually.

"You mean the rice terraces?" I asked, assuming she wasn't talking about the lookout.

"Yes," she replied, indicating some newspaper clippings and pictures pinned to the wall behind her. "Number eight! They are famous, no?"

I said, "I don't know," meaning I'd only just arrived, but then felt slightly ashamed of my stinginess.

"Oh," she said with a little laugh, "you will see, then. You will see."

I recalled that in some popular accounts of the terraces there was a feeling that even the Eighth Wonder ranking wasn't quite adequate for them. "They call it the eighth wonder of the world," one writer had observed, but then continued: "In justice, it should be called the first. For beside it, the pyramids of Egypt, the gardens of Babylon, or the Roman Aqueducts are simple attempts at minor engineering."[14]

I decided to save the lookout for later and set out to walk along the bottom of the valley instead. There was a narrow dirt road, hardly more than a footpath, that led past a few houses and past some stalls selling wood carvings. There were eagles with outstretched wings in a range of sizes but also kangaroos, a bit on the chubby side, giant ornamental spoons and forks, and an assortment of erect penises mounted on ashtrays.

The valley was perhaps half a kilometer wide at the bottom, rice fields flanking the road on either side. These fields on the valley floor were squarish and bounded by low earthen bunds that served as pathways for the field workers or anyone else who wanted to go cross-country. Where they reached the rising ground on either side of the valley they became narrower, accommodating themselves to the incline of the hillsides as they ascended them. Here the bunds separating the terraces became higher and higher until they achieved the fabled staircase effect. On the steepest slopes the bunds seemed to be higher than the width of the fields they supported. You had to wonder how all this effort could actually be worthwhile in terms of crop yield.

Harold Conklin mapped the terraces around Banaue in laborious detail in the 1960s for his authoritative *Ethnographic Atlas of Ifugao*. He estimated there were approximately twenty thousand kilometers of terrace wall in the Ifugao region, seven thousand kilometers of which were of dry stone construction.[15] Conklin studiously avoided hyperbole, but less sober commentators, as early as the 1930s, had begun playing giddy games with terrace statistics. A Philippines journalist claimed they were ten times longer than that rival to Eighth Wonder status, the Great Wall of China.[16] The ethnologist R. F. Barton claimed that "[s]trung end to end, these terraces would reach nearly half-way around the world."[17] I'd never really understood this obsession with length, with laying end to end things that were never intended to be arranged that way. Obviously, if you laid the terraces end to end they wouldn't be terraces any more.

There was no wind in the valley, just an occasional stirring of the air that was enough to set the stands of rice in the fields swaying and rippling. As the afternoon wore on, the sunshine mellowed to a soft golden hue, suggesting the long afternoons of childhood when time seems to slow almost to a stop. One of the 1970s journalists had said that in Banaue, "poetry wells up in the heart, and it recalls the psalmist's 'I will lift up mine eyes unto the hills from whence cometh my help.'"[18] Here you did lift your eyes to the hills; the hills demanded it. You craned your neck as each turn in the path revealed another angle on a ridge of terraces rising skyward.

The road wound in and out of the concavities between the ridges, into and out of the sunlight. On the road's uphill side were terrace walls with mosses and ferns growing on them and moisture seeping everywhere. A stream of clear water spilled down a stone-lined channel in the cleft of a gully and passed gurgling under the road itself and then down into the terraces on the slope below. There were bamboo conduits carrying irrigation water from field to field across ditches. There was the sense of a hugely intricate and largely invisible network of channels and runnels directing and redirecting, dividing and apportioning the flow of water down through the entire valley.

Because wet rice agriculture requires carefully regulated water levels in the fields at certain points in the growing cycle, the fields must necessarily be quite flat. At Banaue, a place where flatness barely existed in its natural state, flatness had to be improvised. It was a place where, in Conklin's words, "[a]lmost all forms of the available earth surface are considered transformable and transportable."[19] It was strangely moving to stand in a valley like this, in such deeply dissected terrain, and to witness all around you evidence of people's desire for perfect flatness. For half my life I'd been living in Australia, a continent that has been quietly working at achieving a perfect flatness for eons and has gone further in that direction than most other places. I was thus no stranger to the reality of flatness, but here in Banaue, where flatness was a human artifact, it was as if a natural order had been reversed. And yet there was still something about the terraces that did appear entirely natural. When I looked up at the hillside I saw the horizontal lines of the terrace walls following the curves of the ridges like contour lines. They *were* contour lines. The terracing accentuated the natural contours of the landscape rather than obliterated them, and it was this, I thought, that lent them their naturalness.

I hardly met anyone on the road and saw only one or two people in the fields. Occasionally a head and shoulders broke the surface of the rice crop away in the distance as somebody straightened his back momentarily before bending again to whatever it was he was doing. Late in the afternoon, on the way back to Banaue village, I ran into Pedro and Juan who had just finished harvesting part of their grandfather's field and were on their way home. They each had big bunches of cut paddy in baskets hanging from either end of carrying poles that were improvised from trimmed pine branches. The grain-heavy stalks of paddy hung over the sides of the baskets and flopped up and down with the motion of their walking, not unlike the way the boys' straight, glossy black hair rose and fell with each footfall. I felt a bit foolish walking beside them with nothing to carry except my camera, but I knew I'd look really foolish if I tried to carry one of those loads. Juan was fourteen and Pedro was sixteen but looked to be in his early twenties. He said that people up there in the mountains got old quickly because they had to work, meaning, I suppose, that they had to work in the fields and on the maintenance of the terraces. "Of course," I heard myself saying, as if it were a fact of nature.

After dinner that evening I walked down to the bottom of the village street and stood leaning on the railing of a small bridge, looking down at the dark, fast-moving stream that passed beneath it. There were fireflies under the bridge, hovering over the water, winking. They were also in the trees. The sound of the river was almost drowned out by the croaking of frogs, so many of them that the sound merged into a continuous racket, as loud as a machine but organic and for that reason somehow sweeter. A boy and girl walked past holding burning torches not much larger than candles. I watched them go along the road holding their torches overhead and then turn off onto a path through the fields. With hardly any moonshine the valley was as dark as it was damp, and the terraces were invisible.

I went back and sat on my bed to write up my journal, then continued reading Scott's books on the history of the Cordillera. Interestingly, the Spanish, the first Westerners to see the rice terraces, seem to have found them unremarkable. Scott quoted a passage from an 1879 publication by Father Juan Villaverde in which the friar seemed to consider them simply a peculiarity of local agriculture: "As the terrain is never, or hardly ever flat, they supply this lack by constructing various terraces of more or less height, called *pilápiles*, all for the purpose of levelling some area a bit in which rice can be planted."[20] The effort that went into the construction and maintenance of the terraces was colossal, Villaverde noted, but he stopped well short of seeing the result as a marvel of primitive ingenuity.

The scant attention given to the terraces by the Spanish so struck the anthropologist Felix Keesing that it encouraged him to think they might have originally been constructed only during the Spanish period.[21] But archaeological excavation of terrace structures in the Banaue valley later indicated they were up to three thousand years old. So why were the Spanish almost silent about a phenomenon that we find so extraordinary? Perhaps, as Scott suggests, they simply preferred not to mention them. The missionaries, being in favor of moving the Igorot population down to the "civilizing" influence of the lowlands, were hardly likely to draw attention to Igorot achievements in the mountains.[22] Or, if they saw the terraces merely as a logical solution to the problem of growing wet rice in steep terrain, then it was something obvious and not worth getting excited about.

By the late nineteenth century, German and other European travelers and naturalists discovered the terraces and they did get excited about them. It was a sentiment echoed by the Americans who began to move through the Cordillera in the opening years of the twentieth century as the United States established its administration in the Philippines. The terraces were becoming a spectacle. The British traveler Henry Savage-Landor wrote in 1904 of "the astounding work of these quaint humans."[23] However, he found the terraced terrain difficult to travel through: "After crossing innumerable terraces we came upon another bit of the trail, which seemed to us like walking in Piccadilly or Broadway after the wretched terrace balancing."[24] What he was referring to was the local custom of traveling the hillslopes by walking along the top of the terrace walls with the rice on one side and a sheer drop on the other.

By 1906 Dean C. Worcester, zoologist turned colonial administrator, was casting his eye over the terraced hillsides at places such as Banaue: "Their agriculture is little short of wonderful, and no one who has seen their dry stone dams, their irrigated ditches running for miles along precipitous hillsides and even crossing the faces of cliffs, and their irrigated terraces extending for thousands of feet up the mountain sides, can fail to be impressed."[25]

But through the early decades of the twentieth century, as the Ifugao began to put on shirts and skirts, as they ceased head-hunting and began to attend church and school, they ceased in the eyes of the West to be the "real" Ifugao that their parents and grandparents had been. They lost their coverage in *National Geographic*. But the terraces remained ostensibly unchanged and increasingly the terraces came to stand for what was real or authentic about Ifugao culture. By the 1970s, at a popular national and international level, people no longer spoke about the Ifugao, they only spoke about the terraces. Things had come full circle from the days when the Spanish looked at the terraces simply as ancillary to Ifugao agriculture: Now the Ifugao were ancillary to the terraces. This situation is exemplified in the government's failure to consult the Ifugao about the 1994 nomination of the terraces for the World Heritage List, but more of that later.

As the terraces broke free of their makers to pursue their career as heritage icons and tourist attractions, the local people all but dropped out of the picture. This was evident in the modern newspaper accounts of the Cordillera that I'd read in Manila. The articles frequently noted the head-hunting past of the Ifugao but had nothing of substance to say about Ifugao society in the present day. Unlike Dean Worcester's pieces, they make no mention of what the Ifugao now looked like, what their rituals were, what you could expect to find inside or underneath their houses. They were not the first people to be elbowed aside by their own heritage nor would they be the last.

It was late by the time I went down to dinner, but when I entered what looked to be the most interesting of the cafés in the street I found all the tables were taken. The waiter found me a place at a table with two Japanese tourists, who, it emerged, were on their first trip out of Japan after graduating from a design school in Tokyo. Mikage stood out among the backpackers at Banaue on account of her short, spiked hair, her smart black dress, and her dark brown biker's jacket. She was interested in silk. They'd been in Thailand looking at silk workshops before coming to the Philippines. Bangkok had been their first stop, and she described their amazement at the bars and the street food and the taxis whose back doors didn't open for you automatically. Her sense of being on a great adventure in the outside world was quite palpable. I asked her boyfriend, Katzuo, what he thought of the terraces, suddenly remembering that they had rice terraces in Japan.

"Ah, very . . . special," he said. His family were farmers, and he grew up with rice fields. "But not like this," he laughed, using his hand to indicate the steepness of the terraced slopes around Banaue. We were drinking San Miguel, a little on the warm side, and we lingered after the food was finished. To my surprise, it began to rain; you could hear big drops of water pounding on the banana leaves outside the window.

As we were leaving, the woman at the counter said they'd heard on the radio that a cyclone was coming. She said we shouldn't worry, though; Banaue wasn't in its path. She was right; we only really caught the outer edge of it, but there was heavy rain and very strong winds for the next two days, making it virtually impossible to leave the hotel. The staff said there'd been slips along the highway to Baguio and Manila, and the buses would not run again until the road had been cleared. During those couple of days the hotel seemed almost to shrink in size. The air was pungent with dampness and marijuana smoke, and the guests started talking to each other in the hallways and on the stairs.

The first night of the storm I lay in bed with my book listening to the rain lashing the windows and feeling the building shudder under the wind. I woke in the night and thought the wind, if anything, sounded stronger. Noticing my feet were strangely cold, I discovered the end of the bed was wet. The power was off so I used my flashlight to search the ceiling for the leak, finding a slow but steady drip. Dragging the bed out of the way, I put a water glass—it was all I could find—on the wooden floor to catch the drops.

Mikage and Katzuo were in the café when I went down in the morning. It was then I discovered the road was closed. I'd been planning to return to Manila that day, but once I realized this wasn't an option, once I appreciated that I was caught up in an act of nature, I stopped worrying. Mikage showed me some postcards she'd bought in Sagada, a village on the other side of Bontoc. They were striking black-and-white pictures taken by a local photographer, Eduardo Masferré, before the Second World War. Mikage pointed to one that showed a young man posed squatting in what might have been a rice field. He wore a short waistcoat of a striped woven fabric, an off-the-shoulder cape of a similar fabric, and a kerchief around his hair. He was crouching with his forearm resting on his raised bare knee, his gaze directed away to the side. Mikage was admiring his clothes and asked if I thought the garland he wore was made of white beads or small shells. I couldn't tell.

Looking at the picture from over my shoulder, she said she thought he was handsome. Entering the spirit of things, I mentioned how the delicacy of the beading along the edges of the waistcoat was offset by the muscles on his exposed shoulders. What really struck me though, was the intense, almost threatening expression in his eyes. Had he been coerced in some way into posing? According to a photocopied flier that she fished out of her bag, Masferré was a local man who had lived as a child at the Episcopalian mission at Sagada in the 1920s and whose photographic inspiration had partly come from seeing Dean Worcester's photographs from half a century earlier.

That afternoon I met up with Mikage and Katzuo again when a young Dutch couple invited me to a party in their room. They had a view down across the valley from folding windows that extended across the whole width of the room. People chatted about places they'd been, the price of hash on Boracay, the best places to stay on Mindoro. The wind was gusting through the valley below, buffeting the palm trees so that the trunks swayed and the fronds tossed wildly, as if desperate to break free.

I looked through Mikage's Masferré postcards again. There was a beautiful view of a terraced hillslope photographed at a time of the year when the terraces were flooded in preparation for the planting of a new crop. There were others of people posed in rice fields, all of them wearing traditional dress. If there was a timelessness about these scenes, it was because time had been neutralized in them. The modern world intruded nowhere and yet the modern world was all around, most tellingly, perhaps, in the person of the local man, Masferré, and his camera (Masferré who, one could pretty safely assume, was not himself wearing traditional mountain garb).

In a photograph taken about the same time (figure 2.2) people seem almost to be flaunting their Western-style clothes, clothes I'd suggest they regarded primarily as modern rather than Western. The boy on the right seems perfectly at home mixing a (cast-off?) formal dark jacket with a traditional woven basket. On the label on the back of the print supplied to me by the National Library of Australia the scene is described as "two boys in conservation (Western dress)," presumably a typographic error. But when I first read it I momentarily thought the original photograph must be in the hands of the library's conservators. My mind then lurched to the bizarre thought it was the boys who were "in conservation" before it settled on the more mundane likelihood that they were "in conversation."

The Masferré photographs marked one of the final moments when the Ifugao would be depicted along with the rice terraces. It was the moment before an order of precedence was reversed and the terraces eclipsed their makers. The terraces were now a sign of precolonial, indigenous achievement in a country that had problems with national identity. Nearly all the sites registered as national historical monuments were Spanish-period churches or birthplaces of revolutionaries. Many Filipinos felt they needed an Angkor Wat, a Pagan, a Borobudur: a place that would help anchor them to a more ancient past.

Figure 2.2.   Two boys in conversation (western dress) (Beyer Collection 47, National Library of Australia)

They turned to the Ifugao rice terraces, but there was a difficulty with this. The terraces were ephemeral agricultural phenomena that had always been in a state of change. Conklin knew this because he took the trouble to find out. He learned, for instance, that on concave slopes it was frequently the case that several small terraces would be combined into a smaller number of larger, wider terraces by building higher walls and in-filling them.[26] It followed that buried beneath the present pattern of terraces were the traces and outlines of former patterns. Even to retain an existing formation of terraces unchanged required the regular weeding of the walls and replacement of missing stones as well as the regular clearing and weeding of irrigation and drainage ditches. The skills necessary for all this were exacting and took time to learn. Conklin observed that Ifugao children would "spend hours at the streamside building miniature terrace systems and waterworks."[27] Outsiders might speak of the terraces as monuments, but they were monuments that never ceased being built.

Once the terraces became iconic they attracted increasing numbers of tourists, and new possibilities for earning a living became available to local people. Some of them built small hotels, like the one I was staying in, and others worked in them as waiters, cooks, and housemaids. And then there were the things tourists would buy: Woodcarving became a small industry, and the wooden eagles and horses that weren't sold locally were sent to shops in the cities. As early as the 1970s outsiders were complaining about the way Banaue was changing. Fields were lying uncultivated as people carved wood. In 1989 a Manila newspaper announced, "the eighth wonder is dying," its "terminal condition" being due to "uncontrolled woodcarving."[28] As evidence emerged of a decline in laborious and time-consuming rice cultivation, a government study recommended the planting of beans in the terraces. However, as provincial officials astutely commented, "Who wants to look at bean terraces?"[29] If we had lost interest in the Ifugao once they stopped head-hunting, we were now suddenly interested in them again. They had a responsibility to us to maintain their rice terraces.

The hillsides were subject to the normal processes of erosion, and unless the terraces were properly maintained they would gradually erode away. Gravity would do its work, and the staircased hillsides would revert to their natural state.

There was also the nagging problem of the corrugated roofing iron that had appeared on many of the lovely old Ifugao huts scattered through the valley, replacing the previously universal thatch. Tourists didn't like the roofing iron. They felt it jarred with the natural primitiveness of the terraces. (Elsewhere in Southeast Asia roofing iron has been driving art historians and historical architects mad for decades.)[30] In the early 1980s an instruction had come from the presidential palace in Manila requiring the municipal government of Banaue to replace iron roofing in the town center with thatch. The local mayor refused to comply.[31] Evidently the locals, while they wanted the income from tourism, also wanted modernity on their own terms. Also, it has been suggested that people such as the Ifugao these days associate vernacular architecture with the hard life of subsistence agriculture and with the "economic deprivation they have suffered for many generations."[32]

This didn't mean, of course, that they rejected their identity as Ifugao, that they didn't still feel authentically Ifugao even with corrugated iron over their heads. Still, I wondered what it would be like to live with the knowledge that the rest of the world believed you were only authentic when you looked and behaved the way you did a century before. To know the world believed all your "great moments were in the past."[33]

On the day the roads reopened I went on an excursion to Kiangan to see the place where the Japanese had formally surrendered to the Allies in September 1945. Several kilometers off the highway, sequestered in its own valley, Kiangan had been the capital of Mountain Province under the American colonial administration. It held its status as capital until 1948 when it was bypassed by the new highway linking Bontoc and Banaue to the lowlands on the northeastern side of Luzon. These days Kiangan was little more than a village, a scattering of old wooden buildings separated by gardens and fields. Some of the houses and municipal buildings, I thought, showed an American influence; some were surrounded by hedges or picket fences and shaded by large old trees. It was a quiet place left alone to mind its own business.

On this warm, still afternoon, with the cyclone already barely a memory, human voices and even one's own thoughts seemed muffled and distant. I walked slowly up the main street of Kiangan and went into the post office to ask directions to the museum. They said to continue up the hill and turn right after the Protestant school. I passed some old two-story houses with large fruit trees and flower gardens running wild. They had casement windows, and the grain stood out in relief on their eroded weatherboards. Organ music drifted out from an old wooden church with a pointed steeple that had a single, round stained-glass window. Then came the Protestant school, the Kiangan Academy, with its large shutters (in lieu of windows) thrown open and children's voices, reciting their lessons, spilling out. I saw their little, bent heads as I walked past, the only person on the street, and I had to suppress an impulse to tiptoe.

Turning at the school, I walked up a street to a large flat field with a concrete monument at one end. At the other end was the Ifugao Museum, a tiny, single-story, modernist building in glass and concrete that was surrounded by long, dry grass. The field was empty and the museum was closed. Peering in through the glass door I could see displays of wooden artifacts and basketry in the dim interior. The monument at the other end of the field took the form of an open-fronted Ifugao house, complete with steeply pitched roof, but the entire thing was in ferro-concrete rather than wood and thatch. On the concrete floor of the monument facing the field stood a low, dusty benchlike concrete table covered with mosaic tiles and pierced by a hole that might once have housed an eternal flame. Next to the hole lay a tattered straw hat, its brim unraveling. There was nothing to suggest that anyone local cared for the place.

A plaque stated that it had been dedicated by President Ferdinand Marcos in 1973 to mark the spot where General Yamashita, commander of the Fourteenth Area of the Imperial Japanese Army, along with his staff, had surrendered. Above the bench and set into the back wall was a massive wooden panel carved in deep relief with the figures of soldiers dying in each other's arms. The Japanese had withdrawn into this part of the Cordillera after the American bombardment of Baguio, the mountain resort to the south, and they held out for several months. I wasn't sure whether the tableau represented the war in the Philippines as a whole or just this final episode.

I approached two young men, Christian missionaries, who were sitting on the front steps of a small house next to a half-built church on the far side of the field. They invited me in for a glass of water, and I sat with them on the polished wooden floor of the front room. The subject of the monument sparked little interest in them, though one of them, Ronaldo, was interested in archaeology and asked what I thought of the Garden of Eden. Was there any archaeological trace of it?

"We have to be reborn again," the other one chimed in, apropos of nothing.

Ronaldo had heard that there was now archaeological evidence of the drowning of the Egyptians during their ill-conceived pursuit of the children of God across the bed of the Red Sea. I confessed that Middle Eastern archaeology wasn't my field.

A little later, as I was passing the museum I saw the door was open and found the part-time curator inside, a local woman who took me around the exhibits in the single room, introducing them as if they were objects in her own home. There was a display of carved wooden *bulbul*, the small figurines she said people still put on their rice granaries. There was a display of harvest ritual paraphernalia, a death blanket, a display of traditional artifacts used in rice growing, and in the center of the single room an area set up to resemble the underneath of an Ifugao house. Here there were a couple of blacksmith's bellows, donated by the Banaue smithy who, she said, still worked bronze.

Against one of the walls was a display of funerary objects. She explained that they used to have a carved wooden coffin—you could see the imprint of where it had rested—donated by a man across the mountain to the northwest after he had removed his father's bones from it and buried them in the Christian manner. But his father had appeared to him in a dream, demanding the return of his "house," and she had no alternative but to give it back, despite the fact, she added wistfully, that the museum had given the family a pig to formalize the original transfer. We both looked silently for a moment at the space left by the absent coffin.

There were some old black-and-white photographs from the time of the Americans, two of them showing Ifugao men in traditional garb standing in front of a substantial stone building. I assumed they must have been taken in Bontoc, but, no, the curator said, it was the old administrative building that stood on this very spot before it was bombed by American airplanes at the end of the Second World War. The Japanese were using it at the time, she explained. I signed the visitors' book and thanked her for her trouble. Outside she pointed me to a path, a shortcut back to the main road. It ran down a spur and onto a clearing where, as she had promised, I found a few concrete foundation piles in the long, dry grass, all that remained of the American governor's house, also destroyed in the war. This spot had been known in wartime as Hill 32, in the way that armies have of reducing things to numbers. It had a nice view down the valley; it was a great spot for a house.

The path led from the hill down past the high school where I stopped to read a painted sign outside the home economics building. It was actually there in that weatherboard classroom, according to the sign, that Yamashita had surrendered. The classroom, still in use, seemed more credible as a surrender site than the spot marked by the unfortunate monument up the hill. Two schoolgirls watched through an open window as I copied the words of the sign into my notebook. The war would seem more remote to them, I supposed, than it did to me, born in the first postwar generation.

One of the missionaries had told me earlier that a group of Japanese veterans came to Kiangan every year to make offerings to their "pagan gods." Ronaldo said they were looking for Yamashita's gold, the legendary bullion the Japanese were said to have hidden in 1945 as MacArthur's forces were closing in on them. The veterans went trekking up into the hills. He said they had special maps, in Japanese, which nobody else could read.

In his book *A History of the Mountain Province*, Howard Fry mentioned Lieutenant Miasaki, the thirty-year-old garrison commander based at Kiangan who was said to have mixed well with the local people and to have departed with tears in his eyes, his friends having hired a band to farewell him.[34] A darker picture of the Japanese experience emerges from the book *Terraced*

Figure 2.3.   Ifugao rice terraces, Luzon, 1890–1923 (Carpenter Collection, Library of Congress, LC-USZ62-98049)

Hell, written by Tetsuro Ogawa, who was a young noncombatant officer in the last desperate months before the surrender. He was one of those, in the years before the city was retaken by MacArthur's forces, who "had enjoyed themselves in the cabarets of Manila in their white suits and rubber-soled shoes." They retreated in front of the American forces into the Cordillera with the remnants of their army. The retreat became a nightmare as they made forced marches up one muddy range of hills after another, being picked off by guerrillas and American planes. Half-starved, not knowing what their enemy had planned for them when they surrendered, they imagined the worst.[35] Ogawa has nothing flattering to say about the rice terraces. They were simply an element of his misery.

Ogawa and his platoon were sent to Banaue to gather rice from terraces that had gone unharvested because the villagers had fled the fighting. Late one afternoon, on entering a seemingly empty hut he found three headless Japanese corpses there. They had each been speared through the stomach, apparently in their sleep. Twenty-four years later he visited Banaue with some of the others who had survived the retreat and with relatives of the dead: "I saw the house where the three beheaded soldiers had been. It was inhabited by Igorots, who looked at us indifferently. The rice terraces and the surrounding scenery were just as they had been twenty-four years before. There was nothing to suggest that nearly a thousand soldiers had died in this area."[36]

On the whole, the mountain people had not treated the Japanese badly, and Ogawa testifies to this. The dead soldiers in the hut had perhaps unwittingly transgressed Ifugao custom in some way, perhaps simply by being in the hut.

Ogawa seemed haunted by the absence of traces, perplexed by a landscape that seemed to deny it had ever been the scene of any catastrophe. Indifference is always difficult to deal with. We are familiar with the monumental landscape, the evocative landscape, the landscape of the heart. Heritage discourse thrives on all of that. But what about the indifferent landscape?

The previous evening I'd told Mikage and Tatsuo that I was going to Kiangan, looking for the site of the 1945 surrender. They'd seemed genuinely surprised the Japanese army had been up there in the mountains during the war. It wasn't that they were unaware that the Philippines had been occupied by Japan; they just hadn't made the connection between that history and this place. I think they assumed their generation of adventurous young Japanese travelers were discovering places like Banaue for the first time.

On the highway I caught a pickup truck taxi to Lagawe, and then found the battered yellow bus that would take me back to Banaue standing in the shade of a huge tree. The bus boys were loading large carved wooden eagles onto the roof, one boy standing on the roof and the other handing them up to him to be tied down. I climbed into the bus and sat in the back near some women who had plastic shopping bags and cardboard boxes arranged around them. The middle-aged woman next to me had bright twinkling eyes, a deeply lined face, and long hair gathered up behind her head. She wore an American football T-shirt with the number 33 on the front of it; she had a double cord of large carnelian beads around her neck and a small, tired girl on her knee.

On the street outside a jeepney pulled up, and a man got out and began attending to a pig lying on the roof of the vehicle's canopy, its legs tied to either end of a bamboo pole. The bus boys, finished with the eagles by now, went over to help get the pig down, an opportunity for a bit of posturing on their part. The head bus boy was making an effort to look tough, I thought, but could not quite pull it off. He didn't have the face for it; he looked more comical than threatening. He had a red sun visor, the band of which kept his longish hair in place. His tight, patched, and faded jeans were half unzipped, his brown check shirt was unbuttoned to the navel, and he seemed determined not to miss any opportunity to parade his sexuality. His face was screwed up as he took the considerable weight of the squealing pig and passed his end of the bamboo pole down to his companion on the ground. The latter had an eye problem that caused him to squint a lot. He wore a black fishnet singlet rolled up to his chest.

I sat there writing my notes, waiting for the bus to go. When I looked up again some people had arrived with a bundle of large wooden horses, all the same and all with holes bored in the rear for the attachment of the wooden tails that were bundled together separately. Evidence of uncontrolled woodcarving, I thought, as the bus boys launched themselves into the task of hauling the horses up onto the roof of the bus and tying them down. The owners of the horses stood back and watched critically, as if they didn't trust the boys not to damage their work. We passengers also watched the horses, their bodies pressing against the window glass as they rose toward the roof.

An ice-cream vendor approached the bus, ringing his bell and handing up brightly colored one-peso icicles and ice creams on sticks to passengers who handed down coins. The girls and boys from Don Bosco High School, wearing white T-shirts with pictures of Don Bosco on the front, drifted by in twos and threes. The general flurry of movement around the bus intensified, and the calls of "Banaue-Banaue-Banaue!" from the bus boys now assumed an urgent, no-nonsense tone as the bus shuddered to life and finally edged away from the curb. Before heading out of town it circled the streets, the bus boys hanging out the front and rear doors, shouting to people we passed, urging them to get on. People didn't miss this bus; they were not given the chance.

Back on Rizal Avenue we picked up speed and set a resolute course for Banaue. We passed some shops and a church, but then, near the edge of town, we began to slow. Something was wrong. The boys were hanging out of the doors fore and aft, pointing to one of the front wheels and shouting. It was a flat tire. The bus made its way slowly back to the tree.

I climbed down and sat on the grass to wait for the wheel to be changed. The old yellow bus, its roof piled with wooden horses and eagles, and the theatrical bus boys, now throwing themselves into the wheel-changing business, made a compelling picture. I thought it was an image that would probably stay with me for a long time. The minutes passed slowly. The increasingly golden light of the low sun shone down on this scene like stage lighting, and it occurred to me that it was this that I'd come for. Ostensibly I'd come looking for the terraces and the surrender site, but the essence of contemporary Ifugao culture—if you believed in the essential—was being played out, as if solely for my benefit, right at this moment and right in front of me.

While the wheel nuts were still being tightened, a jeepney bound for Banaue cruised into the street and pulled up only fifty meters away. Immediately a dozen or so of our laboriously accumulated passengers rushed to get on it. Neither the bus driver nor the boys acknowledged this situation with so much as a glance: They seemed to convey the message that passengers were cheap; that there were plenty more where they came from. Or maybe they weren't even in it for the passengers.

When the wheel was secured I got back on. Two bent old men, supporting themselves on staves, appeared at the last minute and climbed in through the back door. They had a shrunken appearance, not unlike some of the wood carvings of wizened old men you saw in the craft shops of Banaue. They wore T-shirts and blue woven G-strings and they stood in the aisle—there were no vacant seats—cackling to each other and sharing jokes with the bus boys who treated them as familiars; "accomplices" was the word that came to mind.

Once again the bus lurched off and gathered speed for Banaue. The boys hung out the doors and beckoned passing schoolgirls to get on, and the girls either studiously ignored them or threw back insults, to the boys' evident delight. Their brand of machismo was like a parody of male sexuality. I tried to imagine them back in their grandfathers' generation, the generation of the two old men on the bus or the generation before that, strutting around in raffishly tied G-strings and fresh tattoos. They would be the volatile, smoldering force in the village, always pressuring for another head-taking expedition.

By rights, these boys should have been tending their family's rice terraces, soon to be items of World Heritage, rather than chasing schoolgirls through the sleepy streets of Lagawe. But who was I to say? I doubt I'd have lasted half a day planting rice in a paddy field. And why should they want to follow preceding generations into the rice fields, any more than we would want to repeat the experience of our parents and grandparents in bleak factories?

The bus began to ascend the long ridge, stopping occasionally to pick up passengers who climbed onto the roof, the boys throwing up their sacks and bundles after them. The roof was so laden that I half-expected it to sag and then collapse into the already chaotic interior. The sun was making its way down the last few inches of sky above the mountainous horizon. The rice crops were yellow in the fields, fields that, as the terrain steepened, began to form inevitably into terraces. Each time the bus stopped the boy in the net singlet jumped down and ran to put a chock in the form of a river cobble under the front wheel. When the bus began to move again he would grasp the cobble and begin running, reaching out to grab hold of the railing of the moving doorway. It went without saying that he waited for the bus to pick up a bit of speed before making his nonchalant but immaculately timed run for the door.

The road steepened. We stopped for a youth with a long carrying pole, which, once he was on the roof, he let dangle down the side of the bus. From his position hanging from the front doorway, the head bus boy spat into the road, but his spittle, carried by the wind, landed on the dangling pole, causing its owner to start beating him with it from above, evidently trying to dislodge him from the now rapidly moving bus. The bus boy, shrieking, hung on by the fingers of one hand while fending off the blows with the other. All this was taking place as the bus careered around a long bend with a clifflike cutting on one side of the road and a sheer drop to a fabulously terraced valley on the other. The hapless bus boy was suspended out over this valley, the backdrop for his twisting body the lovely soft yellow-green of the distant terraces glowing in the golden-red light of the setting sun.

People looked up from their roadside house yards as the bus passed by and, even as a mere passenger, I couldn't help but feel proud to be associated with such a spectacle. Open-mouthed kids stared, men and women looked up from what they were doing and nodded or smiled. In one yard a man was cutting the hair of a boy who was sitting on a chair with a cloth draped around him and a terraced mountainside behind. When we finally pulled into Banaue I stood for a moment in the square, feeling a pang of loss as the passengers dispersed. In the twilight the bus looked suddenly ordinary, as did the driver and the bus boys as they shuffled off toward a café.

The Ifugao rice terraces were inscribed on the World Heritage List in 1995 as "an outstanding example of living cultural landscapes . . . illustrat[ing] traditional techniques and a remarkable harmony between humankind and the natural environment."[37] They were only the third "cultural landscape" to be given the honor since that category was recognized under the World Heritage Convention in 1992. Less than ten years later, in 2001, they were inscribed on the list of World Heritage in Danger, UNESCO's World Heritage Committee noting at the time that about 25 to 30 percent of the terraces had been abandoned and were deteriorating and that "irregular development" (read: iron roofs and cheap hotels) was occurring.[38] In the committee's view, "the World Heritage Values may be lost unless current trends are reversed within 10 years (maximum)."[39]

Agusto Villalón argues that a successful outcome would need to be based on a cultural revival strategy and an approach that focused more on the cultural practices that produce and maintain the terraces rather than on the terraces as a "tangible" heritage site.[40] Behind all of this is the difficulty that heritage practitioners have with the idea of authenticity. We want "authentic" culture and authentic-looking terraces. But the truly authentic is, of course, always already there in front of us, in the present.

NOTES

1. Scott 1975, 13.
2. Scott 1977, 278.
3. Foucault 1973.
4. Adas 1989.
5. Breckenridge 1989, 202.
6. Hutterer 1978, 145. Howard Fry (1983, 40) reminds us that the 1804 Louisiana Purchase, whose centenary the exposition celebrated, inaugurated the westward expansion of the United States: "It is somewhat curious that the implications behind the decision to include an ambitious Philippine exhibit at this Exposition have been so often overlooked. The decision clearly implied that the acquisition of this faraway archipelago was in no sense intended to be seen as a temporary occupation, the accidental result of war, but rather was to be viewed as a fruit of the latest giant step forward in the westward expansion of the United States."
7. Fry 1983, 40.
8. Scott 1977, vi.
9. Fry 1983, 40.
10. Scott 1975, 2.
11. Jenks 1905, 41.
12. See also Worcester 1906, 827.
13. Spurr 1993, 22.
14. An article in "a Buenos Aires publication" quoted in the *Manila Times*, 29 June 1988.

15. Conklin 1980.
16. *Times Journal*, 11 August 1975.
17. R. F. Barton (1930, 60) attributes the first such calculation to H. Otley Beyer, noting, "My own calculation, independently made, is almost identical with his. Both are probably underestimates." See also T. Inglis Moore (1931, 9). The information that, placed end to end, the terraces would reach halfway around the earth is inscribed on a public monument in the village of Banaue.
18. *Philippines Daily Express*, 22 January 1975.
19. Conklin 1980, 37.
20. See translation from the Spanish by Scott (1977, 322).
21. Keesing 1962.
22. Scott 1977, 279.
23. Savage-Landor 1904, 485.
24. Ibid.
25. Worcester 1906, 829.
26. Conklin (1980, 38) notes, "While the outward appearance of the agricultural landscape in the broader central valleys has probably retained its general form throughout the historic period, any resemblance to a static and unchanging permanent sculpture or construction is misleading."
27. Conklin 1980, 7. See also Conklin's (1980, 26) observation that "after several years without inundation and dike repair a terrace begins to erode and tilt."
28. *Times Journal*, 19 May 1989.
29. *Daily Express*, 7 July 1975.
30. Boutsavath and Chapelier (1973, 12) note that corrugated iron sheets had made their appearance in the countryside of Laos in 1955 and spread like wildfire. Lao villagers found them to be a "huge success" as a replacement for traditional ceramic roof tiles.
31. *Daily Express*, 7 July 1975.
32. Villalón 2005, 93.
33. Said 1985, 35.
34. Fry 1983, 199.
35. Ogawa 1972, 157.
36. Ibid., 163.
37. Report of the 19th session of the UNESCO World Heritage Committee, Berlin, 1995.
38. Report of the 25th session of the UNESCO World Heritage Committee, Helsinki, 2001, 53.
39. Ibid.
40. Villalón 2005.

· 3 ·

Traveling in Karangasem

$\mathscr{I}$n March 1963 it took three days for word of the eruption of Gunung Agung to filter through to the *Straits Times* in Singapore. Dominating the eastern end of Bali, Agung was the island's largest volcano as well as being a key site in the Hindu-animist belief system of the Balinese people. As I reeled through pages of the *Straits Times* on a microfilm reader in the Fisher Library at Sydney University, an image of Agung's almost perfectly symmetrical cone hovered in my mind.

I'd begun my search of the *Straits Times* microfilm at the Sunday, 17 March edition, the day of the eruption, but there was no headline announcing it, nor even a "stop press" item on it. No word of it, either, in the Monday edition, and when I'd scrolled through to the end of the Tuesday edition I was beginning to wonder if I hadn't somehow made a mistake about the date of the event—maybe it had been 17 May or 17 April.

Telecommunications in 1963 were not what they are now, when places like Bali are only as far away as a beam bounced off a satellite. Back then geographical remoteness still meant something. Newspaper stories still carried datelines, like: "Daresalam (Tuesday). Our correspondent reports. . . ." When were datelines dropped from newspapers, I wondered, scrolling onward, and why were they dropped? I noticed that television had only just arrived in Singapore in 1963. The *Straits Times* carried photographs of TV sets with desirable rounded plywood cabinets standing on black stiletto legs with pretty girls posing next to them.

A second after the front page of the edition for Wednesday, 20 March, appeared on the screen my eye jumped on the headline: "Volcano death toll now totals 130."

"Now?" I murmured to myself querulously, but I was already devouring the story. It was a Reuters report, filed from Jakarta and based on information gleaned from "travellers reaching here" ("fleeing there" might have been more accurate). One of those travelers happened to be the chief editor of *National Geographic*.[1] He wrote of how he'd been driving through the Balinese countryside on the morning of the eruption, enjoying the tranquil scenery, when he became aware of a tapping sound on the roof of his car and, climbing out, he found volcanic ash and cinders falling out of a darkening sky.

Ash began falling on the island of Madura and on 18 March clouds of it blacked out the sky over Surabaya and then Jakarta. When correspondents reached Bali some of them chartered light planes and flew with their photographers over the lava flows and the destroyed villages. They sent back descriptions of a "mushroom cloud" standing over the mountain. This was 1963, remember, when nuclear testing hadn't yet gone entirely underground and the mushroom cloud was a symbol both of postwar modernity and the cataclysmic events that brought the war in the Pacific to an end only eighteen years earlier. The airborne observations were followed by firsthand accounts from correspondents who had managed to reach the disaster zone on the ground.

After nearly half a century of mythologizing Bali as an Oriental island paradise, there weren't a lot of people in the West who hadn't read about the place or seen pictures of it.[2] The press now played on the pathos of the situation: the kindly, peaceful inhabitants of an island paradise suffering in the wake of a natural disaster of a kind that was itself only too exotic. The eruption had "made a wilderness of a paradise," the *National Geographic* observed, and in the process had "killed more than 1,500 of some of the world's handsomest and most intelligent people."[3] In the midst of the Cold War, would the magazine's Western readers have been less distressed, I wondered, if they'd known how many of those handsome Balinese were members of the Indonesian Communist Party (Partai Kommunis Indonesia)?

I spent longer with the *Straits Times* that afternoon than I'd expected. Once immersed in the early 1960s, I didn't really want to leave. At one point, when I got up to get another microfilm box from the shelf, it struck me that this library building must date from about that time. The reason I associated the period with lightness and optimism was perhaps that I was a teenager at the time, and the world outside my family, school, and neighborhood was beginning to open up. The names that populated the newspaper pages I was now reading—like Tunku Abdul Rahman and President Sukarno—were names I remember hearing on the radio in the early sixties. They were exotic sounds that seemed to beckon from the big world.

One day in July 1994, a month or so after that afternoon in the library, I locked the bamboo garden gate behind me in Bali and drove toward Candi

Dasa (the *c* pronounced *ch*). This was the small beach resort on the southeast coast of Bali where the lower, gentle slopes of Gunung Agung reached down to the sea. Approaching Agung by road from the western side of the island you first take the inland two-lane highway to Klungkung, cutting across the lower rice-growing slopes of another volcano, Gunung Batur, whose six-kilometer-wide crater lies above you and out of sight in the clouds. The road rises and falls as it cuts across a succession of ridges and intervening valleys etched into the topography by the streams that drain Batur's southern slopes.

You pass slowly through the few busy streets that make up the town of Klungkung and then the road turns and descends steeply to the coast. Immediately the country seems less populated, the traffic is lighter, and there are glimpses of the ocean for the first time in hours. Somewhere over to the left, on the other side of the deeply cut, bush-covered valley of the Yeh Undu River, lies the village of Gèlgèl, the center of a former kingdom (1500–1651) whose influence extended from East Java to the island of Sumbawa. It is from Gèlgèl that most Balinese families trace their descent.[4]

Candi Dasa is situated on the east side of a long bay. The place barely existed in the early 1960s except for a few fishermen's huts. It had been known mainly for the shrine to a local deity that was located in a tiny stone-walled sanctuary on the hill behind the beach. Then in the 1970s it was discovered by young international travelers hankering for the unspoiled and the remote. It was the sort of place you could lie in the sun on a pristine stretch of sand,

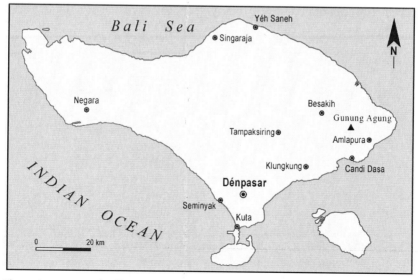

Figure 3.1.   Map of Bali

a fishing canoe at your side, close your eyes and imagine you've left the world behind, perhaps for good. The sound of small waves playing with the pebbles at the waterline would be all that tethered you to reality.

In the 1990s Candi Dasa was still a sleepy place even in the high season, those months of dry and relatively cool weather that followed the end of the monsoon. Its bungalow hotels were squeezed into the narrow strip of flat land at the foot of the parched hills and they faced out onto a sea that saw a light traffic of outrigger sailing canoes and occasionally, further out, an interisland trading *prahu*. At night the young travelers gathered at one or another of the pavilion cafés to watch video films advertised on handbills plastered over the trunks of coconut palms along the sandy laneways and paths. The sound of the music and the voices was swallowed by the darkness and diminished by the sound of the sea. Inland there was the dark backdrop of the foothills and, further in the background, the dark mass of Gunung Agung, which on a moonless night you could sense more than see.

Wanting to be alone, I picked a small hotel under the shelter of the steep ridge that enclosed the bay at its eastern end, a ridge clothed with tinder-dry grass and a scattering of brittle shrubs. From the row of old one-room cottages, each with a veranda, you could look back along Amuk Bay and then beyond to where the coastline disappeared into the haze. The cottages couldn't have dated back beyond the 1970s, but the tropical climate and salt air had aged them prematurely.

I spent what was left of the afternoon on one of the small strips of sand. They were all that were left of the beach after a decade of erosion, triggered by the short-sighted mining of the reef for building material in the years immediately after those first young travelers put Candi Dasa on the map. Later I sat in the hotel's open-sided restaurant that nobody seemed to patronize and waited for the sunset, which, when it came, was disappointing. There weren't enough clouds near the horizon, and the sun, in the end, just slipped into the sea. I went and found the waiter and ordered a bottle of Bintang beer, then sat and watched the last of the light fade from over the bay.

I had come here partly in order to get away from the small world of Seminyak, which was fifty kilometers away as the crow flies back along the coast, down beyond the end of the bay in the gathering darkness. The people I knew there were mainly expatriates. Most of them didn't read much, not even newspapers, and there was little interest in the world outside the small radius in which we lived our lives. I knew that when I got back there nobody apart from Daniel would want to know where I'd been. It was an introverted existence that in some ways mirrored that of the Balinese, whose own universe was closely focused on the village and the *banjar* (the subvillage enclave). When the low-voltage lights came on in the restaurant, the darkness outside seemed complete and thoughts of Seminyak faded into the night.

But I had also come here to look for traces of the 1963 eruption. Not to look in a systematic or, still less, scientific way. What I had in mind, rather, were a few days wandering around eastern Bali thinking about loss and the signature of loss in the landscape. I had just spent four years researching and writing on the subject of heritage management for my doctorate, and a lot of this had involved thinking about deterioration, decay, abandonment, and ruin in relation to "built heritage." Then in the lull following the end of this work I started to think about the ways in which our own lives are also permeated by the experience of loss, even if that only meant the ticking off of passing days that accumulated quietly into irrecoverable years. I had so little to do during this lull that the days merged into each other, and I found that whole weeks passed almost unnoticed. Yet there was always, in the background, a consciousness that this couldn't go on.

One of the ways I filled in the long afternoons was by riding a motor scooter semi-aimlessly around the back roads of the agricultural country to the west of where we lived. It was an intricate mosaic of irrigated rice fields, small villages, and tree-shaded temple compounds; of roads that twisted and turned, branched off, circled back on themselves, sometimes gradually trickling away until they became footpaths through the fields and sometimes leading unexpectedly back to the highway. I never really learned the larger map but I became absorbed in its finer details. So when I first came upon reference to the Gunung Agung eruption, in the form of that dog-eared 1963 *National Geographic*, it was a landscape such as this one that I imagined being partly obliterated. I imagined swaths of it being wiped out the way that strokes of an eraser might cut through closely written text on a blackboard.

The next day I drove east from Candi Dasa, taking the winding road up and over a steep, bush-covered ridge that was one of the spines of high ground radiating out from Gunung Agung. I passed a brick spirit shrine near the crest of the ridge and a stall selling watermelons halfway down the other side, then drove across the flat floor of a valley through an irregular grid of irrigated rice fields. The road went through a village where the house compounds were enclosed by dry stone walls, and it was just on the other side of this that I noticed, off to the left of the road, the remains of a former bridge, ten meters upstream from the small bridge I was crossing. I pulled over and walked back to it. There were the masonry stumps where the bridge had connected with the bank on either side and, leading away from them, strips of old tarmac marking the route of the road as it had been in that former time. Further on, in the Regency of Karangasem, I passed a couple more of these phantom bridges and felt sure they were the first tangible signs of the 1963 eruption.

One of the most remarkable things about the Agung eruption was the extraordinary timing of it. In early March 1963 the Balinese had begun the elaborate and long-planned ceremony, Ekadasa Rudra. The ceremony took place at the island's principal temple, Besakih, situated high on the southwest slope of Gunung Agung, some seven kilometers below and away from the crater. Held according to tradition once every century (a Balinese year having 210 days), this rarest of ceremonies was intended to exorcise the whole island of the evil god, Rudra (the "howler"), by driving it away into the eleven directions of space.[5] The ceremony had last been held in 1848 and was thus well overdue, the lapse being attributable to the upheavals of the Japanese occupation, the nationalist revolution, and the struggle against the Dutch for independence. It was delayed further, apparently, by a failure of the high priests to agree on the most propitious time to hold it.

While not specifically designed to appease the deity of the volcano, the fact that Agung began rumbling during the early stages of the ceremony was regarded by many in Bali as ominous. But the dozens of priests and hundreds of worshippers gathered at Besakih chose to ignore the government's warning to call off the ceremony and get off the mountain. On 17 March, while the priests were still enacting the drawn-out rites in the terraced temple complex to the accompaniment of a gamelan orchestra, the mountain above their heads exploded. The temple, like all those on the island, consisted of individual shrines set inside a series of walled compounds. It sustained damage from ash and rock showers, but although it stood high on the mountain, it was situated along the spine of a ridge and when the lava began to spill over the lip of the crater it flowed around the temple rather than over it. Amazingly few casualties were sustained at Besakih on the eastern slopes of Agung. Not so fortunate were a number of villages high on the southern slopes whose inhabitants died as their homes were suddenly engulfed by lava or perished in the clouds of searing hot gas that cascaded down out of the crater.

The whole eastern end of Bali was cut off from the rest of the island for weeks on end by lava flows and rivers of hot mud and ash. There were no airfields there and no ports. Apart from the movement of outrigger canoes, the isolation was quite real.

A few kilometers past the relict bridge the road veered inland along a broad valley until it arrived at the village of Subagan. Subagan, I thought, should be an ideal place to really start looking for traces of the eruption. The newspapers in March 1963 had carried photographs of a street in the village where the shops and houses were half submerged below a deposit of ash and volcanic rock that had settled around them, spilling in through doors and windows. Torrential rain had fallen on the higher slopes of Gunung Agung, loosening the accumulation of hot ash and rock that had fallen there and bringing it down the mountainside in a steaming torrent, more than half a kilometer wide. The torrent gradually slowed in momentum until, when it reached Sub-agan, it merely filled the village up instead of carrying it away. But it was no less lethal for that. Two hundred people praying at a village temple were killed when it struck. The Malay word *lahar* describes these mobile, rain-saturated deposits of hot ash and rock. In that part of the world *lahar* was considered to be far more dangerous than lava.

Thick clouds of steam were still rising over the village when the press reached Subagan a few days after the *lahar* had hit. Howling dogs roamed the streets. "Most of it is buried under six to 10 feet of black mud that fills its houses up to the roof and makes its roads unrecognisable," the *Sydney Morning Herald* reported on 25 March. "Thousands of boulders, some the size of cars litter the surface of the mud, next to crumbled walls, splintered telephone poles." Eight of those who died at Subagan were found on the roof of the village's small mosque, one of them with minor burns but the others lacking any outward sign of physical injury.[6] It was determined they had died of shock. On the nearby coast, crowds of women were described as standing, naked to the waist, knee-deep in the ocean, "praying to appease their gods and goddesses."

With a picture of the devastated street on the seat next to me—it was a photocopy from microfilm and hence somewhat blurred—I drove into Subagan at that time of day when most people were either sleeping off the heat or sitting in deep shadow playing cards or checkers and listening to the radio. It looked pretty much like any other Balinese village that happened to be on a major road. There was a main street lined with single-story shops and white-washed bungalows, clouds of red and orange bougainvillea hanging over their garden walls. A motorcycle repair shop opened onto the pavement like a grease-blackened grotto. There were no car-sized volcanic boulders lying in the streets, of course, but I looked closely at the shops and houses, comparing them to the ones in the picture. None of them seemed to match, so I left the main street and drove slowly along a smaller road that led up a gentle slope behind the center of the village. Here there were fewer shops and the houses were spaced further apart with rice fields visible immediately behind them. A little further along, the rice fields began to appear in between the houses as well, and I realized I'd left the village behind. The sealed road became a dirt track that petered out at the edge of a steeper, bush-covered slope. I stopped the car and got out.

Large gray rocks in the fields to my left and right were surrounded by expanses of luminous green rice growing in wide terraces that stepped down the slope. The neatly trimmed earth embankments of one of the terraces curved around an obtruding boulder and I wondered which had been there first, the terrace or the boulder. If the *lahar* had passed this way, and surely it had, then the terraces would have been rebuilt in its aftermath, people having no choice but to live with those rocks that were too big to shift. There were several boulders in the fields themselves, protruding above the green surface of the crop, a crop that was like some kind of green fluid that made islands out of anything it couldn't submerge. The level surface of the ripening rice was broken here and there, suggesting there might be smaller boulders present there, out of sight below the crop. The minutes passed while I stood interrogating the fields, enveloped by the heat. The trouble with the heat was not that it distracted you from your purpose but that, like a narcotic, it could all too easily lead you to fasten on some insignificant detail while the afternoon slipped away and the big picture eluded you. I noticed some women working in one of the fields, weeding, their faces unreadable in the shade of their conical straw hats. They were looking over at me and laughing. One of them waved at me, or I thought she did, so I waved back.

The eruption had not, then, been completely disguised by the passage of three decades. There were traces. Back down the road I stopped and looked over the low wall of an empty schoolyard. Projecting from the smooth dirt surface were several boulders too big to have been cleared away when the school was built or rebuilt following the eruption. Now that I had my eye in, I began to notice rocks and boulders everywhere. Freshly washed clothes had been spread to dry over some big ones that lay in an uncultivated field of dry grass. On another road I came upon a field that looked as if it hadn't been cleaned up at all after the eruption: A few small vegetable gardens had been fitted into the irregular spaces between boulders, and a thatch-roofed hut with woven bamboo walls stood on a rocky promontory. Back down near the main road I stopped outside the bungalow-style office of some government department, which was set in a carefully tended compound where the tops of boulders broke the surface of a smooth lawn like carefully arranged features in a Japanese garden.

The survivors of the eruption, upon returning to Subagan, had obviously begun life again and gradually restored the landscape to something closely resembling what it had been. The event that had so suddenly effaced their neighborhood was effaced in its turn. But the continued presence of the partly submerged boulders illustrated the limits of this process of undoing. Unable to be moved and impractical to break up, they merged into the restored topography. Rice crops and lawn flowed around them; garments that people wore on their bodies were laid out to dry on the surface of rocks that thirty years previously may have crushed other bodies. I wondered if the boulders were now such a familiar presence that people didn't often reflect on how they got there.

"Something confusing?" A young man was standing behind me looking helpful.

"No," I replied, nodding my thanks, "I'm just looking."

Then on the spur of the moment I thought of showing him my photo-copied photograph of the ruined street. I placed it on the bonnet of the car, explaining that it had been taken just after the 1963 eruption, indicating with my eyes the direction of the mountain. You couldn't actually see Agung from where we stood because of the trees and houses. I wondered if his English was good enough to have understood me, but he nodded and said he knew about 1963 and Gunung Agung. He said it as if the eruption were an item of universal knowledge, although he was obviously too young to have been born at that time.

He stood there looking with interest at the picture of the ruined street as motor scooters puttered past us and high school students in uniform walked by in twos and threes.

"Where?" he asked.

I was momentarily thrown by his solicitous, sympathetic tone, and then I realized he hadn't understood that this picture was of Subagan, the village where we both now stood.

"Here," I replied. "Subagan!"

"Ya, Subagan?" He picked the picture up now and looked at it more closely, but he shook his head. "I think not Subagan," he said, handing it back to me as if to rid himself of it. But I wasn't to be put off quite that easily.

"See, here, it says Subagan," I said, picking up the picture and pointing to the caption, suddenly conscious of the amount of faith I put in the printed word. He glanced skeptically in the direction of my finger, but just then a small bus coming down the hill slowed to a stop in front of us, and he quickly apologized and hurried off to board it, leaving me holding the picture. I watched the bus as it moved off again down the hill. I was a bit nonplussed by the way he'd shrugged off the photograph, as if the eruption were my history and my problem rather than his.

Back in the car, I glanced at the picture again as I began driving slowly back along the main road in the direction of Candi Dasa. I now looked more carefully at the facades and roofs of the buildings I was passing. The tiled roofs all looked comparable in shape to the ones in the photograph, and the black stains on the tiles, left by wet-season fungal growth, gave all of them an appearance of age. But that could happen almost overnight in this climate. Two of the shops in the photograph had facades in the *kantor* or "office" style favored by the Dutch administration in the first half of the twentieth century, but I could see nothing in front of me that quite matched them. I stopped the car and walked back along the street, pausing every few meters to take a close look at the buildings on the opposite side, trying to distinguish recent additions and renovations from older elements. In March 1963 an AAP correspondent had written, "Today Subagan is a dead town. Only vultures, and a few dogs and chickens and a number of looters are interested in it. Subagan is about as thoroughly destroyed as a town could be."[7]

And yet the present village looked as if it had always been there. It was a picture of solid and uninterrupted continuity.

Apart from the boulders I'd been observing, the 1963 eruption, as a historical event, had little or no visibility in today's landscape. At least not to my eyes. The landscape seemed to have grown over the evidence, like skin growing back over a graze, almost as though it were colluding in a form of censorship, encouraging a certain illusion. Was that what a cultural landscape was? A kind of template that simply reproduces itself, or another version of itself, to cover over any gaps or lesions?

I wondered how older people remembered the terrain that had been buried and semi-obliterated. Surely even today they would still carry a picture of it in their minds. I imagined sixty-year-olds out in the fields planting rice seedlings, standing up to straighten their backs, and looking over at a hill slope covered in lush bush. Did they see the neatly trimmed rice terraces that had been buried there, terraces they'd worked in all through their youth? Fields where after school they sat under a palm frond shelter, scaring the birds away from the ripening rice by pulling strings tied with tin cans that were strung across it. When they glanced in passing at a vacant piece of land did they sometimes see an afterimage of the house that had been there and the people who'd lived in it, people who numbered among the lost? Or standing in the compound of one of the village's temples during a ceremony did they sometimes visualize the old temple that had stood on the same spot and whose remains were buried down there below their feet?

Back on the streets of Subagan, meanwhile, my problem lay in deciding what in the streetscape dated from before the eruption and what from after. I knew it must have been possible to assign approximate dates to the structures on stylistic grounds, but, frustratingly, I didn't know enough about modern Balinese secular architecture to make such discriminations.

When I left Subagan half an hour later and passed through Jasri, a village a few kilometers back down the highway toward Candi Dasa, my attention was caught by the rough stone walls standing shoulder-high in front of most of the houses. Was this where the smaller rocks deposited by the eruption had ended up? In the gardens of some of the houses there were ferroconcrete imitation rockeries that took the form of small cliffs, sometimes with waterfalls and often with niches for growing ferns and trailing plants. These rockeries featured sham boulders, cleverly shaped and finished in cement tinted a charcoal gray. You'd have thought there were enough rocks in this landscape without the need to fabricate more.

Back at the hotel in Candi Dasa I sat on the veranda and looked down along the curve of the bay. There was enough light left to see a few people still sitting on the small aprons of white sand. Closer to me, on a surviving remnant of the old beach, a fisherman was unloading a double-outrigger canoe. A slight figure burned dark brown by the sun, he walked up the slope of the beach toward the coconut palms, carrying his folded net over one shoulder and a string of small silver fish in his hand. It seemed a pathetically small reward for a day spent at sea. Like the youths seen trolling along Kuta Beach day in, day out, hawking fake Rolexes that were next to impossible to sell, it was a small insight into the economics of poverty.

I was still sitting there when night fell, not rapidly, in the manner described by northern European writers used to that gradual fading of the sun peculiar to the northern latitudes, but at a pace normal to what was probably the greater portion of the globe. The boy who was watering the garden with a low-pressure hose, working his way down the strip of shrubs in front of the cottages, had finished and gone away. I thought about my own day and the little I had to show for it. But mostly I just looked at the waves breaking over what was left of the reef and at the much smaller order of waves coming over the lagoon.

I was woken in the night by the noise of a motorbike somewhere nearby. Its engine died and was followed by the sound of footfalls scrunching along the gravel path. I lay on the hard mattress, conscious of the stickiness of my skin and the coarseness of the sheets, and when I knew I wouldn't sleep again for a while I got up and went back to the seat outside. The moon lit up the scalloped edges of the clouds as it passed behind them. I could sense no movement in the air, but, even so, salt-laden moisture was rising off the breaking waves and settling in a film on the tiles of the veranda, leaving them tacky underfoot. It settled invisibly on my bare arms. After a while a door closed somewhere nearby, and a young Balinese guy with the Rasta look of the Candi Dasa gigolos came back down the path, nodded to me as he passed, and rode away on a motorbike.

I picked up the folder of 1963 press stories and sat reading them on the bed with my back against the cool masonry wall. My eyes wandered to the news stories that shared space on the same pages as reports of the Agung eruption. In Singapore in March 1963 they were talking about water rationing and the upcoming meeting in Washington between the Malayan deputy prime minister and John Kennedy. The Profumo affair was breaking news in London, and in Tokyo Crown Princess Michiko had had an abortion. France had just detonated a nuclear device under the Sahara Desert; students in Algiers were protesting against the test, and the United States was expressing a wish that the French would carry out their experiments in the Pacific instead.

In March 1963, in Sydney, the government had chosen a contractor to demolish the historic Rocks area on the waterfront adjacent to the central business district in order to redevelop it with office towers and hotels. This dangerous moment in the city's history was averted when the builder's laborers union refused to engage in such vandalism. Meanwhile, Queen Elizabeth II was making her way majestically down the Western Australian coast in the royal yacht, Britannica, and had stopped off to visit a remote mining town. Like me, she might have lain awake in the night, listening to the sea and wondering if she was getting the most out of life. The *Straits Times* reported that in Bandung, Java, seventy-five thousand students had marched on the residence of the military governor, protesting rising prices and demanding Communist representation in Sukarno's cabinet.

The following morning I decided to move to the town of Amlapura, the old seat of the rajas of Karangasem and only a kilometer or so further to the east of Subagan. When I reached it, I found a place of quiet tree-lined streets and swept sidewalks whose commercial center consisted of a single strip of two- and three-story shop houses, mostly Chinese-owned. But it was the only place in the Regency of Karangasem larger than a village, and if it had gone largely undamaged during the eruption—it had been unaffected by lava or *lahu,* and the prevailing monsoon wind took most of the ash away westward toward Java—it had also been bypassed by the tourism and development boom.

I'd been told that they rented out rooms to travelers at the Puri Agung Karangasem, the old raja's palace, but when I parked the car on the street outside and climbed the steps up to the first of a series of walled courtyards, this hardly seemed likely. The palace extended along the top of a ridge, and the courtyards were terraced into its flanks. Just inside the monumental brick gateway to the first courtyard was a small table on which lay a ledger book and a block of admission tickets. There was nobody around so I took the steps up to the main courtyard, passing through another monumental gateway, this one in the form of a square tower with three pagoda-like diminishing tiers rising over the passageway itself. Most of the space in the large level compound was taken up by a rectangular carp pool that was half covered with lotuses and in the center of which was an island pavilion reached by a small causeway supported by arches. It was a delightful space, but there was no sign or promise of hotel accommodation. When I went back down to the first courtyard the ticket seller was sitting at his table. Over the next couple of days I learned that the trickle of tourists who found their way to the palace often dried up for hours on end, and during these spells the ticket seller, who introduced himself as Madé, could stretch out and nap in a small *balé* (a raised, open-sided pavilion) nearby. Madé had several fighting cocks, lined up on the gravel in light rattan cages shaped like bell jars. They needed a lot of handling and pampering and moving in and out of the shade, and this also took up a lot of his time.

The Puri Agung Karangasem did indeed have rooms for guests, Madé assured me, and he led me off to see them, up to the second compound and past the lotus pond to a smaller gateway at the southern end. Beyond this stretched a dirt path hemmed in by the outer walls of the succession of small courtyards that opened off it and to which it provided access. Down along this path we passed two of the courtyard gateways, which, similar to those found in temple compounds, were like ornate brick bookends placed close together. As always, there were a couple of brick steps on either side of the actual door, so you stepped up through the gate and then down into the courtyard, this marking the crossing of a particular liminal threshold. Since the typical Balinese house consisted not of bulky single buildings but of freestanding rooms and open pavilions distributed around the enclosed spaces of walled courtyards, the entry gateway took on the significance that a front door would in a Western building. Even the simplest of gateways on the island had winged doors that opened inward from the middle so that you always passed through the center of the opening rather than somewhat toward the left as you would with a single-wing door.

In the courtyards we passed, nothing seemed to move except the leaves of the trees. I took in the bare, weatherworn wood of the doors and the exfoliating plaster through which patches of orange brickwork were visible: There was a suggestion of gradual decline here. Madé showed me into the courtyard containing the guestrooms, none of which was occupied. Following him, I slipped off my sandals, stepped up onto a paved veranda, and then passed into the dim space of one of the rooms. It was hotel accommodation at its most basic but entirely in keeping with the mood of the *puri*.

When Madé left I strolled around looking at the plants but was then drawn back out to the dirt pathway I'd come in along. The surface looked as if it had been recently swept with one of those bunches of stiff straw (*sapu lidi*) people used. You could see the brush strokes even around the trunks of the hibiscus and the stems of the smaller shrubs growing in rows along the base of the walls. A line of tiny tracks from what I thought might be a lizard were visible on the path's velvet surface. The straw broom would gather up the brick dust and plaster fragments from the exfoliating wall, along with fallen blossoms, leaves, and cigarette butts. Like the Thais, the Burmese, the Javanese, and others of the region, the Balinese were meticulous in sweeping around structures, leaving the structures themselves to get on with the business of deterioration.[8]

The white plastered surfaces of the walls on either side of the path were cracked and discolored by grey and green mold, which had spread in patterns that mapped underlying inconsistencies in the layer of render. The unplastered orange-colored bricks of which the gateways were built were about half the size of conventional "Western" bricks and they were laid with almost no mortar, so that from a distance the joins were almost imperceptible. The low-fired nature of these unglazed bricks, which caused them to erode relatively quickly, lends Balinese architecture one of its characteristic aspects. A portion of them always erodes more rapidly than the others to produce rectangular concavities like rock shelters in the otherwise smooth orange surfaces of walls and pillars. Three or four such "soft" bricks were eroding on the outside face of the gateway to my courtyard, spilling a small cone of bright orange powder onto the step a few feet below. I squatted down to get a better look, thinking I might actually see some brick particles fall.

There was traffic noise in the distance and the tinny sound of a radio floated over the wall of one of the nearby courtyards. No particles fell, but squatting there by the gateway I was conscious for a moment of how this whole complex of buildings was breaking down. It was not to be thought of as regrettable; rather, it was integral to the life and meaning of the place. Buildings all over the island were decaying in the same manner—the hourglass of falling brick dust calibrating the pace of attrition—and rarely was anything done to interfere. People lived with a level of decay that, though it seemed rapid, was entirely sustainable, matched as it was by their ability to rebuild.

I had a shower in the poorly lit bathroom, kneeling on the concrete floor and using a pink plastic scoop to pour over my head cool water from the pastel-blue tiled tub in the corner. Then, sitting on the edge of the veranda, I poured a glass of tea from a Chinese tin thermos that had appeared on a low bamboo table. I then got out the Nelles Verlag 1:180,000 touring map. I wanted to have a look for signs of the eruption on the higher slopes of Gunung Agung, so I traced a route up there with my finger and memorized the turns in the road. The courtyard was quiet, the invisible radio had been turned off. The ground was covered with a bed of loose, flat pebbles; no lawn nor even any flower beds as such, just trees and shrubs rising up out of the pebbles and the terra-cotta and brightly painted concrete pots standing on the pebbles. There was a small dining pavilion in one corner and a gate in the far wall with a few steps down into the garden of an adjoining courtyard at a lower level. A cylindrical goldfish tank stood partly shaded by a fruit tree, its cement walls softened with moss, its sides pierced by four small round glass windows, exactly like portholes in a ship except that here the water was on the inside. I supposed the tank had been one of the innovations of Gusti Bagus Jlantik (1887–1967), the previous raja and a well-known modernist.

Figure 3.2.   Fish pond at Puri Agung Karangasem, Amlapura, Bali, 1990s (Denis Byrne)

Collecting my camera, map, and sheaf of photocopies, I left the court-yard and set off back up the path. Entering the large plaza with the lotus pool, I noticed there was an unobstructed view of the Gunung Agung's volcanic cone, over to the left, its outline softened by the haze. It stopped me in my tracks. I'd missed it on the way in, too absorbed in what was in front of me to have bothered turning around. Amlapura occupied somewhat higher ground than the surrounding terrain, and the *puri* seemed to occupy the highest ground in town. From the *puri* I looked straight across the countryside to the mountain.

What would it be like, I wondered, to behold a view like that every morning of your life? Would it caution you to remember that the ground you stood on, like the weather, was volatile? Or would it be so familiar that you would simply not see it? It was not just a mountain, though, to these people; nor just a volcano: It was inseparable from the Hindu-Balinese deities that dwelt there, a fact that, I supposed, gave it more presence. It also meant you weren't helpless in the face of nature; you could intercede with that presence, or at least try to. Pura Besakih played a key role in this.[9]

Once out of Amlapura I backtracked along the highway to Subagan then took a road that climbed across the southern foothills of Gunung Agung. Within ten kilometers there appeared on either side of the road trellises of split bam-boo, covered with creepers and backed by hedges to form green walls. I slowed down. Every so often very narrow lanes of swept earth, bordered by high hedges, led back off the road and ended in front of closed bamboo gates. A heavy haze hung around these slopes, accentuating their containment and privacy.

Passing through the villages of Sibetan, Pesangkan, and Duda, I then came to Selat. In March 1963 a lava flow had approached Selat from upslope, but it followed the deeply incised river channels on either side of the village, leaving the village itself isolated and untouched. But later a wave of *lahar* had swept over everything. A *National Geographic* reporter walked several kilometers to get to the area and found starving dogs prowling through the remains of the place: "There wasn't a sound—not even a bird. Smoke rose here and there from the ash. The ground was almost too hot to touch, and the smell of sulphur made me dizzy."[10] The magazine published a photograph showing an expanse of what had once been rice fields, now nearly ten meters deep in steaming ash.[11]

Like Subagan, the much smaller village of Selat now seemed not to own up to this past. Most of its shops and houses, the afternoon I was there, had the appearance of being long established. The rice terraces surrounding the village were a picture of neatness and had that aspect of naturalness that came from shadowing the land's natural contours. But I noticed there was also an unusual amount of uncultivated land around the village. It was forested or covered with tangled brush, and I thought these might be the areas worst affected by the eruption.

I took a road leading directly uphill from the village, passing groves of giant bamboo. On one side of the road was an expanse of rocky, uneven ground vegetated with large ferns and shrubs. Was that the aftermath of a *lahar* torrent? The higher I drove the more marginal was the land for agriculture. The irrigated terraces ceased and were replaced by fields of maize. In 1963 a reporter for the *Straits Times* had seen "maize fields where the leaves had disappeared and only the scorched ears remained on the stalk. The corn was roasted."[12] Driving back down the road I acknowledged to myself that I wouldn't really have known what a volcanic ash deposit or even a lava flow would look like after thirty years, certainly not in an environment so extraordinarily favorable to plant growth.

In the distance a man was coming down the road with a large black rock on his shoulder, quite bent under its weight. Seeing him turn into the entrance of the concrete shell of an unfinished building, I stopped the car and walked over. The floor of the structure was mounded with blocks and chips of this black stone. It resembled a coal depot but, in fact, was a stone-carving workshop where blocks of basalt were being shaped into spirit shrines. The dozens of individual carved blocks that made up one of the pedestal-like shrines (*palinggih*, meaning place or seat) had been assembled in a corner, perhaps awaiting a customer, whereupon it would be disassembled and carted off to a temple or house compound. Shrines just like this, perhaps a little less ornate, also stood in rice fields, and hundreds of them must have been buried during the eruption. There was something poetic in the idea that the lava and rock that had come down out of the volcano, destroying the shrines and temples, had now become the raw material of new shrines and temples. The spirits of the Balinese pantheon to whom these shrines belonged, along with the spirits of the people's ancestors, outlived worldly events like the 1963 eruption. To a great extent they were spirits of place and they would still be "in place" even after an ash shower or lava flow added to the place's surface.

The Western press had played to the religious dimension of the Agung eruption. They reported on the people who had defied official warnings and stayed praying in their temples as the mountain rumbled in the days before it erupted: "Hundreds were roasted alive in three villages just south of the mountain as they knelt in prayer."[13] They reported on the women who were seen carrying their colorful propitiatory offerings of flowers and fruit to the temples and the spirits of the sea even while the eruption was in progress and ash floated down upon them. There was no getting off the hook for the poor Balinese: Even in the midst of disaster they still had to provide the West with its fix of exotica.

Figure 3.3.   Gunung Agung from Puri Agung Karangasem, Amlapura, Bali, 1990s (Denis Byrne)

When I got back to Amlapura, Madé and two of his friends were sitting on the pavement opposite the main gate of the *puri* eating fruit salad. The fruit vendor's barrow was one of those glass-sided boxes on wheels (they are all over Southeast Asia) in which fruit is stacked, glistening in its different colors, waiting to be chopped and served with sweet syrup and crushed ice. Eyeing the car, they asked if I'd like to see a cockfight that was being held in Madé's home village that day. They assured me it wasn't too far away.

We took the road to Amed, which is a small fishing village on the coast to the east, but before Tirtaganga we turned off the road onto a smaller road heading directly up the slopes of Gunung Agung. We climbed steadily up the gentle incline that comprised the volcano's first thousand meters' elevation. It was late in the afternoon, and people were coming home from the fields with hoes over their shoulders or baskets on their heads. They sat in gateways or stood talking in the roadway, holding their bicycles: the end of another day in the Regency of Karangasem. It turned out that all three of the boys were originally from the same village, and as we drew near to it they began to pay closer attention to the people along the road, waving and calling out to some of them, merely passing comment on others as we drove by.

The cockfight had been going since the morning and was just finishing as we arrived. People were drifting away from the area under the trees where it had taken place. The boys might have known this was on the cards even before we left but just couldn't pass up the chance for a ride back home. It didn't matter to me, either; I was happy just to see the village in their company. We walked up a path into the compound of Madé's uncle where I shook hands with some men sitting together on the steps of a pavilion. Most of the adult male population of the village seemed to be drunk on palm wine, the sweet, cloying smell of which hung in the air. There was a lot of laughing and back-slapping and stumbling around; the boys looked a bit askance and suddenly decided we should go to see another of Madé's uncles who lived just up the road. The atmosphere there was calmer, except for the twenty or so cocks that stood in their cages in two neat rows across the dirt courtyard, scratching the dust and crowing. There were two old men, some middle-aged men and women, and several children, but nobody between the ages of about fifteen and thirty. They all seemed to be aunts, uncles, or cousins of the boys.

Squatting on the ground, one of Madé's younger uncles had taken a bird out of its cage and was holding it, gently squeezing its thighs and stroking its beautiful orange neck feathers. He looked inquiringly up at Madé who was standing looking critically down at the creature. Without understanding what he said, I sensed this was an occasion for an honest opinion rather than flattery. Later, as we were driving up the road, he said he'd heard that some Australians didn't like cock fighting, and I said this was true. It wasn't a custom of ours. "Always in Bali we do it," he said with an air of inevitability and closure, as if it were something that couldn't be helped.

The boys thought there was just enough daylight left for us to drive further up the side of the mountain to where there was a good "panorama" of the landscape below. For my part, I thought it might be my best chance to see the cone of the volcano up close. A kilometer or so up the road from the village we turned and crossed a dry riverbed by way of a concrete ford. Unlike the deeply incised beds of most of the rivers and streams on the island, this one was shallow and wide, and I wondered if in March 1963 a preexisting gully here had carried a lava flow that had solidified in place. The surface was now covered with gray rocks. Across the riverbed the road turned uphill again, and soon the vegetation began to thin out and we were on a gentle slope that ran up to the foot of the immense cone. The boys suggested we stop here because there was cloud rolling down the mountain and the light was fading.

I asked if they had ever walked up to the crater. "No, no, we have never," Madé replied, and the three of them laughed quietly. Wayan, looking more serious, added in a quiet voice, "We cannot." The others nodded. Perhaps because of the nature of the deities present there, most people seemed not to venture far above the zone of arable land, which extended not much higher than Pura Besakih at 950 meters. Foreign tourists, though, seemed to have little trouble finding guides to lead them through the bush and over the scoria slopes to the chilly summit. Perhaps the tourists felt the need to climb it simply because it was there, like the thousands every year who opt to climb the monolithic Uluru in Central Australia, despite signs erected by local Aboriginal custodians politely asking them not to climb a rock that is sacred to them. Apart from the ordinary tourists who climbed Gunung Agung, there were New Agers from many parts of the world who believed the mountain was a key point of convergence on the globe's geopsychic energy grid. Its vibrations, apparently, were exceptionally strong. Some had gone up the mountain without guides and some of those, rumor had it, had not come down again. This was the sort of talk you heard late at night in Seminyak, sitting on the floor around somebody's bamboo coffee table drinking the cheap local vodka.

The land on which we stood had been good farmland before the eruption, Madé assured me. Now it was a lava field beginning to be colonized by tough shrubs and a resilient variety of grass. There were some stunted trees, but the place was desolate and dry. Another type of tree was being grown from cuttings that had been stuck in the ground at regular intervals in a grid pattern. At first I didn't see the grid, I just saw two or three of the sprouting sticks; then I saw more of them, and the grid pattern snapped into focus. A solitary old man was gathering regular-sized rocks, placing them in neat piles. This wasn't for himself. It couldn't be. Surely he would be long dead before this austere terrain was ever productive again. For his descendants then, or for the sake of something that was out of my grasp. For a moment I was appalled by the time span of what he was involved in.

The clouds moved away from the cone, and I stood looking at it for a while. Then turning to look downhill it occurred to me for the first time that when Agung had erupted, the boys' home village must have been inside the zone of major impact. It was very quiet up there, above the realm of everyday life. The boys were thinking about going back to Amlapura, "the city," as Wayan called it. You could see it in the distance looking like a handful of gravel dropped on a lawn. They pointed out items of interest in the landscape below us, the "panorama" that extended to the edge of the sea, about fifteen kilometers away. It was this they'd brought me to see, not the view of the mountain behind us. They had spent virtually the whole of their lives within the space of this vista.

It was cold for them up there, they told me. "Yes, of course," I said, and we climbed back into the car. It must have been all of twenty-five degrees Celsius. Riding back down the mountain we listened to a Pretenders cassette I had and then to Nat King Cole. There were children running about at the side of the road and ducks that looked like they might cross in front of the car or might not; I had to keep my eyes peeled and make an effort not to be distracted by the sights. The fact that you rarely got to drive faster than forty kilometers an hour on Bali was one of the reasons the island seemed so much larger than it really was.

It was almost dark when we got back to Amlapura. I spent an hour or so at the table in the dining pavilion writing my journal. In one corner of the pavilion there was a white refrigerator still standing on the form-fitted white styrofoam pallet it had been delivered in. It wasn't plugged in. When I opened it earlier in the day it was empty except for a large praying mantis, which clung in its perfect greenness to the white plastic icebox door. I tried to pick it up, but it jumped down and stood on one of the racks below, waving its long antennae at me. I'd left the door open a little so it could come out, but in the meantime somebody must have closed it and now, when I opened it again, the mantis was still there but one of its back legs was missing. The leg was lying on the glass shelf below. It still wouldn't come out.

The only book I had with me was a new translation of semiautobiographical short stories by Osamu Dazai (1909–1948) that a friend had lent me.[14] In the story "One Hundred Views of Mount Fuji,"[15] Dazai describes his stay at a teahouse on a mountain pass near Fuji, a place that had accommodation for guests and where he was trying to work on a novel. The mountain strikes him as disappointingly short: "Any mountain with a base that size should be half again as tall," he writes.[16] A friend comes to visit and they stand by a window of the teahouse smoking cigarettes and poking fun at Fuji:

"Awfully crass, isn't it? It's like 'Ah, Honorable Mount Fuji.'"

"I know. It's embarrassing to look at."[17]

Masao Miyoshi characterizes the Buraiha (vagabond) group of writers to which Dazai belonged as posturing decadents, which they may well have been, but I sympathized with Dazai's impulse to make fun of Fuji.[18] I assumed that the modernist Buraiha had either put aside or simply lost their belief in Shinto and hence the belief in Fuji as *kami* (a locus of divine power). And once you stop believing in the divine aspect of a place—which, anyway, is never an aspect or facet of it but rather its embodiment—and, let's say, you fall back on a purely aesthetic appreciation, then Fuji really is only one step removed from being crass. For Dazai, Fuji's overrepresentation turned it into a vulgarity: "It was a wall painting in a public bath. Scenery on a stage. So precisely made to order it was mortifying to behold."[19]

The *puri*'s public areas were deserted when I went out for dinner at about seven-thirty. Walking back down the swept dirt pathway, I indulged myself in the fantasy that I lived here and walked this pathway every day. There were a couple of palace dogs lying on the cool cracked terrazzo of the pavilion floors next to the lotus pool, one of them giving a token growl as I went past. When I came back an hour later the old wooden door to my courtyard had been locked from the inside. After knocking on it a few times and calling out over the wall, I retraced my steps to the compound on the lower terrace, between the *puri*'s two entrance gates, and called Madé's name outside what I hoped was his little room. He came in his singlet and sarong and had to climb over the wall to unbar the door, saying the people in the courtyards beyond mine must have thought I was already inside, implying, I thought, that there was no reason to be "outside" at such an hour.

While I was having coffee the next morning, an elderly woman in an exquisite and very faded brown batik sarong was using a long bamboo pole to shake the branches of a jambu tree at the other end of the courtyard, bringing down a shower of small bright pink fruit. They ran down the old tiled roof and landed on the gray pebble bed where the morning sun, shining through the leaves, illuminated some of them and left others in a shade so deep you could barely distinguish them from the pebbles. She brought over a dish of them, freshly washed. The fruit was white and watery inside, almost like an apple but tasting of the pinkness (I can't think of a more adequate word) of the skin. The pinker the skin, the stronger the taste.

Before going out for the day I spent a while exploring the *puri*. Most of the current buildings had been erected by the late raja, Gusti Bagus Jlantik, after he came to the throne of Karangasem in 1908 at the age of twenty-one.

These structures included the lotus pool with its island pavilion and the arched causeway leading out to it. At the northern end was a colonial-style villa he had built perhaps a little later and that was now unoccupied. I walked down its cool central hallway, through the back doorway, and around the side where a sign invited me to peer into the darkened rooms through the barred windows. Dusty gongs and xylophones of an old gamelan lay in one of them, an elaborate wrought-iron bed in another.

It was hard to believe that Gusti Bagus would have wanted to dwell in this structure when he had the choice of any number of courtyard pavilions, infinitely more gracious and more suited to the climate. The explanation no doubt lay in his relationship with the Dutch. The former raja, Gusti Gedé Jlantik, had ceded control of Karangasem to the Dutch in 1895 after the latter had conquered the island of Lombok, a dependency of Karangasem and the source of much of its wealth. By the time Gusti Bagus became raja, thirteen years later, the Dutch were in control of the whole of Bali. The defining moment in this power shift had come on the morning of 20 September 1906. In an act of ritual mass suicide, or *puputan*, the entire court of the powerful kingdom of Badung in southern Bali (centered on present-day Denpasar), along with their followers, in ceremonial dress and to the accompaniment of the court gamelan, had marched out of their *puri* and into the fire of the assembled Dutch troops. More than one thousand men, women, and children were killed. Gusti Bagus retained his prestige under the Dutch, and the villa he built in his *puri* may have represented an effort to be taken seriously as a modern regent. There exists a photograph of Gusti Bagus and his family, in the company of Dutch officials and their wives, taken on the veranda of the villa at Amlapura in the early twentieth century.[20]

I spent the next few days exploring the coast on the northeast side of Gunung Agung where the lower slopes of the mountain fall directly into the Lombok Strait. The country there was surprisingly arid, and most people lived off the sea, fishing from small double-outrigger sailing canoes called *jukung*. The white-painted dugout hulls were trimmed in bright blue and yellow; the prows were shaped like swordfish with open jaws, and they had bulging eyes carved on each side for night vision.

Gunung Agung was no further away, but its presence was less noticeable here: On this side of the mountain one seemed always to be facing the sea. The one occasion when I ventured into the sea—in the *jukung* of two young fishermen I'd met—I was surprised at how the order of things was instantly reversed. As the triangular sail pulled us out beyond the breaking waves, the narrow coastal strip quickly shrank to insignificance and the volcano loomed up out of the haze. Alit and Wingan, the fishermen, had that slender, economical build that I supposed was suited to clambering around on small boats at sea. They wore cotton *ikat* sarongs rather than the bright rayon sarongs patterned with stars and turtles that young people were wearing in south Bali. When we accidentally ran across a fishing line from another canoe, Alit snaked out along the curved outrigger boom to free it and then slithered back again. The nylon hand lines with which they, too, made their living lay in the bottom of the one-piece hull. Along with a pink plastic bailer the lines were all the boat contained.

Back on shore, Alit and Wingan invited me back to their home on a rugged, boulder-encrusted hillside. The two-room house of unpainted concrete blocks was quite new, and facing it on the other side of a shaded dirt

Figure 3.4.   Fisherman near Amed, Bali, 1990s (Denis Byrne)

court, like a before-and-after illustration, was an old hut of woven palm leaves with an earthen floor and strings of garlic and chilis hanging from the eaves. Living here with Alit were his wife and young daughter and Wingan, with his parents and younger brothers. Wingan's mother made tea and brought out bowls of floury popcorn made from their own maize.

The inside of the new house and even part of the outside wall under the veranda were papered with pages from the *Bali Post,* and I found my eyes wandering to headlines about car accidents and photographs of footballers. Somebody had painted "I love film sex," in English, on one of the wooden shutters. I accompanied them that night to a gamelan and dance performance at a fishing village a little further down the coast. Wingan and Alit changed out of their sarongs and into jeans and polo shirts, which Wingan's mother handed out from a low cupboard, neatly folded, afterward securing the cupboard door with a small padlock. There seemed to be no suggestion of any of the others coming with us.

Situated on a sandy flat just above a beach, the performance space was covered by a canopy of striped sails lashed onto a framework of detachable *jukung* outrigger floats. These consisted of lengths of thick bamboo painted white with the blue and red trim carried by the canoes of this village. More sails were spread across the ground. We arrived early, when the place was almost deserted, but by the time the two twenty-piece gamelans sat down facing each other across the plastic sheets, a solid wall of people surrounded the stage, small children sitting avidly in front, adults receding into the darkness behind.

The satin jackets and sarongs of the musicians, yellow at one side of the floor, puce at the other, shone under the naked lightbulbs suspended over them. Each was from a different area, and they played in half-hour spells with that violent and sudden oscillation between delicacy and controlled frenzy for which the Balinese gamelan is known. The crowd pressed in, but the musicians seemed oblivious to anything except the music and they sat crosslegged, heads erect, eyes cast down. They ignored the men of the organizing committee who stood shouting at the crowd to move back. The crowd only pressed in further.

Sudden gusts of wind from the sea made the canopy billow, and then, in the middle of the performance, one side of the rig gave way and a dozen raised arms were left holding the weight of the outrigger floats as the sails flapped loudly and came loose. Three men from the crowd began dragging at the sails and retying them onto the bamboo, a task that necessitated them walking in among the gamelan players who, apparently entranced by now, barely seemed to notice them. The men stood with legs apart as the music surged around them, intent upon what their outstretched arms and hands were doing. This would be normal for them, I thought; they'd be accustomed to crises at sea. For a moment it was almost as if we *were* at sea, being pulled along through the darkness by those currents and whirlpools for which the Strait of Lombok was so notorious.

Perhaps it was a mistake to go to that coast because in doing so I lost my focus on 1963 and the eruption. Driving back home, away from Gunung Agung, I resolved to try to remember that I was living on a volcanic island with violent past. But as the traffic on the highway grew heavier and the southern beach enclaves grew closer, I felt this certainty slipping away.

NOTES

1. Booth 1963.
2. Vickers 1989.
3. Booth 1963, 436.
4. Vickers 1989, 166.
5. Eiseman 1990, 236.
6. Eastern Bali has a small but significant population of Muslims whose presence there dates from the period prior to the mid-nineteenth century when the predominantly Muslim island of Lombok was ruled by the rajas of Karangasem.
7. AAP report in the *Sydney Morning Herald*, 26 March 1963.
8. In reference to Thailand, it has been pointed out that it is not part of the Buddhist ethic to try to forestall the decay of material things and that the inevitability of decay is central to Buddhist teaching (e.g., Sharp and Hanks 1978, 22; O'Connor 1978, 177).
9. In 1995 the Balinese successfully resisted a proposal by the Indonesian government to nominate Besakih for the World Heritage List; they opposed it being referred to as an object rather than a being (Tanudirdjo 2006).
10. Mathews 1963, 453.
11. Ibid., 449.
12. *Straits Times*, 26 March 1993.
13. AAP report in the *Sydney Morning Herald*, 23 March 1963.
14. Dazai 1991.
15. The title of Dazai's "One Hundred Views of Mount Fuji" is a reference to Hokusai's famous collection of *ukiyoe* prints of the same name (Dazai 1991).
16. Ibid., 71.
17. Ibid., 75.
18. Miyoshi 1991, 116–22.
19. Dazai 1991, 75.
20. Photograph by Tilly Weissenborn, reproduced in Vickers 1989.

· 4 ·

Traces of 1965–1966

$\mathcal{I}$ spent a lot of time down at the beach during the wet season. Mostly the sky would be low and uniformly gray, just like everywhere else on the island, but I felt less closed in there. The beach was a slow half-hour walk from the bungalow, under that low ceiling of cloud, along a road bordered by flooded rice fields whose surfaces reflected the sky. The air smelled of mud and the warm, wet road. There was no escape from this world of moisture where the walls and the bed linen smelled of dampness, where the pages of books buckled and sagged, and where people withdrew into themselves.

At the corner of the road, just where it turned and ran east along the back of the small bush-covered dune, was the stone gateway to one of the first luxury hotels built on the island. You couldn't see the single-story buildings from the road, only the garden, which was long established and which in places was almost wild. Nature in the form of the weather, the insects, and the mosses and mold seemed to be pulling it toward a jungle state. Pitted against this force were the gardeners as they methodically clipped and trimmed. They took sickles to the greenery, the same ones they used for harvesting rice, but the growth rate of the vegetation was impressive, even disturbing.

Just past the hotel gate was a path leading over the dune to the beach, passing in front of the small walled compound of the village's *pura dalem* (temple of death). This in turn was next to the overgrown cemetery. Both of them were situated at the *kelod* end of the village territory in a cosmological system in which spatial orientation was always in relation to two poles of purity and impurity, *kaja* and *kelod*. *Kaja* was the direction of the volcanoes, the dwelling place of gods, and the realm of everything good and sacred. *Kelod* was the direction of the sea, the dwelling place of malevolent spirits, and the realm of all that is low and impure.

The storms washed a lot of seaweed and driftwood up onto the beach, along with plastic drinking straws and lengths of thin nylon rope, unraveling, fading, and tangled up with dry seaweed. There were pieces of water-worn bamboo, low-wattage light bulbs, green plastic turtles that once contained a sticky-sweet soft drink, instant noodle packets, coconuts, and toothbrushes with worn, splayed bristles. Here a stiletto heel, there mango seeds with the fur washed off. Sometimes there were items of clothing: a torn pair of check shorts half submerged in the sand, a football sock with blue-and-white stripes. On the beach in front of the hotel the garden staff raked all of this up every morning and buried it in shallow pits on the beach from which it would be pulled out and spread around again by the next high tide.

One year a great tree stump was washed up, its roots reaching out like the arms of some kind of sea creature. It had been in the ocean so long that shellfish had fastened themselves to the water-blackened wood. Local people said it must have come from Australia.

It wasn't until my second monsoon season on Bali that I became interested, through my reading, in the 1965 coup that had brought General Soeharto to power and in the events that formed the aftermath of the coup. The climate of that season seemed appropriate to the nature of the events of that earlier time. Like many other things in Indonesia, the attempted coup, or whatever

Figure 4.1.   Hotel terrace, Bali, 1990s (Denis Byrne)

it was, had become known by an acronym, G30S (Gerakan Tiga Puluh September, the 30 September Movement).[1] I learned that following G30S an ominous calm had fallen over the country for a period of some three weeks during which Soeharto and the army consolidated their power and effectively sidelined President Sukarno, who had held office ever since Indonesia gained its independence from the Netherlands in 1949. In Java, the lull following the coup was followed in turn by the rounding up of PKI (Partai Kommunis Indonesia) cadres, party members, and even relatives and associates of party members. They were either killed or imprisoned. The roundups and the killing then spread outward from Java, the death toll for the country as a whole reaching somewhere in the vicinity of half a million people, concentrated, apart from Java, mainly in Bali, north Sumatra, and West Kalimantan (Indonesian Borneo).[2] It is thought that about one hundred thousand Balinese were killed in late 1965 and the early months of 1966.

In Bali the killings began on a significant scale only in early December 1965 with the arrival on the island at that time of the same para-commandos who had been orchestrating the massacre of Communists in East Java.[3] Mostly the Balinese victims were trucked to army depots or villages controlled by the PNI (Partai Nationalis Indonesia), where they were shot, stabbed, or beaten to death. Many civilians participated in the killings, either convinced by propaganda that the PKI were the enemies of Balinese religion or trapped by an army-imposed logic that held there could be no neutrality in this matter: You were either for the government (represented by the army) or you were PKI.[4]

Thousands of people lived those days in dread that their names existed on some list, in dread of marauding gangs of PNI youths in black shirts,[5] and even in dread of the sound that trucks made.[6] The bodies of the dead were tossed into the sea, thrown down wells, or buried in mass graves at least some of which were situated near the island's beaches. One of the most infamous death sites was a village on the road from Denpasar to Tabanan, an ordinary-looking place I'd ridden my motor scooter through numerous times with barely a sideways glance.

A peculiar silence had quickly settled over the events of 1965–1966, a silence that was a product of shock, fear, censorship, and the complete disappearance (by death and imprisonment) of the country's Left intelligentsia. Internationally, the same press that diligently covered the 1963 Gunung Agung eruption chose by and large to turn its head from the 1965–1966 killings. Even Western anthropologists subsequently working in Bali rarely mentioned them.[7] The killings were almost never referred to publicly in Indonesia in the period from 1992 to 1995, when I was living there, except obliquely in government warnings about the dangers of communism and instability (the two were elided). The impression was encouraged that the murkiness of this lit-tle-visited realm of history was somehow natural to it rather than a product of systematic official obfuscation and censorship.

So there was this discursive silence, but there was also the muteness of a tight-lipped tropical landscape that seemed so adept at swallowing up the traces of major events. When I had gone looking for traces of the 1963 Agung eruption, I'd taken with me copies of press photographs from the time that showed the sites of devastation. As far as I was aware, no press photographs of the more lethal catastrophe that visited the island two years later had ever appeared. There were no photographs that could lead me to particular streets, fields, or riverbanks where certain things had happened. Without pictorial testimony, the silence surrounding this event deepened considerably, espe-cially for an outsider like myself.

There was, though, a photo without provenance that appeared in the book *Ten Years' Military Terror in Indonesia.*[8] The caption read: "As two men await certain death, a soldier bayonets those at his feet. (October 1965)." This photo was more likely to be from Java than from Bali, but from the moment I saw it I felt it said everything. It shows a young man standing with his back to the soldier who is bayoneting a figure on the ground. The young man is roped around the neck and wrists to this fallen figure behind him, and the rope is pulling him backward toward what is being done to that person. He cannot see what is being done but he must be able to hear it and must know that the same thing is about to happen to him. That photograph was repro-duced in Robert Cribb's volume *The Indonesian Killings 1965–1966*, a book that I had with me in Bali.[9] I remember becoming acutely conscious of its presence on my bamboo bookshelf one afternoon when some policemen called to collect "donations" for their football team. I sensed it shimmering there like an obvious piece of contraband.

The history of these events, once I became conscious of it, proved im-possible to put aside and, given that it changed my experience of living in Bali and led me to write these pages, perhaps I should try to explain what this consciousness consisted of. It was a somberness that was also informed by outrage that the same regime that had orchestrated the killings was still in power.[10] To say this, though, may seem to imply a level of bravado on my part to which I can have no claim. On the contrary, it was knowledge that made me nervous. I moved around in a state of mild paranoia. There was no comparison, of course, between my nervousness and the fear that must have been felt by millions of Indonesians who had lived through the killings. Still, after having lived for more than a year in an island paradise, it was as if a door had now opened onto a previously invisible version of the same place. It was a door to another country, a place that for the previous three decades had been, in the words of a student on the streets of Jakarta in May 1998, "an archipelago of fear."

Not that learning about the killings rendered me immune to the beauty of Bali. I was still lulled by the palm trees, the flowers, and the warmth of the sea, things I've always had a weakness for. The candles in the garden at night, raindrops dripping from the fringe of the thatched roof and the sound of them hitting the fronds of the umbrella palms down below, these things still lulled me. When it was fine, the open-sided bungalow basked in the stillness of its walled garden. The distant sound of the road filtered through, but with it came the closer sound of wooden cowbells from beyond the garden gate and the occasional shrill shout from over the hedge where small boys were chasing birds from the rice crop. We cleaned our teeth at night over a bathroom sink made from a giant clamshell and showered standing under the stars in the outdoor bathroom, surrounded by the enormous leaves of the plant that had climbed all over the wall. A significant part of me was still convinced I was in paradise.

One of the points of similarity between the Agung eruption and the events of 1965–1966 was that in both cases whole villages were destroyed. In John Hughes's book *The End of Sukarno*, he provides the only firsthand account by a Westerner who was present in Bali around the time of the killings. He depicts the scene in the vicinity of the Bali Beach Hotel, Sanur, in late 1965.

> Almost in view of the big new luxury hotel the government had built to woo tourists to Bali stand the charred and blackened ruins of one such village. For their Communist affiliations the menfolk were killed. The women and children fared better; they were driven screaming away. The village itself was put to the torch.
>
> Night after night the sky flared red over Bali as villages went up in flames and thousands of Communists, or people said to be Communists, were hunted down and killed.[11]

It was upon reading Hughes's account that I first began to ponder the issue of the destroyed villages. The fate of the village described by Hughes was not unique. According to one Western historian the countryside of Bali following the killings had been "pock-marked with the blackened shells of former settlements."[12] Another historian describes "a landscape of blackened areas where entire villages had been burnt to the ground."[13] The expression "burnt to the ground" would not apply in a literal sense to most of the Balinese villages in question: Thatch roofs, woven bamboo walls, and wooden structural elements might well have "burnt down," but the brick and *paras*[14] walls of the houses and compounds would not, nor would the stone-and-brick pedestals of the spirit shrines in the household and village temples. It was elements such as these that you might have expected to still mark the sites of destroyed villages. In my travels around the island I had never seen anything resembling such a site.

Had the remains been demolished and recycled? Had the sites been resettled by people who, perhaps living with a sense of guilt at having benefited from the misfortune of others, added their silence to the general silence (Catherine Merridale records this having occurred during the famine of 1933 in Russia).[15] In cases where they had not been burned, had wooden houses simply been dismantled and removed? There is mention of this happening in 1965, near Jakarta, where the houses of victims were taken apart and transported elsewhere, with nothing remaining of certain villages "except stripped trees and gardens."[16] Built without nails or screws and with only pegs locking the joinery together, the portability of many old-style wooden houses in Southeast Asia is well-known.[17] But surely the Balinese village temples had not been dismantled. As anthropologist James Boon observes, in Bali "the Sanskritic concept of dharma pertains more to location than to individuals or groups"; it is a "dharma of space."[18] In other words, no matter to whom the temples had "belonged," they were sacred sites. And, again, it was not easy to imagine the temples being destroyed by the PNI gangs who were, after all, the self-styled defenders of Hindu-Bali religion against the supposed threat of communism. Perhaps newcomers had simply adopted (or been adopted by) the temples of those who had died.

And what of the mass graves? Robert Cribb found it "a little puzzling" that in the years after 1965–1966 there had been no reports of mass graves being discovered in Indonesia.[19] He speculated that the sites were known but were avoided by new construction projects and he mentioned "sporadic accounts" from Central Java of rice fields no longer tilled because they concealed mass graves. Anyone who happened to come upon such a place, he observed, would "think carefully" before reporting it.[20] In such situations, it is not merely the mention of certain past events that is proscribed, the archaeology of these events must also remain unnoticed. Yet it is not as simple as that. The authorities actually banked on the assumption that people would notice because the noticing kept alive the fear that in turn produced compliance. We should never underestimate the subtlety of people's relationship with the material past as they maneuver around it in the course of everyday life.

One January night I was sitting in a bar in Seminyak, gazing absently at the wet street through the open front of the pavilion-like building. Motor scooters were passing by, the bare legs of their riders glistening wet and sticking out from under plastic rain capes. The cavernous space had begun to fill with ex-pats from a range of countries who supported themselves on the island by running small export businesses trading in cheap clothes and "tribal" accessories. There was also the somewhat younger population of Indonesians who patronized the bar, most of them Javanese. Many of them were in flight from wealthy families, but some of them were workers in the export clothing factories. Some others lived by trading on their looks. In his imperfect English, a young ethnic Chinese man in the group at my table had just referred to a large Westerner sitting by himself a few tables away as a "voyager" (presumably he meant "voyeur"). The Westerner was dreamily eyeing a group of handsome young Javanese. I pictured a cruise ship sailing through the tepid monsoonal sea somewhere in the islands to the east of us, leaving behind it a wake of oil, cigarette packets, and the fading sound of dance music and engine noise. Into this reverie drifted a comment from elsewhere at the table that brought me to my senses. A tall blond woman, a friend of a friend, had mentioned (as part of a conversation I hadn't been attending to) that two thousand Communists lay buried beneath a five-star beachside hotel that had been built by the government in the early 1970s and then subsequently privatized. This was the hotel whose garden I passed when I walked to the beach.

I'd never previously heard the subject of mass graves raised in public and I half expected ripples of stunned silence to spread through the bar. The woman was a Greek Australian who had lived on the island on and off for the better part of twenty years. She had been married to a Balinese and now lived alone with their teenage son. She was speaking about ghosts and how the grounds of the hotel had been renowned for them when she lived there in the mid-1970s with her ex-husband, who'd been the manager. Some local women had told her that thousands of Communists killed in 1965–1966 had been buried in the space between the sea and the fields that had become the site of the hotel. I could think of no good reason why she would have made this up.

I wondered if it was possible that in Bali, unlike in Java, some of the mass grave sites, rather than being avoided, had actually been targeted by government construction projects as a way of permanently sealing them off. Some time later I mentioned what I'd heard about the hotel to a young Balinese whose circle of friends I knew to be privately critical of Soeharto's New Order government. He told me that quantities of human bone were discovered only a few years previously, when the foundations for a large hotel were being excavated on another part of the island. Among the Balinese it had been common knowledge, he said, that human bones were being found on that site. He said that everyone knew what the bones meant.

Late in the afternoon, the day after hearing the woman speak of the mass grave, I walked slowly along the sand in front of the hotel. On the terrace I saw the waiters in their white jackets and blue sarongs stooping to gather freshly fallen frangipani blossoms to place on the white linen-covered tables they were setting for dinner. The hotel sat beautifully upon its large site. The individual guest cottages with their courtyard gardens, the reception area and lobby with its sweeping thatched roofs, the great trees: all had that sense of "fit" that often strikes you in the rural villages of Southeast Asia, that appearance of having grown slowly out of the ground. Many monsoon seasons had softened the hotel's architecture. Mosses had been allowed to colonize a thousand crannies in the rough limestone masonry. And, of course, there were the gardens, suspended on the brink of a reversion to jungle.

That afternoon and on subsequent occasions I found myself looking for some sign, some sinister detail previously missed, that might hint at what lay beneath the surface. I saw nothing of that kind. Yet, if the woman in the bar had been correct, the Balinese themselves must always have been aware of what was under the hotel, stratified below the gardens and the low thatched buildings. They must have lived, like the survivors of the Agung eruption, with the intimate knowledge of what was "down there."[21] One afternoon I strolled along a stream that ran through the dune immediately adjacent to the hotel grounds, furtively scanning the sand embankment for any sign of exposed bones. None were visible. Eventually I came to realize that my quest for obvious physical traces of the killings was misguided. It was in the period before this that I went to Negara.

My interest in Negara dated from the day I'd read of how in late 1965 the palace of the rajas of Jembrana, the capital of Negara, had been "destroyed" and "reduced to rubble."[22] Located near the western end of the island and set in the middle of a sliver of irrigated rice land between the mountains and the sea, the small town of Negara had historically been regarded by other Balinese as a wilderness, a place to which people were sometimes banished. It happened that the postindependence governor of Bali, Anak Agung Bagus Sutedja, was a member of the royal house of Jembrana. As a left-leaning reformist backed by Sukarno, Sutèja attracted the enmity of the traditionalist part of the (nationalist) PNI. The leader of the (communist) PKI in Bali, I Gede Puger, was also from Negara and was a friend of Sutèja. It thus transpired that, as one of the strongholds of PKI support in Bali, Negara became a focus of anticommunist violence in 1965–1966. According to Hughes, "The worst violence was in Governor Sutedja's own county of Jembrana, where crowds ran amok in the main town of Negara, and killed several thousand people. Communist leader Puger was killed and his house sacked. The palace of Sutedja's father was destroyed, the family thereafter consigned to live in outbuildings."[23]

While I saw the folly of trying to find traces of Balinese villages destroyed in 1965–1966, a destroyed palace, it seemed to me, might be a different matter. A *puri* (palace) would tend to occupy a dominant position in the central and oldest part of a town, and even if it were reduced to rubble, you might still expect to find surviving portions of the perimeter walls, or perhaps just a large telltale gap in the streetscape, overgrown with weeds. If I couldn't find the site of the Negara *puri*, I told myself, then what was the point of being an archaeologist.

So one weekend I drove with Daniel to Negara in his car, stopping on the way to spend the night at a beach that had a small hotel and a few cabins for rent, the only accommodation along that sparsely populated stretch of coast. The beach was almost deserted when we arrived. There was a café where sand blew across the concrete floor and where there never seemed to be any food. Listless Japanese surfers lounged on the terrace throughout the afternoon, watching the sea. The whole place had a bleached appearance, from the weathered wood of the tables and chairs to the tobacco-colored hair of the surfers and the worn-out cotton board shorts of the young Balinese boys who sat with them. Even conversation at this beach seemed rare and muted. In the hotel room, Daniel read his stories of flying swordsmen in premodern China, stories he had become addicted to as a youth in West Kalimantan. I went for a long walk up the beach. It was less than an hour's drive from Negara.

We left the beach in the morning and got back onto the highway, that two-lane conduit between central Bali and Java (the world's most romanticized island and the world's most densely populated island are separated by a narrow strait plied by vehicular ferries). In Negara we drove around for half an hour looking for traces of the old *puri*. Not finding any, we began asking directions and Daniel eventually found a Chinese shopkeeper who said the *puri* was only a few blocks away. She said it had a banyan tree outside, you couldn't miss it. We found the tree standing in front of a set of padlocked wrought-iron gates, behind which were two solid Dutch colonial-style bungalows of brick and plaster. An old teak house next door seemed to be part of the same complex, so we went in there and spoke to a calm young man with long frizzy hair who wore an army camouflage shirt. He was sitting on the steps of a dilapidated porch, deep in the shadow of an enormous tree. His name was Ari. He offered to show us around and led the way down a path behind the house. I caught a glimpse of the words "No Woman No Cry" painted on the aged teak weatherboards. We passed through a gap in a brick wall and entered a large open space directly behind the bungalows, partly shaded by another great tree.

Aside from the fact that they were supposed to have been reduced to rubble in 1965, these two bungalows seemed too recent and ordinary to have been the main buildings of the *puri*. Perhaps the latter had stood in the open compound Ari had brought us to—that, however, seemed too small. I interrogated the dusty surface of the ground while Daniel sat under the tree with Ari, who had begun quizzing him about who we were and where we came from. I saw a few lines of brick that were level with the surface of the well-trodden ground and wondered if they could have been the foundations of a previous structure. But nothing else. There was a surreptitious aspect to this scrutiny that stemmed from my reluctance to broach with Ari the events of 1965–1966. I didn't want to make him an accomplice, however indirectly, to my little "investigation."

Back on the street, as we were saying goodbye, Ari mentioned that there had been another *puri* at Negara, belonging to another branch of the same royal house. He said it was a little way out of town at a place called Mendoyo. "Of course," I thought, "we've got the wrong *puri*."

Two hours later we were parked under a tree somewhere near Mendoyo, taking a break. Mendoyo had turned out to be nothing more than a small village strung thinly out along the highway: a school, a police station, a government office, all single-storied, and a scattering of small houses. The village was surrounded on three sides by rice fields. Failing to pick up any sign of a *puri* after slowly driving through the place, we had turned back and asked at a gas station. Nobody there had heard of any *puri* in those parts. We drove down a meandering side road and spoke to some men playing cards on a raised bamboo platform beneath a tree. They discussed our query among themselves in Balinese and then said in Indonesian that the place we probably wanted was more toward town, on the other side of a certain bridge. But we found only fields in the place they seemed to be indicating, fields that had the look of having been there for a very long time. Then another side road, more questions, more peering through trees.

I looked out at the country beside the car, marveling at how everything seemed to fit together so perfectly. The terraces with their green, recently planted rice crops began at the edges of the houses and stepped down the slopes to where large trees and thickets of bamboo cloaked the streams. I imagined these rice terraces, like the sliding leaves of a dining table, extending out over the ruins of a destroyed palace or a burned-out village with remorseless neutrality.

It was steamy and my motivation to go on was ebbing away. I examined the Nelles 1:1,000,000 map of Bali, trying to read more into it than was there to be read, the way one does with maps of that scale. Daniel lit an Ardath Mild and threw the match out the window. "It's like looking for a needle in a sack," he said.

"If you want my opinion, we're never going to find this place," he continued, gazing out across the countryside.

A pause followed, one of those pauses that in the tropics seems to hang in the air, opening up a space that slowly fills with halfhearted and unpursued lines of thought. The sweet, thick smoke from a smoldering pile of weeds was drifting down the road toward us.

". . . and I can't see the point of it," he concluded in a softer voice.

"But it's obvious," I said, turning to him from my scrutiny of the map.

"No," he said quickly, drawing on the cigarette, and I realized then that he must have been harboring this skepticism for some time but had been allowing me, the *bule* (Westerner), to run my course.

"It's not obvious," he went on. "You tell yourself that you have to find this place, but really you are just picking at people's wounds."

"Wait a minute. . . ," I started, unnerved at the way he'd gone so deftly to the core of my own half-formed anxiety about this project.

"That's what you're doing," he said with finality, his face set and directed up the road away from me.

We drove back home, mostly in silence. The weather closed in and it began to rain lightly. In the grayness of the afternoon, looking out at the passing countryside, for the first time Bali seemed banal to me, drained of any hint of romance. The sort of place you could imagine as a setting for the occurrence described in Geoffrey Robinson's book, *The Darker Side of Paradise*, which I read only later.

> In Negara, Jembrana . . . where the Java-based troops first landed in early December, eyewitnesses have reported that dozens of Army trucks, loaded with alleged communists picked up from the surrounding villages, formed a slow and orderly procession down the main street for several days. At a large warehouse the prisoners were unloaded one by one, hands bound, and taken inside, where they were shot with automatic weapons.[24]

It was around this time that I discovered an abandoned bungalow down at the beach. I'd been sitting on the sand in the shade of some bushes when I became aware of a clanging noise that intermittently cut through the sound of the waves. It was coming from a little distance behind me where a loose sheet of iron in a fence was being pulled at by the breeze. I'd noticed this fence before. It was painted a nice pale green and was leaning forward under the weight of a mass of blue-flowering creeper the Balinese called *pelung-pelung*. Looking at the loose sheet of iron, I realized that if I pulled it back further I'd be able to slip through the gap.

On the other side of the fence I saw only what I'd expected to see: a piece of land covered with long grass, weeds, and a tangle of trees, shrubs, and creepers. Perhaps it was a site earmarked for a new hotel but left to languish because the finance had slipped away. It was only when I'd gone a little way along a narrow sandy path through the grass that I realized that what I'd taken to be a large tree, colonized by more of the blue-flowered creeper, was actually a built structure of some kind. It was two stories high, half-finished, and camouflaged not merely by the creepers but by wet-season moss that grew on the concrete pillars and walls. A bungalow, evidently, abandoned during construction.

Looking around more carefully, I noticed a pit-like depression in the ground between the derelict bungalow and the fence. Making my way over there I saw that it was nothing more sinister than a half-realized swimming pool. Plant life spilled down its sides, and timber offcuts and leaves floated in a stagnant pond at the bottom. I'd never had much time for swimming pools, having failed to learn to swim in one as a child, and I was struck now by how much better they looked in a state of abandonment. Aqua blue mosaic tiles were visible through the screen of hanging plants around the sides, but there was no sign of an overgrown stainless steel ladder leading down into the deep end, and I looked in vain for one of those porthole-like lights in the wall.

The house itself had been conceived on quite an elaborate scale, with several formwork concrete balconies on the upper floor and a cylindrical lobby with a vine-hung spiral staircase. Unlike our own rustic bungalow, this place had evidently been designed to have proper windows rather than shuttered glassless openings. But the window frames had never been installed. I peered through the frameless windows into the downstairs rooms: They looked dank, and the black-stained bare concrete floor was littered with broken roof tiles and twisted, rusting lengths of steel reinforcing.

When I climbed the rough, unplastered staircase, I was surprised to find that the upper floor was clean, as if recently swept. Two thin kapok mattresses, partly covered with batik sarongs, lay on the concrete floor, and some clothes, neatly folded, lay on a length of wood. There was a spiral of ash on the floor from a burned mosquito coil. Apart from the sea, the only sound came from the rustling of the trees outside—the wind had freshened, and when I walked out onto the balcony the first drops of rain began to fall. The rain, I felt, gave me an alibi for being there, so I sat down on a bamboo mat with my back against the cool concrete and looked out over the parapet to what had been intended as a garden.

Next to me on the mat, well out of the rain, was a guide to the eastern archipelago, the serious one with anthropological insights in the introduction and better-than-average photography. I felt a sudden admiration for whoever the travelers were who had found this place and had the nerve to camp here. Under the guide was a paperback copy of Virginia Woolf's *The Waves*, on the cover of which was a detail from a Whistler painting called *Cliffs and Breakers*. Looking at the picture, I thought how little difference there was in appearance between the cold sea of northern Europe and the warm sea of the tropics. I opened it and read some pages while waiting for the rain to stop.

> After quarrelling and reconciliation I need privacy—to be alone with you, to set this hubbub in order. For I am as neat as a cat in my habits. We must oppose the waste and deformity of the world, its crowds eddying round and round disgorged and trampling. One must slip paper-knives, even, exactly through the pages of novels, and tie up packets of letters neatly with green silk, and brush up the cinders with a hearth broom. Everything must be done to rebuke the horror of deformity.[25]

I wondered how old this bungalow was. Two years, perhaps three? Certainly no more than five. And yet it was already well advanced in ruin and had almost disappeared under the vegetation. What chance was there of finding on this island traces of the events of twenty-eight years ago?

When it stopped raining I went back downstairs and made my way around the back of the house. Near what would have been the back door was a tiled foot pool designed for people to wash beach sand off themselves before going inside. The shower had never been connected. There was a blue plastic bucket and a plastic dipper, a small mirror hanging from a nail driven into a frangipani tree, and, in a fork of the tree, a dark-green plastic soap box. Armani for Men. I opened it and the musky aroma of the green soap momentarily overwhelmed the smell of the rotting leaves and the sea air.

Perhaps my background led me to crave objectively legible physical traces when, for most people, it was their memory that led them to find the past in the landscape around them. Most Balinese now above the age of forty-five or fifty are likely to have witnessed at least some of the events of 1965–1966, if not the actual killings themselves. Thousands still alive today must have lost children, husbands, lovers, friends, and relatives; thousands of others must have actually participated in the executions. Surely the land must still be replete with traces visible to them in the same way that many of the traces of the Agung eruption, which had eluded me during my travels in eastern Bali, would have been quite legible to survivors of that disaster.[26]

The most eloquent relics need not be the products or debris, in a direct sense, of that which they signify. Would the gateway through which a lover or child was glimpsed for the last time as he or she was being taken away not be imprinted thereafter, for those left behind, with intimations of loss? We all know how, in cases of deep personal loss, ordinary objects and places can trigger real pain; we know how these objects and places can lie in quiet ambush for us as we move gingerly across the terrain of each new day.[27] The gateway,

Figure 4.2.   Abandoned bungalow, Bali, 1990s (Denis Byrne)

yes, but also perhaps every laneway and riverbank, a detail here, a detail there, until the familiar local landscape becomes for the survivor a minefield of memory sites.

The way people signify things and landscapes, privately, locally, intimately, animates them in ways that are likely to be invisible to outsiders. This invisibility, this localized activity taking place "below the thresholds at which visibility begins," to use Michel de Certeau's words, can be a form of resistance in the face of larger, national narratives that aim to impose their own ultravisible truth claims.[28] While not suggesting that memory is static or immune to decay, or that it remains the same with every recall, it is nevertheless possible to see how the memory of individuals can preserve an account of events that is subversive to the official version. Not available to surveillance, these private memories constitute a type of "noise" in the officially imposed silence. In post-1966 Bali this "noise" must have been almost deafening for locals and yet quite inaudible to the generations of tourists who subsequently wandered the beaches and foothills of the island.[29]

There is a sense, then, in which even those people who escaped the fate of those in the mass graves were nonetheless buried alive. A few years after I left Bali a friend passed on to me an article by Erik Mueggler in which he described how many victims of the Cultural Revolution in southwest China subsequently became socially invisible and inaudible, incarcerated as they were within the space of their own memories.[30] His particular use of the word "encrypted" led me to realize that it could stand for the crypt as a burial site while simultaneously referencing the hidden meaning of an encoded message. It reminded me how tenuous the distinction was between the surface and the subsurface, the aboveground and the underground.

Even if outsiders are unable to quite penetrate this world of local knowledge, designated a "traumascape," it is possible for them to come very close.[31] The invisible border zone between the outside and inside hums with the kind of tension described by Indonesian journalist Maskun Iskander in an account of his visit to the Purwodadi area of Central Java in 1969 to investigate persistent rumors of a renewed bout of killings there.[32] He was on dangerous ground, given the climate of political oppression, as, obviously, were the locals he hoped to speak to. In this local landscape he finds that facts are hard to come by; facts are dangerous. But he does what he can: He gathers and records rumors of death and torture, rumors of trucks taking people away in the night, whispers that people are missing from each of the villages he visits. Iskander seeks something definite, something objectively tangible, and he does come very close. He senses what had occurred but cannot quite see it.

Village people wouldn't respond to direct questions about what had happened. What he gathers and what his article succeeds so well in conveying is more than anything else a scattering of absences and silences. Coming into one particular village his jeep was surrounded by small children:

I approached one of them and asked in low Javanese, "Do you have a sister?" He was silent. "Where is your mother?", I asked again. He remained silent, making circles in the sand with his big toe. "Is your father here?" I asked at random. The child raised his eyes. They were brimming over. Then he ran away into the narrow streets of the kampung.[33]

For an example of the exercise of discretion in relation to such absences it is difficult to go past Norman Lewis's account of his experience in East Timor in the 1970s, in the years immediately after the Indonesian invasion. He had been staying with some nuns at a small mission in the village of Venilale, in the hills of central East Timor, and had been accompanied on his walks in the surrounding countryside by a young man, a local, who always carried a guitar:

> He was an unobtrusive and diffident presence, tailing along behind at a distance of three or four yards and occasionally twanging urgently on his guitar to draw our attention to some feature of the sinister wilderness through which we were trudging that had sparked off strong emotion.... A twang of the guitar might be a signal for the eyebrows to shoot up over widened eyes and the corners of the mouth to droop in a sort of depressed smirk. We followed his eye, wondering what could have happened to provide fury or grief among a largely featureless spread of thickets, cunningly pruned trees, and sallow rocks at this particular spot.... Once only were we able to identify the cause of Thomas's excitement, when a spar of charred wood poked through the undergrowth on a ridge over a shallow valley. This had been a village, but no more of it remained than the Romans had left of Carthage.[34]

The "structures of forgetting" the Indonesian state put in place to cover the events of 1965–1966, to cover the absences, had a counterpart at the international level in the distancing effect of the Cold War.[35] In 1965 the West saw Sukarno's Indonesia as a domino waiting to fall to communism. The fact or supposition that those who were being killed in Indonesia in 1965–1966 were communists quarantined them from the West's compassion, the sort of compassion eloquently expressed three years earlier for the Balinese victims of the Gunung Agung eruption. The "geopolitical abstraction" of the Cold War that neatly divided the planet into the Soviet Bloc and the Free World enabled this distancing, a distancing that in itself was a form of violence.[36]

If Iskander strove to see what had happened in Purwodadi through the eyes of local survivors rendered mute by fear and if Lewis, more passively, allowed his eyes to be opened by the urgent strumming of his silent companion's guitar, most of the rest of us are content to go to places like Bali and maintain our strange distance from the things that have happened there, the things that people there know. In the warm evening air we linger over dinner on the hotel terrace, perhaps conversing with the charming young Balinese waiters who are gracious, never servile. When it is quite dark they turn on floodlights, mounted high on the palm trees, that throw light on the incoming waves. Two men in temple clothes sit under a tree playing a flute and a gamelan xylophone, softly, so that the music comes and goes in different parts of the garden depending on small movements in the air. Away along the beach, in the darkness beyond the floodlights, some fishermen stand on the dark, wet sand preparing their hand-casting nets. We stroll through the gardens of the hotel, this hotel that looks as if it has always been there, and then retire to our rooms where we lie down to sleep just a few meters above the dead of 1965–1966.

NOTES

1. The G30S "coup attempt" is widely attributed to elements in the Indonesian Communist Party, and this was certainly the line proclaimed by Soeharto's regime. But there are some who suggest it was staged by a discontented faction within the military itself. The first Western scholars to question the Soeharto regime's version of events were Benedict Anderson and Ruth McVey (1971) of Cornell's Modern Indonesia Project. The many still-unanswered questions surrounding G30S and the events that followed it have also been discussed, among others, by Crouch (1973), Van der Kroef (1972), and the authors in the volume edited by Cribb (1990).

2. For a discussion of the difficulty of arriving at a reliable estimate of the death toll, see Robert Cribb's (1990) introduction to *The Indonesian Killings, 1965–1966*.

3. Robinson 1995, 281–85. My other main sources of information on the killings in Bali are Cribb 1990, 241–48; Hanna 1990, 125–26; Hughes 1968; Soe Hok Gie 1990; and Vickers 1989, 168–73. Robinson's book represents the most detailed study, relying on contemporary Balinese newspaper reporting, unpublished documents, and interviews conducted in Bali in the 1980s and 1990s.

4. Robinson 1995, 293; Hughes 1968.

5. Hughes 1968.

6. Robinson (1995, 298) refers to a Balinese newspaper account that claimed it was enough for people associated with the PKI to hear the roar of a truck for their hearts to beat wildly with fear.

7. See Robinson (1995) for a discussion of this omission.

8. Caldwell 1975.

9. I am grateful to Robert Cribb for informing me of the earlier, 1975, publication of this photograph.

10. The Soeharto regime fell in 1998, a victim of the East Asian economic meltdown of that year.

11. Hughes 1968, 175.

12. See Cribb's (1990, 241) "editor's introduction" to *The Indonesian Killings*.

13. Vickers 1989, 170.

14. *Paras* is the volcanic tuff commonly used in Bali as a building material. It is cut into small blocks for walls and its softness, when wet, lends itself to being carved.

15. Merridale 1996, 1–18.

16. McKie 1969, 94. This may be based on hearsay, as McKie does not cite sources for his information.

17. Waterson 1990, 78.

18. Boon 1977, 100. See also Boon 1979.

19. Cribb 1990, 9.

20. Ibid., 10.

21. See Read (1996, 75–78) for an account of a community in Australia who kept alive the memory of their original homes after these had been submerged by a hydro lake.

22. Hughes 1968, 180; Vickers 1989, 171.

23. Hughes 1968.

24. Robinson 1995, 297–98.

25. Woolf 1992, 137.

26. "Understandably, few Balinese want to relive this time in conversation and most, like survivors of other conflicts, prefer to block it out of their memories" (Vickers 1989, 172). Living as I was in an expatriate enclave, I was not in a position to know whether Balinese spoke about the killings among themselves or not.

27. For traumatized people, as Tumarkin observes, "[t]he past enters the present as an intruder, not a welcome guest" (2005, 12).

28. De Certeau 1984, 93.

29. This is illustrated by failure of the Australian artist Donald Friend (1915–1989) to mention the recent killings in his otherwise detailed diaries recording his sojourn in Bali that began in late 1966 (Friend 2006).

30. Mueggler 1998. My thanks to Heather Goodall for drawing my attention to this article.

31. Tumarkin 2005.

32. Iskander 1990.

33. Ibid., 207.

34. Lewis 1995, 160–61.

35. For a discussion of "the structures of forgetting," see Hamilton (1994, 13).

36. Connery 1995, 37.

· 5 ·

Shalimar and Sukarno

$\mathcal{A}$ bottle of Shalimar de Guerlain was among the few personal possessions of Sukarno, Indonesia's first president, that were recovered by his son, Guntur, after his father died on 21 June 1970 in a Jakarta hospital. A broken man, Sukarno had been under house arrest since formally relinquishing power in February 1967 to the military leaders who had orchestrated his demise.[1] Several objects popularly believed to be magically empowered and to have contributed to Sukarno's charismatic power mysteriously disappeared at the time of his death.[2] They included a *kris* from his Balinese great-grandmother that was believed to have been dipped in the blood of Dutchmen.

This information can be found in a 1981 conference paper by Pierre Labrousse, an English translation of which was published in the Cornell journal *Indonesia* in 1994.[3] On first reading it, I imagined the bottle of Shalimar, half empty and dusty, standing on a dresser in a large, dimly lit bedroom in a quiet colonial-era villa in Jakarta. Along with the bottle of Shalimar, described as "his cologne," the other objects salvaged by Guntur were his father's pen, his razor, and his *kopiah*, a cap worn by Malay Muslims.[4] A partial rehabilitation of Sukarno's memory occurred in 1978 when a funerary complex was constructed for him in Blitar in East Java. But the climate of fear created in Indonesia by the mass killings of 1965–1966 and the way Soeharto's New Order government played on this fear to foster compliance ensured the continued effacement of Bung Karno[5] until the regime's own demise in 1998.

In the aftermath of my own "discovery" of the events of 1965–1966, as I continued to live on an island that, though it had been a key site of these events, maintained its silence about them, I found myself giving a lot of thought to the question of what constitutes an archaeological trace. In particular, I wondered what subtle forms such traces might take under blackout conditions. We are used to thinking of the archaeological as being that which is primarily, literally, under the ground. But we know that under circumstances of censorship, traces that are in the category of the forbidden might exist and circulate in a kind of underground that is part of our existence here on the surface. And as elements of this "underground," we can think of them as archaeological.

The idea of a (surface) underground that I am trying to convey, and that is central to the project of this book, is suggested by the "ghostly silhouettes" that began to appear around Buenos Aires in 1983.[6] Painted by relatives of those who had disappeared during the 1976–1983 military dictatorship in Argentina, these silhouettes contained the names of the disappeared and the dates of their disappearance. If the disappearances, the disappeared, and those who search for traces of the disappeared all exist in a kind of twilight zone, then the painted silhouettes can be seen as an attempt to connect or anchor this floating zone to the physical surface of the city. The insistence by the Association of Mothers that their children continue to be regarded as disappeared rather than dead reinforces this idea of a twilight zone.[7]

So it was that I started thinking about that bottle of Shalimar de Guerlain. The anthropologist Anna Tsing writes that the oppressive politics of the New Order "fostered a turn to a personal spirituality and mysticism in both national and regional cultural expression." In this climate of political silence, "mysticism thrived."[8] I wonder, in retrospect, whether in attempting to follow the trail of a perfume back through the decades to the former president I was not indulging in a kind of mysticism myself. On balance, though, I think not. The Sukarno-Shalimar connection, however thin, was real. It seemed impossible to dwell on the events of 1965–1966 without allowing Sukarno into your life. And since public discussion of him was banned in Soeharto's Indonesia, I had elected, as a mild kind of protest against this form of effacement, to come at him via a perfume that I regarded as a trace. The perfume, like the "ghostly silhouettes" of Buenos Aires, would, for me at least, ground Sukarno in the contemporary terrain of Bali. Like ancestor busts in ancient Egypt, the silhouettes and the perfume would act as "a mnemonic to reactivate the presence of a known individual."[9]

Jacques Guerlain completed development of his new perfume, Shalimar, in September 1924. The company launched it in Paris in April the following year at the International Exhibition of Decorative Arts in a distinctive fluted bottle with a large sapphire-blue glass stopper. The name Shalimar is a Sanskrit word glossed as "garden of love," an appropriate enough name for what would come to be acknowledged as a benchmark Oriental perfume.[10]

One night in Bali, shortly after reading the Labrousse paper, I was visiting my friend Peggy in a bungalow located down the end of a long laneway, barely wide enough to ride a motor scooter. When I was telling her about Sukarno and Shalimar she remembered that the name of the perfume occurred in the Van Morrison song "Madame George."[11] She dug out a bootleg tape cassette of *Astral Weeks,* and the two of us lay on the cool tiled floor, listening to it with the ceiling fan stirring the warm humid air above us. The room filled with the sound of violins and double bass and that ageless voice singing about the backstreets of Belfast, the rain, history books, and the smell of a sweet perfume that drifted "on the cool night air." All of which seemed a long way from where we were in some ways, but not so far in others.

I rode the scooter into Denpasar one day to find a bottle of Shalimar, but the department store didn't have it. They had the other Guerlain Orientals, Samsara and Mitsouko, but no Shalimar, which seemed odd, but I wasn't inclined to read too much into it. So it wasn't until I was back in Sydney for a few weeks that I had my first physical encounter with Shalimar. It was on an afternoon in midwinter that I walked down through the park to David Jones on Elizabeth Street and made my way across the marble floor to the Guerlain counter. Shalimar was there on the glass countertop among a cluster of tester bottles. The bottle was something of a disappointment. Its neutral, modernistic lines were quite devoid of any Oriental reference (I didn't know then that in Paris at that very moment Guerlain was bringing out a new "retro" bottle for the perfume based on Raymond Guerlain's design for the 1925 Baccarat original).

As I reached for the Shalimar bottle a smallish woman in her fifties, older than most of the other sales staff on the floor but just as carefully made up, approached me on the other side of the counter. She asked in a fairly heavy French accent if she could help me. I was interested in the Shalimar.

"Well, yes, it's classic," she replied authoritatively, seeming to draw back a little, as if to regard the bottle from a greater distance. Making an effort to rise above the sense of personal dishevelment I always feel in the cosmetics section of department stores, I asked her if she knew when the perfume first came out. She did, but she moved directly into a detailed discourse on its structure that left me floundering. The dominant element was vanilla; I gathered that much.

"But you first notice the scent of iris, the top note, as they say."

She was reaching now for the bottle. She sprayed some on a card, waved it dry and held it out for me to smell. I wasn't sure if I recognized iris, but I was immediately conscious of vanilla.[12] It came at you directly, almost aggressively, like a suppressed memory broken free. Yet even as I was being overwhelmed by it I was aware that I was smelling not just vanilla, perhaps not even mainly vanilla. The moment I tried to put my finger, so to speak, on its particularity, it withdrew into an orchestration of smells that to my untrained nose were inseparable one from another. I was out of my depth here, but I was fascinated.

People talk about their first smell of the Orient. The moment, for instance, when the door of the plane is unsealed at Bangkok airport and a wave of warm air comes rolling down the aisle bearing the aroma of flowers, aviation fuel, fish sauce, frying chilis, incense, and stagnant canals. As I stood there holding the card to my nose, the voices around me fell away and the bronze mirrors and faux-marble pillars slipped out of focus. I was caught up in an act of recognition. I was fairly certain that I had never had occasion to smell this perfume previously, but—and this was its genius, perhaps the genius of all great perfumes—it connected with something in me that seemed already to know it. The smell of Shalimar had reached into some remote part of my being where it was recognized.

So this was the moment, in the winter of 1995, when I first smelled Shalimar. On reflection I'm pleased I hadn't been able to track down a bottle in Bali, which, after all, is the Orient. As a representation of the Orient, Shalimar should, if possible, be first experienced in the West or, at least, the quasi-West of somewhere like Australia. These are the spaces it was originally designed for. To smell it in the Orient itself was, I subsequently discovered, quite confusing.

"What else is in it?" I asked the woman, recovering myself. She mentioned bergamot, patchouli, sandalwood, and she sprayed some onto a card for herself, as if to refresh her memory. As she was wrapping a bottle up for me she commented on my interest in Shalimar. I said that I'd read about it recently and had been looking forward to smelling it.

"You know President Sukarno of Indonesia?" I asked.

"Yes. From the 1950s I think."

"They say he had a bottle of Shalimar in his possession when he died."

"Really," she replied evenly, handing me the package. "Sukarno?" A slight raising of the eyebrows.

We stood looking at each other for what seemed like an awkward moment. I thought she might be wondering where this was leading and I'd like to have said something about Sukarno's archaeological signature but couldn't find the words.[13]

A couple of days later, in the chemistry shelves of the Fisher Library at the University of Sydney, I found Calkin and Jellinek's book, *Perfumery: Practice and Principles*, and was able to add coumarin, civet, and vetiver to the list of Shalimar's ingredients. The authors had devoted a whole section to Shalimar, describing it as "one of the greatest and most aesthetically satisfying perfumes ever made."[14] Evidently, the spicy aspect of Shalimar was built on a foundation of cinnamon bark oil, nutmeg, and clove. All of these, I realized with a quickening of my pulse, were indigenous to the "spice islands" in the east of the Indonesian archipelago. Would it be too much to suppose that in possessing a bottle of Shalimar, Sukarno, a leader of the Non-Aligned Movement, had been involved in a political act? An act of reappropriation; a previously overlooked manifestation of his postcoloniality?

Later that night I had dinner with my friend Ross at the Thainesia on Oxford Street and then walked down the cold windswept street to Taylor Square and the Oxford pub. Just inside the door Ross ran into a man he'd worked with once but hadn't seen for a long time. It was a Friday night and the place was packed. The air was thick with cigarette smoke, and dance music pumping out over the hundreds of raised voices. We talked about this and that until the subject of Indonesia eventually came up, and I mentioned that I'd been reading about Sukarno.

"Speaking of which," I said, reaching into my pocket for the Shalimar tester card I had just remembered I was carrying, "do you know what this is?" I handed the card to Ross with the brand name facing away from him and he smelled it but after a moment of thought shook his head. He handed it to his friend who sniffed at it and, obviously stalling for time, asked how long I'd had it in my pocket. He had another sniff:

"Well, I *can* say this is not a male fragrance. It isn't Opium, is it?"[15]

For the West, Asia had become a site of decadence and eroticism as early as the Middle Ages.[16] Shalimar, however, sits within a particular tradition of western manufacturing representations of the East for the West's own consumption. In addition to a fascination with imports from Asia of commodities not produced in Europe, such as silks and porcelain from China, by the eighteenth century Europe's aristocracy and middle class were seeking to create what they imagined to be an Oriental atmosphere in their houses and gardens. Chinoiserie and Japonesque were styles that deployed "authentic" imports of Asian art and antiquities but, in tapestries, paintings, and wallpapers, they also depicted the social and natural landscapes in which they imagined these objects might originally have existed.

In the bedrooms and dressing rooms of London and Paris, the East was presented as an intimate, somewhat feminized space. In this sensual, passive, timeless zone whose inhabitants wallowed in laziness there was no room for the colonial reality of the rubber and tea plantations with their machinelike exploitation of native bodies. Another reality was also masked, one the West had difficulty accepting even while partly encouraging: Asia was modernizing. The Edo period (1603–1868) woodcut prints by Japanese artists such as Hiroshige, Hokusai, and Katsukawa, which poured out of Japan and into the collections of Western collectors in the early decades of the twentieth century,[17] depicted geisha, samurai, and antique landscapes (where no trace of the machine age intruded) at the very time Japan was feverishly industrializing and was on the brink of producing, among other modern products, the Zero fighter plane.[18]

At the moment when the West was beginning to disengage from its colonial domination of the East, substituting direct enslavement for enslavement by capital, Guerlain was announcing that it was no longer necessary to be physically present in the East in order to experience the sensual allure of its women. Shalimar would transpose that allure onto the bodies of the women of the West. To that extent, the East, in its physicality, would be rendered redundant. Something similar to cross-dressing may be at play here. Is it possible, one wonders, that the Shalimar consumers are turned on more by the slightly "bent" experience of the (imaginary) aroma of the East on the body of a Westerner than they would be by the body of an Easterner taken, as it were, "straight"? After all, does the frisson derived from creating an Oriental atmosphere in one's Paris apartment not come precisely from the fact that it *is* in Paris rather than in Shanghai?

It was always clear that the presence of the "Chinese" room in the apartment did not stem from a sense of inferiority or lack in our own culture. On the contrary, it expressed confidence in our cultural dominance. This assurance tends to blind us to the fact that other people might just as readily play similar games with Western material culture. Even now, if we enter the Bangkok apartment of a Thai acquaintance and find it filled with Alvar Aalto furniture and Littala glassware we might find ourselves wincing at the inauthenticity of their taste and commiserating with their desire to be Western. We don't see that the last thing they want is actually to *be* in Finland or actually *be* Western. What amuses them is to have Finland in Bangkok.

From the beginning there were people in the East who were conscious of the West's appetite, not merely for Eastern products but for products that represented the East as the West liked to imagine it. Chinese porcelain manufacturing centers in Guangdong and elsewhere, for instance, began producing items specifically designed for the European market virtually the moment the demand was detected in the sixteenth century.[19] The famous Willow Pattern motif, developed in England in the late eighteenth century, consisted of an imagined Chinese landscape. Willow Pattern ware was subsequently imported into China where it was copied by Chinese potteries for export back to Europe.

There has long been a curiosity by inhabitants of the East about the way we have dreamed them, and this curiosity has created a reverse flow of commodities. Asia has turned with something like nostalgia to the Chinoiserie and Japonesque that lulled the West in earlier times. Marilyn Ivy draws our attention to Japan's third postwar generation, the so-called *shinjinrui* (new humans), who, while fascinated by Taisho (1912–1926) and early Showa (1926–1989) mass culture, are equally avid consumers of neo-Japonesque imported from the West.[20] Ivy describes this phenomenon as "the repetitively ever-new domestic (re)appropriation of what the French did to Japanese style, now retrofitted for hip Japanese delectation."[21] In the Australian short film *Hell Bento!!*, the young Japanese woman who hangs out with the members of a punk Tokyo band called The Jet Boys says she is attracted to the kitsch products of America's 1950s "misconception" of Japan.[22] These plastic rickshaws and miniature parasols are cool, she says. She collects them.

So I found myself wondering if Sukarno was similarly a collector of Western dream objects. From what we know of Sukarno, the meanings he derived from Shalimar might have been quite complex.

I was in the garden at night in Bali with my cupped hands over my face, inhaling. Shalimar smelled older here and blunter. Its enactment of the "Orient," while actually situated in the Orient, set up a sort of olfactory noise, not unlike feedback in a PA system. I thought I detected a very faint mustiness that I hadn't noticed in the perfume previously. It could have been an olfactory allusion to a room long closed up, perhaps a reference to tropical humidity and the way it accelerated the decay of brickwork, upholstery, and books.

Figure 5.1.   Field kit

The air in the bedroom of the bungalow of Sukarno's last years might have been like that. The aroma of house arrest.

He had come to Bali often during his time in office. There would be local dignitaries at the Tuban airfield, and then the motorcade would set off to travel up the long road into the foothills, passing rice fields, temple compounds, and schools with children in white shirts waving to him. The end point of this journey was the palace he had built on the hillside at Tampak Siring.

Sukarno was hugely charismatic, but he had little use for Indonesian parliamentary democracy, whose demise in the late 1950s was in large part his responsibility. Indeed, the authoritarian rule he instituted in 1959, in the form of Guided Democracy, could be said to have laid the groundwork for Soeharto's subsequent dictatorship. And yet, given the darkness that descended with the massacres of 1965–1966, I found myself associating Sukarno with a "lightness" I attributed to the period that went before. The public commemoration of Sukarno was discouraged in Indonesia partly because any remembering of him would be impossible to uncouple from a remembering of the events of 1965–1966, and any remembering of that would help delegitimize the Soeharto regime. I think it had worked in reverse for me: A dislike of the Soeharto regime had led me to 1965–1966, which in turn led me to Sukarno.

My interest in him was only sharpened by the fact that his image, which must have been everywhere on the island prior to 1965, seemed subsequently to have been scoured off the face of the landscape. The new regime's writ did not, however, extend to the lunar landscape. The Australian artist Donald Friend, living at Sanur, made the following diary entry for 30 January 1967: "Last night, according to excited talk all over Bali, villagers in masses stood about viewing, on the face of the moon, President Sukarno's portrait. What could it mean?"[23] Perhaps it meant that effacement has its limits. At a time when it would have been dangerous to exhibit a picture of Sukarno in Bali, where he had been enormously popular, the authorities could hardly prevent people from witnessing an apparition of his image on the moon. I had a more prosaic encounter with him myself when, one day, riding the scooter down to the beach, I came around a corner to be suddenly confronted by his face painted, larger than life, on the wooden tailgate of a truck parked beside the road. It was from Madura and it was unloading fake antique (*antik baru*) furniture.[24] The scooter wobbled and continued on.

The association of Shalimar with Sukarno is tenuous, I know. But in Soeharto's Indonesia, with its tightly controlled media, there were always more rumors than verifiable facts. Shalimar was a rumor that I cultivated in my mind and through my senses. But eventually this wasn't enough: I wanted to find it in the actual landscape of Sukarno's Bali. I decided to visit the palace he had built at Tampak Siring.

The roads in that region mostly run along the tops of the long ridges that radiate down toward the sea from the crater of Mount Batur. Rather than taking one of these roads up from the town of Denpasar, I cut across from the southeast, partly for the pleasure of riding on the narrow roads that link the ridge roads. Turning off onto one of these, the road almost immediately plunges down into a deep, heart-melting gully full of trees and ferns where the road cuttings are covered with moss. Suddenly there is cool air washing over my face and bare arms, the road levels momentarily, crosses a bridge above a fast-flowing stream, and then is climbing again into the world of sunlight. Finally I reach the ridge road that I figure is the one Sukarno's motorcade would have taken on the way from the airport. I slow down. The president is in the back of a big American car, wearing his trademark dark glasses, looking at the passing scenery as he turns over in his mind the uncertain loyalty of the army, the spiraling inflation, the failing balance between the forces of Islam, communism, and liberal nationalism, forces he has always attempted to keep in balance. There are afterimages of the beautiful Balinese girls dancing for him on the tarmac of the airfield at his arrival. And somewhere in the car the faintest trace of Shalimar de Guerlain; it is impossible to tell if it is an actual trace or a memory.

Figure 5.2.   President Sukarno in Washington, DC, 1956 (Warren K. Leffler, Library of Congress, Prints & Photographs Division, U.S. News & World Report Magazine Collection, LC-USZ62-134160)

I am conscious of riding in the jet stream of the presidential limousine. My eyes are mainly on the approaching road surface, watching for holes and bumps, while somewhere in my consciousness I sense, or remember, the aroma of Shalimar. In the discourse of perfumery one speaks of the afterlife of a scent, meaning the perceptible changes it undergoes in the time after it is applied to the skin and its ability to retain a distinct signature long after the fading of its initial intensity. Reading Lynn Meskell's *Object Worlds* years after that ride to Tampak Siring, I thought of Shalimar as I took in her suggestion that we attend to the affective afterlives of objects, the afterlives, for instance, of statues and other images in ancient Egypt that could "extend the biography and trajectory of the individual through time."[25] A perfume is not a statue, of course, nor was Shalimar created with the intention of giving "individual permanence" to Sukarno.[26] But his association with the perfume, whatever its nature, undeniably had a "residual force" for me during those months in Bali.[27]

Sukarno's palace, which was more in the way of a large villa, had been constructed in 1954 in the grounds of a Dutch rest house. It was situated on a steep ridge overlooking, in the gully below, a complex of shrines and pools that marked the site a sacred spring. This arrangement breached Balinese religious protocol that maintained a house should not overlook a temple. But there were large trees around the temple and from its picturesque courtyards with their moss-covered walls you couldn't quite see the villa perched just out of sight above.

Sukarno, whose mother was Balinese, spent a great deal of time at Tampak Siring. He entertained, at different times, Ho Chi Minh, Robert Kennedy, and Jawaharlal Nehru there. Nehru, during his visit, referred to Bali as the "morning of the world," an expression later picked up by the tourism industry. Tampak Siring also served as a base for Sukarno's project of incorporating Balinese art, dance, and music into the national culture of Indonesia.[28]

After visiting the temple I took a road that led up the ridge to the entrance of the original rest-house compound. Parking the scooter in front of a ceremonial wrought-iron gateway that guarded the grounds, I peered in across the lawns and gardens. From here, too, Sukarno's villa was out of sight, too far down the side of the ridge to be visible. The bolt and the hinges on the gate were rusted up, suggesting it hadn't been opened for a long while and implying no expectation it would need to be opened anytime soon. I'd heard that Soeharto very rarely visited this place. Bali was perhaps too much for his dour temperament, or was it that Tampak Siring was too imbued with the spirit of his predecessor for him ever to be entirely comfortable there?

I found another entrance, further up the street, which apparently provided everyday access for the gardeners and maintenance staff, but I was stopped there by a guard and told I could only look from the outside. This was disappointing. I retired to a *warung* across the road and drank cold tea while an elderly woman invited me to buy a carved wooden frog. Then a boy came selling paintings and drawings of mountain scenes in the style of the 1970s Ubud artists. The lush vegetation they depicted spilled over onto wooden frames elaborately carved with leaves and vines, as if nature were truly irrepressible.

It was perfectly understandable they would not want foreign tourists poking around in a presidential residence. I could appreciate that. But I just wanted to see Sukarno's villa, even from a distance, so I turned to consider the topography. Logically there should have been another ridge to the east of this one and unless it were covered in trees it should have been possible to look across from there to the villa. I followed the road back down the hill to the temple turn-off and continued on until I came to the top of the neighboring ridge. There was a road along the ridgeline, but it was lined with houses and small shops and you couldn't see out. But eventually I found a path that led between two buildings to a temple located in the rice fields behind. The land fell quickly away from the ridgetop into the deep bush-filled gully that separated this ridge from the Sukarno ridge. The rice fields were terraced. I had to climb down to the second terrace to get a view because the top one had a dense hedgelike band of shrubs along its edge.

And there it was, Sukarno's villa, on the side of the opposite ridge just about level with where I stood and surrounded by smooth, empty lawns. It was a study in 1950s Third World modernism. The single-story, L-shaped structure was by no means monumental in scale. Its long axis was built partly into the slope, and the projecting wing hung in the air, supported on slender concrete stilts. The main access seemed to be via a walkway elevated above a ravine to the south. There were large windows and an uncomplicated wrought-iron balcony. The walls were a pale powder pink, nicely offset by the gray tiles on the high gabled roof.

I sat down in the grass on the edge of the terrace, conscious that I had entered the space of the Sukarno underground. Curtains were drawn behind the windows over there, which made it easier to imagine him in residence. The place seemed impeccably maintained, as if time had stood still since 1965. I thought of myself an hour ago sitting at the *warung*, staring across the street at the iron fence and feeling frustrated by the villa's invisibility when all the while it was exposed to view from this other ridge. Well, I thought, that's how it is with these sites of the underground: They're always there, under our noses; we just choose not to see them. Or perhaps it's a case of needing to be cued to the particular dimension in which they exist?

Figure 5.3.   Sukarno's former villa, Tampak Siring, Bali, 1990s (Denis Byrne)

Somewhere in the distance a siren sounded, and I wondered if there was some regulation against gazing upon Sukarno's villa. What would happen if I were discovered here with a bottle of Shalimar in my pocket (a miniature bottle, convenient for fieldwork, that someone had acquired for me from a duty-free shop)?

When I got back to the scooter drops of rain had begun to fall, spotting the hot surface of the road. I rode back home as quickly as I could, keeping just ahead of the rain that was pouring out of the mass of dark clouds behind me. Down the ridge roads and across the deep, cool gullies, I was managing to stay just in front of it, though the smell of it was in the air and the air itself, stirred up by its proximity, was bending the trees and swirling through the rice crop. Back down to the coast and up onto the surface of the everyday.

NOTES

1. Although Sukarno delegated authority to General Soeharto in March 1966 in the crisis following the failed coup attempt, it was not until the following February that he "signed away all administrative powers" to the general, who took up the presidency on 27 March 1968 (Brooks 1995, 65). Sukarno was under house arrest at first in Bogor and later in the house of one of his wives in Jakarta.

2. Benedict Anderson (1990, 78–93) critiques the use of the concept of charisma in the contemporary social sciences as an attribute of certain demagogic, irrational, and dangerous non-Western leaders. He contrasts this with Max Weber's characterization of charisma as a transhistorical, transcultural quality of extraordinary people, a quality that could have redemptive value in a modern world of advanced/extreme rationalization, secularization, and bureaucratization. He also contrasts it with the traditional-popular Javanese discourse of power that conceives the power of human leaders as continuous with, and derived from, divine power.

3. Labrousse 1994.

4. Ibid., 180–81.

5. *Bung Karno*, a popular term of affection widely used to refer to Sukarno during his presidency (*bung* meaning brother).

6. Crossland 2002, 123.

7. Bosco 2004, 390.

8. Tsing 1993, 298.

9. Meskell 2004, 81.

10. The Shalimar gardens were constructed in Lahore in 1619 by the Mugal emperor of India, Shah Jahangir.

11. Van Morrison's *Astral Weeks*, released by Warner Brothers, 1968.

12. Instead of naturally occurring vanilla, Guerlain used ethyl vanillin, a synthetic compound discovered around the turn of the century, about four times stronger than vanillin, the principle extract of the vanilla orchid (Calkin and Jellinek 1994, 124). Guerlain supplemented the ethyl vanillin in Shalimar with an alcoholic tincture of vanilla to lend a feeling of naturalness to the synthetic.

13. "A perfume should not announce your arrival, it should leave your signature," a statement popularly attributed to Coco Chanel.

14. Calkin and Jellinek 1994, 124.

15. In fact there now is a "masculinized" version of Opium, Opium Pour Homme (1995), about which Robert Frampton, writing in *Attitude* magazine (December 1995, 16), has the following to say: "Eighteen years ago, YSL created Opium, a rather sticky, choking confection; but his male version is a triumph, both sexy and intoxicating. Fresh bourbon vanilla provides warmth and sensuality whilst the star anise, Chinese galanga and piper nigrum spice up the bottom woody notes. Comforting yet dangerous, this scent is so sinful that I am prepared to forgive YSL his Kouros, worn by just about every queen in the Eighties." Ignoring for a moment the impulse to slip away and empty one's drawers of Kouros, one may notice here the association of Opium/Asia with sinfulness.

16. Jordan and Weedon 1995, 263.

17. The hundreds of prints acquired in Japan by Frank Lloyd Wright went into the collections of various American industrialists and businessmen who were the drivers of American modernity (Meech 1995).

18. The first version of the Mitsubishi Zero fighter was introduced in 1939. Its superiority to Western fighter planes and the confidence this gave to the Japanese is likely to have been a factor in the decision to go to war against the United States (Mikesh 1981, 23).

19. Craig Clunas observes that the imagery present on such mass-produced products both "formed and reinforced European visual stereotypes of China" (1997, 199).
20. Ivy 1995.
21. Ibid., 57.
22. *Hell Bento!!*, directed by Anna Broinowski and Andrew Sully, Ronin Films, 56 mins., 1995.
23. Friend 2006, 21.
24. Madura is a large island off the northeast coast of Java.
25. Meskell 2004, 7.
26. Ibid.
27. Ibid., 10.
28. For Sukarno's exploitation of Balinese arts for the project of national identity formation, see Vickers (1989, 182–83).

· 6 ·

Spectral Coastline

The sea off the northern coast of Bali is fished by people whose fragile villages are almost on the beach and whose brightly painted *jukung* outriggers sail the comparatively shallow waters covering the Sahul Shelf. During the Pleistocene, when much of the earth's water was stacked up in ice sheets, you would have been able to walk northward across the horizon from the present coastline all the way to the Kangean Archipelago and then on to what are now the islands of Sulawesi and Borneo. Nowadays it is what oceanographers call a "low-energy" coastline of smallish waves, in contrast to Bali's south coast, where large breakers roll in against the cliffs and beaches.

Bali is only some eighty kilometers wide, north to south, but to reach the north coast from the south of the island you have to climb a thousand meters in elevation in order to cross the volcanoes. As you begin the downhill run from the top you have glimpses, through the treetops, of the north coast and the sea far below, and it is easy to imagine you are entering another land. There is hardly any alluvial plain there, just a narrow strip of flat land between the sea and the lower slopes of the mountains.

Adji, who came from Java, and David, a Canadian, had built a house on this less-settled, less-visited north coast, near a place called Yéh Saneh. The piece of land they bought was at a point where the coast road runs within a hundred meters of the sea. The stone wall they built along the margin of the road insulated them from the noise of the little traffic that passed along that way. On the seaward side there was a four-meter-high alluvial cliff below which small waves broke onto a narrow beach of glittering black sand and pebbles. Over a period of a few years they built a series of three single-room pavilions whose pitched roofs were thatched with lontar palm fronds, less expensive than the grass thatch used on the south side of the island.

113

The first and largest structure they built was the closest to the sea. It was an open-sided pavilion of dressed coconut-palm pillars with a split-level polished wooden floor. A surrounding balustrade was filled in by a grid of thin batons, and there were cane blinds that could be lowered when it rained. The second structure, a bedroom, was directly behind the pavilion and connected to it by a stone path. Unlike the pavilion, it had brick walls with proper windows and French doors. But it had the same lontar roof, as did the freestanding guest room that was further back toward the road. They put in a bathroom of country rock with a view of the sea and a kitchen hut behind a row of frangipanis. The garden was divided into a series of partly paved courtyards separated by waist-high walls of undressed local basalt. These rough walls, the sun-bleached lontar thatch, and the plants chosen because they could go without water and tolerated the salt air all were in keeping with the austerity of that coastline.

On the lower level of the front pavilion there were a couple of cane deck chairs and a dining table consisting of an old door with an unpainted plywood surface, resting on two wooden boxes. From there you looked out across the wide expanse of the sea. At night it was like looking into a void. Sitting there in the dusk on the day we arrived I remembered, several years earlier, sitting with a friend in a café on the banks of the Mekong at Chiang Saen in northern Thailand. The café, built of piles, extended out over the great slow-moving river, and we sat at a table by the wooden railing looking across to Laos, which was about a kilometer away on the other side. A screen of trees and scrub grew along the shore over there, and the only signs of life we could see were some children who'd brought buffaloes down to the water and who seemed to be playing along its edge. A radio was playing Thai country music, and the red cellophane lanterns grew brighter as the sun set and the daylight quickly drained from the sky. The darkness was then so thick as to seem two-dimensional. Laos disappeared—even the river was invisible—and then a single flickering light, perhaps a campfire, appeared like a star in the darkness over where Laos had been.

At Adji and David's place, instead of the roar of the ocean or the silent passage of a great river, there was just the irregular breaking of small waves onto the black sand. And it was that sound, or rather the spacing of it, that established the rhythm of life there.

A few years after the buildings were finished David's car collided with a truck while he was coming down the mountain road one night after work. He was in the hospital for two weeks. That was the year the kitchen burned down, which is to say that a forgotten candle ignited a fire that consumed everything but the stone half-walls and the tiled floor. It was lucky the thatch of the nearby roofs didn't catch. It was also the year the sea came in and took half their garden.

It was not as if they didn't know from the beginning that the beach cliff was eroding. During high tides the waves lapped at its base, undermining the compacted soil that had been built up partly from the ash of past volcanic eruptions. A centimeter or two at a time, the cliff collapsed onto the beach in buff-colored lumps and slabs that were dissolved and carried away by the sea. But the year the kitchen burned the monsoon tides were higher than usual. Or was it that those of the preceding years had been unusually low? Anyway,

Figure 6.1. House on the coast near Yéh Saneh, Bali, 1990s (Denis Byrne)

they lost several meters of the cliff-top garden, until the front pavilion stood almost at the cliff's very edge, enjoying "panoramic, absolute water-front views," David joked weakly.

We heard all this after dinner when we were sitting on the floor in that front pavilion. The floorboards had been rubbed with sand to bring up the grain and were laid slightly apart to allow the sea air to come through. A young Chinese woman with two thickset, shy young Chinese men had dropped in. The woman owned a small hotel along the beach for which Adji was designing an extension. She had brought a bottle of cognac, the way you might bring a bottle of wine, and David had gone away and come back with a tray of tiny glasses. After they left it began to rain heavily, and we talked against the noise of raindrops hammering on the lontar thatch. In his slightly hesitant English, Adji told us that after the fire, and especially after the front part of the garden was eaten away by the sea, they'd lost heart. The place had been their dream for too long for them to be able to accept what had happened, what *was* happening. They rented a house at Sanur, on the other side of the island, closer to work, and hardly came here for a year and a half. They tried not to think about it. Somebody from the village down the beach kept an eye on the place. The sea took another meter of the garden.

The conversation turned to termites and ways of preventing them from climbing up the foundation poles. David mentioned that he had a colony of tiny ants living in his computer. "What would they live on?" he wondered. "Memory?"

I woke in the night trying to hold onto the threads of a dream I had been having about a professor of archaeology who had just published a book on the prehistory of Polynesia. All I could recall was that the book designers had turned the maps of the individual island groups into pop-up origami constructions. When you opened the pages these pale blue maps blossomed forth in three dimensions, in such a way that the pattern of lines inscribed by the voyages of the trading canoes extended out like starbursts to the outlying islands of the group and then obediently withdrew again into themselves as you closed the page. Nobody had seen anything like it before and there was contention within the discipline on the question of whether it was a mere gimmick or a brilliant innovation.

In the morning the sky was clear, and for a while sunlight fell across the floorboards of the pavilion. The tide was in, pushing a small canoe up against the bottom of the cliff. For some distance out the sea was stained a light brown color beyond which, quite suddenly, it became blue. It was not an unattractive brown, and the sun sparkled off the brown waves and the ripples just as it did off the blue. David said the brown must have been sediment washed down by the adjacent stream, but the stream, I thought, didn't seem big enough for that. And besides, you could see how the waves even now were licking at the base of the cliff right below us.

David poured coffee from an old porcelain pot that had a wad of banana leaves jammed in where the lid was missing. He pointed out to sea, just past the band of brown water, saying he'd been told by the locals that there'd been a coastal road out there once. We looked mutely out and sipped our coffee, the beans for which came from the mountain behind us. I thought about how the brown sea out there represented so many cubic centimeters of land in liquid form. When Adji joined us he spoke about his plans for a sea wall and began sketching a pattern of pyramidal concrete blocks that would be set a few meters out from the cliff, the cliff itself to be protected by a rock wall. Even he didn't seem convinced either that they could afford it or that it would work. I asked Adji if I could look at his sketchbook, and after they'd gone to buy a fish for lunch I sat for a while flicking through it. There were early sketches for the pavilion, a whole page of different ideas for the railing around its sides, and pages of layout concepts for the garden and its stone walls. Everything disintegrates in the end, of course, including us ourselves, and in most cases we're gone long before the buildings we create. In their case, however, it was as if the picture were breaking up even as they were dreaming it.

When the tide began to recede I climbed down to the beach and walked along under the cliff. In places you had to walk out into the water to avoid fishing canoes that had been drawn high up on the sand. In the cliff face, at one point, I saw layers of brickwork and concrete, traces of houses whose spectral forms I imagined extending out over my head, hovering over the sea. I thought of Karangasem and the aftermath of the Gunung Agung eruption and wondered if local people walking up this beach saw these traces and remembered the former landform and the life it supported. I wondered whether they felt the strangeness of this reversal in which the past was a ghostly surface they now walked beneath rather than upon, a faint topography animated by a life that was supported now only by their memories.[1] In normal situations it is the experience of walking on the landscape that brings back emplaced memories of past lives and events; here it was a case of memory having to conjure a vanished landform out of the stump it was once connected to. In a future of global warming and sea-level rise, these spectral coastlines, and perhaps a longing for lost places, would be common experience for many millions of us.

Further along I stood looking at the outline, in section, of what I thought was a silted-up well. There were coconut palms here whose curved trunks leaned out over the cliff. The roots of some of them were exposed and undermined by erosion, and the leaning trunks seemed about to fall onto the beach.

I passed teenage boys in batik-print sarongs who were lashing an outrigger onto a very small canoe. The pebbles lying on the glittering black beach were thin and flat, as if designed for children to skim along the water. They tumbled against each other in the wash of each small wave, producing a sound like a round of polite applause.

Also in the cliff face, if you looked carefully, was the odd shard of Chinese porcelain, blue and white, along with shards of the local earthenware. A few kilometers away to the east a Balinese archaeologist whom I knew had excavated a prehistoric village site and recovered from his trenches, at a depth of about three and a half meters below the surface, shards of a rouletted ware, a distinctive Indian trade pottery that must have reached Bali some two thousand years ago.[2] Beads of glass and carnelian at the site were also thought to have been imported from India in the late first millennium BC. As the coastline eroded it steadily consumed the archaeological record: The past was going out to sea.

We left late that afternoon, driving along the coast and then up the winding mountain road where the low sun illuminated the treetops but left the undergrowth in deep shadow. We were almost at the summit when I remembered I'd left a book behind. I remembered it lying on the battered old dresser in the bedroom, waiting to be put in my bag. A small wave of anxiety washed through me as I foresaw them finding it and assuming I'd left it deliberately to make some kind of point. The book was Marguerite Duras's *The Sea Wall*, a novel set in 1930s Vietnam.[3] It tells the story of a French woman whose schoolteacher husband has died, leaving her with two children whom she supports by working in Saigon as a piano teacher. She has dreams of being a successful farmer, and when she is granted a land concession on a low-lying coastal plain far from the city, she sinks her savings into the venture, hoping to make a new life for herself and her teenage son and daughter. But she discovers when it is too late that half the land, the part that is adjacent to an estuarine wetland (*rac*), is regularly inundated by the monsoon tides. Using the last of her money and mortgaging her bungalow, she constructs a dike to keep the tides out and make it possible to grow rice on the low land closest to the sea and the *rac*. The dike is an earth embankment shored up by a palisade of mangrove logs. Come the July tides in the year after construction, when the land has been cultivated and sown with rice by her native laborers and the villagers who themselves have been infected by her mad optimism, the sea wall crumbles in a single night. Financially ruined, her life becomes a pattern of alternating rage and hopeless despair, and the novel is woven around her efforts to sell a valuable diamond ring given to her indifferent daughter as an expression of love by the ugly but wealthy son of a French planter.

I didn't see Adji and David again for several months, by which time they were renting a house in Ubud. David described how things had deteriorated even further at the dream house. When a hotel renovation project that Adji was working on fell through at the last minute, they'd had to fire some workers from their local village whom they had hired in anticipation. There was bad feeling. Somebody nailed a dead duck to the gate. Boys called out abuse from down on the beach. More of the cliff fell away, undermining the pavilion. Late one afternoon while David was staying there alone, having paced around all day with a drink in his hand confronting in maudlin detail the futility of it all, he saw that the only option was to burn the place down. He went and got a can of the kerosene they used for the lamps and, still with a glass in his hand, poured it around the floor of the pavilion. But when he went to light it he found the matches were damp, as often happens in the humid tropics, and they wouldn't strike. There was no getting free of the place. He said he'd read the Duras book and found it interesting. It was in a packing case down in the basement with the things they'd moved from the house after they had decided to put it on the market.

Bombs fall from a B-52 and sail serenely through the air before detonating in a procession of expanding percussion rings that shadow the plane's progress across the surface of the lush Vietnamese landscape. The rumbling sound of explosions fills the screening room in the basement of the Reunification Palace in Saigon, seeming almost to shake the walls. Built in the early 1960s as the official residence of South Vietnam's president, the basement level formerly housed the war room, an emergency communications center, and a map room. Making provision for the worst of all possible scenarios, it also featured an escape tunnel leading to the basement of another public building several blocks away, though in the end it was the rooftop helipad that proved to be the exit point. The audience is comprised of neatly dressed Vietnamese whom I watch from the corner of my eye, sometimes catching them in the act of watching me. Each wondering, perhaps, how the other is taking this.

I've been here before, a couple of days ago. What starts as a stroll up Dong Khoi Boulevard from downtown, past the Catholic cathedral and through the park, seems inevitably to end here in the screening room. I buy my ticket at the front gate and walk the hallways of the palace, stopping at roped-off doorways to look in at the various rooms: the grand dining room, the credentials presentation room, the first lady's sitting room. All of them have evidently been maintained in the state they were in at that moment in April 1975 when a North Vietnamese army tank broke down the wrought-iron gate and a soldier raced up the stairs to raise the winning flag (gold star on a red field) from the rooftop flagpole. Some of the interiors are decorated with heavy ornate furniture and wildlife trophy heads in a style *Wallpaper* magazine calls "dictator kitsch." Others are expressions of 1960s modernism: light airy spaces with streamlined furniture.

Now they are showing footage of how it was on the ground in Hanoi during the bombing raids. We see hospitals, air-raid shelters, and antiaircraft gun crews. Then there are enemy jets and helicopters shot down in rice fields. The film ends and then starts over again, and I'm walking down a corridor with the sound of exploding bombs receding behind me.

Half an hour later, sitting on my bed on the sixth floor of a very narrow hotel (it is only one room wide), I am looking at a map of Vietnam. Printed on glossy paper, it has a different pastel color for each province of the country and blue dashed lines to represent shipping connections along the coast. I've been in Saigon for five days and I know I'm now just marking time here, putting off making a decision. I am supposed to be on a journey to find the setting of *The Sea Wall*, an idea that seemed straightforward enough when I conceived it in Bali but that now, in Saigon, seems somewhat insubstantial.[4] The problem with chasing ephemera is that you easily become vulnerable to doubts. I now feel the project slipping away from me, the way the days slip away as I watch war documentaries in the basement projection room and waste hours at the sidewalk cafés mesmerized by the endless flow of motorbikes and bicycles.

On the map my eye progresses up the coast from Saigon: Nha Trang, Qui Nhon, Da Nang, Hoi An, Hue. Marguerite Duras describes the farm in *The Sea Wall* as being eight hundred kilometers from Saigon, but the local place-names she uses are fictional. I tear a page out of my notebook, mark onto its edge the scale printed at the bottom of the map, and then mark out eight hundred kilometers in a line north from Saigon. This puts the farm somewhere just south of Da Nang, where the coastal strip between the sea and the mountains is particularly narrow, just as she describes it being. As the crow flies, the farm would have been closer to Savannakhet in Laos or even to Ubon in northeast Thailand than it was to Saigon. I didn't have to resort to the scale to see that eight hundred kilometers south of Saigon would have put the farm out in the ocean, well on the way to Borneo. So, it is Da Nang that should be my next stop. But I have been to Da Nang on a previous visit to Vietnam and hadn't liked it. Ideally, you might think, this is where one's sense of discipline would kick in: Liking Da Nang or not liking it is beside the point; the project requires Da Nang. Yes, but on the other hand, isn't rigidity antithetical to an inquiry of this kind? Shouldn't I be feeling my way along intuitively rather than knuckling down to a fixed itinerary?

My goal or destination is not the actual geographic setting of the novel—always supposing Duras had a real place in mind—but a generic set-

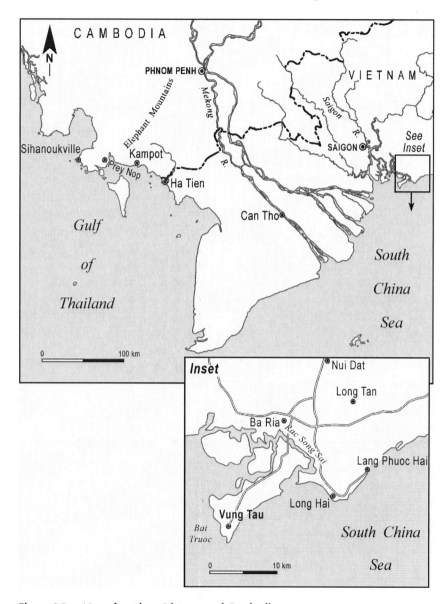

Figure 6.2.   Map of southern Vietnam and Cambodia

ting, somewhere that would evoke *The Sea Wall*'s central scenario of reclamation and eventual loss. When I was reading this novel in Bali, its scenario of a coastal situation in which the sea periodically inundated the lower lands and then withdrew again seemed congruent with the idea of Bali's ostensibly solid surface being a permeable twilight zone (of effaced events, elusive traces, forbidden memories). The French woman in the novel makes the mistake of believing "her" coastline to be a hard line rather than an unstable zone, just as archaeologists may be inclined to make a too-strict distinction between the surface and the underground. I wanted a journey that would help me to think about all that rather than one that would simply take me to a destination.

An alternative to Da Nang was Vung Tau, but to explain the Vung Tau option I need to provide some background. One winter afternoon I was window-shopping in downtown Auckland, New Zealand, the city in which I'd grown up and gone to university. On the gallery level of an old shopping arcade near the harbor I stopped to look at a map taped to the inside of the window of a military memorabilia shop. There were old infantry helmets in the window display along with medals and gas masks that appeared to date from the First World War. So as I stooped down to examine the map, my face close to the glass, I assumed I was looking at the terrain of one of the Great War battlefields: Flanders, Ypres, or the Somme. Looking at the brown and yellow topography I expected to see European place-names, and it was a moment before it registered that names like Au Tug, No Chi Vein, and Din-Co could only mean I was looking at a map of Vietnam. I went in to inquire and was told by the middle-aged shopkeeper that the map was of the countryside immediately to the north of the Vung Tau peninsula, to the southeast of Saigon. He retrieved it from the window and spread it on the counter, saying it belonged to a friend of his who had served with the New Zealand infantry battalion in the Vietnam War. The map showed the area where the joint Australian–New Zealand force had operated in the mid-1960s and early 1970s. It wasn't for sale.

The map was sufficiently detailed to show individual houses and buildings (tiny black squares and rectangles). It also showed individual rice fields, cemeteries, fish ponds, mangrove swamps, "abandoned buildings," and "ruins." Whether the latter were the outcome of gradual decay or were ruins produced by artillery or aerial bombing, the key didn't specify. Superimposed on the base map—stratified over it, so to speak—was a layer of other information in red numbers and symbols. This superimposed detail was thicker and more crudely drawn than the finely etched lines and subtle colors of the base map and had clearly been added later, together with an accompanying legend, also in red. According to the inked-in legend, the small circles indicated "antipersonnel mine incidents," and the single numerals inside these circles indicated the individual years of the late 1960s in which the incidents occurred. There were a few eights, a great many nines, and numerous zeros (representing 1970). An area surrounded by a broken red line was a minefield, a heavy red circle was a base camp, and one of these circles with a cross in it had been "hit by air/arty" (artillery?). "T" stood for tunnel; "RWF" stood for enemy caches of rice, weapons, and food.

Even while my attention was on the map I was aware of the shopkeeper's eyes on me. The Vietnam War and, by extension, this map were unlikely even now to be a subject of neutral interest by a person of my age in a country that had been a participant in that war. When I was an undergraduate student in this city during the war, there had been virtually no middle ground: You either strongly supported the war or you strongly opposed it. He would have been right to assume I'd been in the latter camp, but what was on my mind right now was not that. Rather it was the question of what this map, this detailed representation of a piece of Vietnam's surface as it was in the late 1960s, stood for in the context of this shop. There seemed to be something tentative, even defensive in the shopkeeper's attitude, as if whatever it was that the map meant to his friend (and perhaps to himself) he did not want defiled. Ultimately, their efforts to save Phuoc Tuy province from communism had been futile, but the map predated that failure and so, perhaps, the map was part of an effort to hold on to a lost place. By preserving the map, were they attempting to freeze Vietnam at a certain moment in time?

I said I thought it would be interesting to visit the area and see what traces there were of the military infrastructure. This seemed to decide him. To my surprise he told me that, although he couldn't sell me the map, I could take it to be photocopied at a shop down the street. The color photocopies of the map were with me now in Saigon, in a brown envelope in my bag.

Out in the street, in Saigon, it had started to rain. When the first peals of thunder crackled over the rooftops I went out onto the tiny balcony. The motorbikes were disappearing off the streets and those that remained were accelerating madly for their destinations. The rain hammered on the awnings below me; water poured from downpipes and broken gutters directly onto the sidewalk. Back inside I picked up *The Sea Wall*, leaving the door open to let the scent of rain infiltrate the room.

Later, when the rain had moved away across the rusting roofscape to some other part of the city, I went out into the streets again, but as I was leaving my key at the reception desk I noticed a stack of brochures for a hydrofoil service. A color picture on the cover showed two long white craft cruising at speed along a river. They had windows along the side that curved over at the top, allowing the passengers to see up as well as out. Even on the glossy brochure they looked decades old, like something off the set of a 1970s James Bond film, but it was still difficult to believe they existed in low-tech Vietnam. The receptionist said that one of the boats departed every morning for Vung Tau from a point on the riverfront just beyond the end of the same street the hotel was on. I could stroll there in ten minutes. When I said I might go down to the dock and have a look, the young bellboy, obviously a fan of hydrofoils, nodded his head enthusiastically.

The hydrofoil was tied up to a small quay opposite the Customs House on the outside of a bend in the Saigon River. Even this far upstream the river was deep enough to accommodate the passenger liners that in colonial days used to dock at the quays just across the riverside road from the urbane hotels, shops, and offices of the city center. Downstream, as it neared the coast, the river formed a delta, similar to but very much smaller than the vast delta of the Cuu Long, better known to us as the Mekong.[5]

At the ticket booth on the quay I was told there were still seats left for next morning's run down to Vung Tau, but they were selling fast. I hesitated for a moment, thinking of *The Sea Wall* project and knowing this was a decisive moment. Was I ready to turn my back on Da Nang? Another glance at the hydrofoil lying on the other side of the dock was enough to nudge me over the edge. I gave the man my ten dollars and walked away, looking at the large ticket with its background picture of the actual hydrofoil and feeling sure, now, that I was on the right path. Crossing the esplanade I walked up Nguyen Hue Boulevard and passed under the colonnade of the restored Hotel de Ville. There was a shop that seemed to sell nothing but white embroidered tablecloths and napkins. I gazed in the window and then went in and bought a white tablecloth, undecorated apart from a series of small, exquisitely worked seashells widely spaced along the border. There were several antique shops along the street, all of which had a stock of mid-century wristwatches. In one of them I looked at some Rolexes and was handed a magnifying glass for closer examination. They were fakes, but they were well made. Peering through the lens at the painted face and the gold Rolex crown, I wondered what sort of equipment you'd need to produce, or reproduce, something like this. I would have bought one if they hadn't been so expensive. Far too expensive for fakes and far too cheap to be the genuine article, I wondered who actually did buy them.

In a shop closer to my hotel I was looking into a cabinet full of old bric-a-brac when my eye came to rest, with a small jolt, on an old bottle of Shalimar de Guerlain. The bottle was empty, as far as it was possible to tell given its grimy condition. The woman shopkeeper must have noticed my interest because she suddenly materialized behind the cabinet and delicately lifted the dusty old thing out with a delicacy quite out of proportion to its value.

Once I had it in my hand I saw that it was more than just dusty; there were encrustations of actual dirt between the fluted ridges of the glass, as if it had been excavated from a colonial-era garbage dump. It was one of the fluted flask-like bottles made by Baccarat for the perfume's release in 1925, and at first it seemed extraordinary that it should have been present there among the old lighters, watches, and chipped celadon bowls. But, on reflection, I realized that Saigon would be one of the more likely places in the world to find such a thing. The chances were that the perfume it contained had been worn by one of the fashionable white women of the 1930s who frequented the boutiques and smart cafés on this very street, Le Loi Boulevard, then the Rue Catinat, probably the most fashionable street in French Indochina. But that first bottle design had been in production for decades, so the one in my hand was just as likely to have dated to the 1960s. Fowler, the English journalist in *The Quiet American*, noticed a shop selling Guerlain perfume on his first walk up the Rue Catinat and "comforted . . . [himself] with the thought that, after all, Europe was only distant thirty hours."[6]

"You like?" the woman asked, as I turned it over in my hands.

"Not really," I replied, but without moving to put it down.

First I had to smell it. I removed the blue glass stopper, held the bottle to my nose and inhaled slowly, trying to focus my senses. But I could smell nothing. Not a trace. I tried again, sure that some residue of the perfume, however faint, must remain, though clearly I was in danger of conjuring up the scent of Shalimar out of my recent past rather than out of the bottle. But all I could smell was dust and the more distant background odor of vehicle fumes and cooking.

"I will give you for thirty dollar," the woman said. I shook my head and put it down on the glass counter.

"It's empty," I said.

"It's old," she replied. "Twenty dollar!"

I was tempted, but then context is everything. If I took it away it would be just another displaced perfume bottle. Its significance to me lay in having discovered its presence there in that city, and it would be nice to think of it still gathering dust there in ten years' time. Which surely it would be, I thought when I stepped back out on the street, maneuvering around a boy selling postcards. Who the hell would buy it if I wouldn't?

I took a shortcut back to the hotel along a backstreet lined with electrical shops. The sidewalk outside the open-fronted stores was stacked with televisions, air conditioners, and rice cookers, so that you were forced to walk in the street. Halfway along I noticed a young woman was coming toward me, standing on the side of a slowly moving, wobbling bicycle with one foot on the pedal. I stepped sideways to avoid her, but the bicycle made one last wobble and its front wheel lodged between my legs. All of this in slow motion. I wasn't at all hurt but neither could I move. The woman sort of fell into me, and in the confusion I suddenly realized she was trying to pull my wristwatch off. It was an aluminum Swatch that may have looked more expensive than it was. I grabbed my wrist and for a strangely intimate moment our fingers wrestled for control of the object. Even while this struggle was going on I was thinking what a brilliant ruse it was but also how stupid I must look straddling the front of the bicycle as if I were trying to mount it the wrong way around. And then almost before I knew it the bicycle and the woman were gone and I still had the watch. A moment later I realized the wallet in my back pocket was gone, but it was an old one, containing only a few dollars; I'd left anything of value in the hotel's safety-deposit box.

As I stood there in the street recomposing myself, I glanced around. Everyone was going about their business as if nothing had happened. Whatever rupture had just occurred to the normal flow of life in this street, the waters had immediately closed back over it. But for me it was, in a sense, the first time I had broken the surface of Vietnam: For a brief moment I was more than just an observer. I was the victim in the piece, sure, but even that limited role had dragged me momentarily deeper than I'd been before.

That night after dinner I went for a drink at a bar a few blocks away, a place called Apocalypse Now. It was a very toned-down representation of Kurtz's jungle base, patronized mostly by ex-pats and sex workers. I sat on a barstool watching them dance to old mainstream rock music. I wondered whether it was also an attempt to recreate a Saigon GI girlie bar circa 1967 and whether the girls here were schooled to act in the role of war-era Saigon bar girls.[7] As I was leaving it struck me that the war-era bars would have had netting across the entrance to stop locals from throwing in grenades. Well before midnight I returned to the hotel and found the night manager sitting at a coffee table reading a magazine. I settled my bill and asked him to wake me at six in the morning. He carefully wrote a note for himself.

I woke at half past six and only had time to wash my face before hurrying downstairs with my bag. Coming out of the elevator I was momentarily disoriented: The foyer was dark as night, and yet my room had been flooded with morning sunlight. A metal shutter had been pulled down across the entire glass front of the hotel, blacking it out. There was no sign of the night manager, but a small figure in shorts and T-shirt rose from a banana lounge that hadn't been there before and went across to the reception counter, pointing. I joined him there and we both peered down at the night manager who was still asleep on a mattress affair on the floor on the other side. He didn't respond to my hello, and even when the boy went around and shook him he barely reacted. I could relate to this, as I was still only half awake myself. So I stood there silently while the boy shook his shoulder again and the night manager turned away, a trace of protest on his face but his eyes still closed. He had really beautiful skin, I noticed. His eyelids were a small miracle in their own right, but in the world of harsh realities his sleeping habits were threatening to spoil my rendezvous with the Vung Tau hydrofoil. Just as I was thinking I'd have to start shaking him myself he opened his eyes and focused blearily on my face.

"What you want?" he asked irritably.

I pointed to the door and he reluctantly got up and opened it for me. I got to the jetty just as the last passengers were having their tickets checked at the gangplank. As I sank back into my seat, the boat backed out into the river and then roared away through the sampans and rusting freighters. The windows had a blue film stuck onto the inside, and this was scratched and blistered and quite difficult to see through. In places, the original paintwork of the boat's interior had been badly painted over with a coarse brush that had left black bristles behind. It was a pity, I thought, but the world is a flawed place. I closed my eyes and went back to sleep.

NOTES

1. This section owes an influence to Colm Tóibín's (1992) novel, *The Blazing Heather*, which is set on a part of the southeast coast of Ireland where the cliffs are consumed by erosion and where locals and summer visitors remember, or try to remember, houses and fields that have disappeared as the cliff has moved inland. The same motif occurs in his later book, *The Blackwater Lightship* (1999).

2. Ardika 1991.

3. Duras 1985.

4. Ibid.

5. Cuu Long, the Nine Dragons River, a reference to its nine principal estuarine branches each of which is believed to embody a water dragon.

6. Greene 1974, 23.

7. See Schwenkel (2006, 9–10) for a brief commentary on the Apocalypse Now nightclub that situates it among a raft of other attractions, privately financed but condoned by the government, that help foreign tourists to imagine and vicariously experience wartime Vietnam.

· 7 ·

Vung Tau

$\mathcal{V}$ung Tau is situated at the end of a ten-kilometer-long peninsula, actually a tombolo, that lies on the north side of the Dong Nai Delta. It had been a beach resort during the days of the French, who had named it Cap Saint Jacques. Now it was a holiday destination for the citizens of Saigon, who could reach it by bus or motorbike in a couple of hours. The boat docked at a naval base on the edge of Vung Tau where minibuses waited to take us into town. The one I was in stopped at a series of medium-rise hotels, but when we turned onto the esplanade I asked to get out and found myself standing on the footpath looking at the sea through a gap between two shack-like kiosks, a row of which had been built at the top of a narrow strip of sand on which several small fishing boats were stranded.

This was Bai Truoc Beach. It was good to see the sea, even if what I was looking at was not quite the sea as such but the broad waters of the Dong Nai Delta. Standing there with my bag and my map I was beginning to attract the attention of cyclo drivers, so I crossed the road and went through a garden into the entrance of a drab hotel. I asked to see a room and was shown one on the ground floor that was dim and musty and where a rickety metal bed stood on a painted concrete floor. The woman who showed it to me seemed as unimpressed with it as I was and she simply nodded when I declined. Back on the esplanade I walked north toward the hill at the end of the beach, passing yellow stucco colonnaded buildings with great, spreading trees in their forecourts and gardens. One was a school, another the office of an oil company. A drilling rig anchored a couple of kilometers out in the delta held the promise of a prosperity that hadn't yet arrived on shore.

The sun was filtered through a thin layer of cloud making it quite pleasant to walk, and my bag was light so there was nothing to prevent me strolling around the place for a couple of hours before I would need to get serious about finding somewhere to stay. As it turned out, though, I quickly stumbled upon what I wanted on a tree-lined street running back from the beach and up the side of a hill. The two-story hotel, built into the slope and surrounded by large frangipani trees, had geometric concrete formwork features suggestive of the 1960s. I climbed the steep driveway and stood admiring the concrete "period" staircase in the open-sided lobby as I waited for somebody to come to the reception desk behind which, on the wall, was a row of key hooks, all with keys hanging from them. I took a first-floor room that opened onto the narrow balcony that ran the length of the building and overlooked the street. The room was large and light-filled. It had a floor tiled with terra-cotta and a table under the window next to the door.

I picked up what appeared to be a 1950s bent plywood chair to take out onto the balcony and was surprised by how heavy it was. The "plywood" seat and backrest turned out to be composed of two single pieces of solid tropical hardwood, hewn down into the required bent shape. I'd seen this type of furniture before, in Indonesia, and had wondered if it stemmed from a desire to achieve the modern look of Scandinavian bent ply in a place where plywood or the technology for bending it hadn't yet become available. It was a genre of furniture targeted by collectors who fancy the simulacrum over the original. Arne Jacobsen would surely have loved these curiosities too if he'd known about them.[1]

Once I got the thing out onto the balcony I sat down and put my bare feet up on the concrete parapet. It was mid-afternoon. The street below, which seemed mainly residential, was quite deserted, and such noise as there was came mostly from insects. The balcony was level with the tops of the street trees, so it wasn't possible to actually see the town spread out below on the flat land that extended perhaps a kilometer between the two hills forming the heel and the toe of the boot-shaped peninsula. The hotel was on the south side of the hill that formed the toe. The flat land was bounded by the long beach to the east, which formed the Achilles' heel, and, on the other side, by the narrow beach, Bai Truoc, which lay down at the end of my street and formed the sole. Having taken the trouble to work all that out, I decided to dispense with the foot metaphor for a while.

The town may have been larger now than it was in the late 1960s, during the war. Or was it smaller now? Back then it had been populated by bars and nightclubs catering to American and allied military personnel, either based here or on R & R from bases elsewhere in the region. My hotel might have been one of those built for the officers and troops. It was about the right age. I looked along the balcony and at the series of door, opening onto it. Perhaps soldiers had sat just as I was sitting now, with their chairs tilted back and their feet up on the parapet.

Later in the afternoon I went back down to the esplanade and walked toward the south end of the beach where the road curved around a bush-covered headland. The road ran along the top of a stone sea wall from which small boys and some older men were fishing with rods. A warm wind was blowing in off the South China Sea, a sea for which the Vietnamese no doubt had their own name. The French woman in *The Sea Wall* called it the Pacific Ocean because that was the sea she had dreamed of in France when she was young and also because the name "China Sea" was to her mind "somewhat trifling and provincial."[2] So it was the Pacific Ocean, rather than some provincial sea, that battered down the sea wall she had built from mangrove logs and that ruined her.

The cyclo that had been shadowing me finally turned and headed back toward town. Open-air cafés had been terraced into the hillside above the road, enjoying great views out over the sea. A long stairway that ascended from an arched gateway decorated with gaudy lions and dragons seemed to lead to a pagoda that was up above the zone of cafés, hidden by the trees. The few small houses in pastel stucco, dotted here and there on the lower part of the hill, were also almost hidden by the greenery. They were reached by their own narrow stone and concrete stairways that climbed steeply up from the road, maneuvering around boulders and overhung by bushes. I imagined the houses would have paved terraces and gnarled old frangipanis and canna lilies growing in the stony soil of their gardens and I thought of myself living in one of them. If you were expecting visitors at night, you'd put candles or paper lanterns on the stairs to guide them up.

As I rounded the sharp curve of the headland, a beach came into view at the foot of another hillside where small hotels clung to the slope and a larger, modern hotel stood below, next to the road. When I reached the beach I looked down at the sand from the height of the footpath at the top of the sea wall. Canvas deck chairs were stacked up there; a woman and a boy presided over a row of very faded blue and yellow beach umbrellas, each of which sheltered a deck chair and small table. They had no customers. She looked up and beckoned me down, but I sat instead at the top of some concrete steps looking out at the sea. Two elderly and distinguished-looking men walked slowly down the steps, quietly conversing. They left their towels under one of the umbrellas and walked very slowly into the water, still talking, then swam out a few strokes and floated on their backs, continuing the conversation. Not a bad way to be old, I thought.

I started to walk back but had only reached the headland, half a kilometer or so from the beach, when a young man on a motorbike pulled up next to me. He seemed tall for a Vietnamese but was very slender. He asked if I wanted a ride, but I said I was walking.

Figure 7.1.   Beach and esplanade, Vung Tau, Vietnam, 1990s (Denis Byrne)

"Sure," he said, knitting his brows. "But I think you will get wet."

I looked over my shoulder and saw what he meant. There'd been a murmuring of thunder back there for some time, but the rain clouds had now crept forward, claiming most of the sky. It was as if they were gathering themselves to break over us like a wave. I turned back to him and saw he was smiling. He had an open enough face. Bad teeth.

"Sure," he said again. "Wet!"

I wasn't going to stand there and argue so I got on the back of the bike and he took off, hunching forward over the handlebars. The rain came less than a minute later, falling as a curtain that registered like a physical blow as we rode into it. I tried to hunch down behind him but he was hunched down even further and there wasn't enough of him. A moment later we swerved across the wet road and stopped in front of a food stall. I got off and he rode the bike up onto the sidewalk, putting it on its stand under an awning. An overweight Chinese man in singlet and shorts came bustling down and set up a table for us.

I ordered tea. The motorbike man, whose name was Tan, asked for beer. His black hair was plastered over his forehead and his spare angular frame, much like my own, was clearly visible through his thin wet T-shirt. We dried ourselves with an old towel that the solicitous Chinese man brought to us, and Tan produced a notebook containing brief handwritten testimonials to his reliability as a cyclo driver. That was from when he had a cyclo, he explained; now he had the motorbike. I had some inkling of how momentous an advancement this might be and warmed to him the way one does to success stories.

He was twenty-seven. I mentally calculated his birth date as two years before the end of the war. He grew up in a small town inland from Quy Nhon in Central Vietnam, four hundred miles or so south of the Demilitarized Zone. He trained to be a schoolteacher and qualified to teach mathematics but couldn't get a decent job because of some political blemish on his family's history. So he traveled to the coastal town of Nha Trang, which in the early 1990s had become a beach resort and a key point on the country's recently developed backpacker trail. He pedaled cyclos there for a couple of years before making the move to Vung Tau, which was similarly booming. He was thus moving south, from resort to resort, along the tourists' map of Vietnam. He said he'd never spent a night in Saigon, as if that were some kind of virtue. Vung Tau had been good to him for a couple of years, but then the flow of tourists, even the backpackers, slowed to a trickle. He asked me if I knew why. I said I didn't. He said he thought it was because too many people had been "ripped off."

So the last couple of years had been tough. But it might improve, he thought. We were in the wet season now, so of course things were slow, and by December, who knew? It was odd to think that Tan and thousands of others in his position would be spending their days pondering what was in the minds of young people in Paris, Hamburg, Milan, Osaka, and Seattle. Would these poorly dressed but nevertheless comparatively rich youngsters even now be putting money aside for a trip to Vietnam, or were poisonous rumors of rip-offs in Vung Tau, Hue, and Hanoi circulating out there?

Tan gave me a ride back to the hotel. When I got off the bike he declined to take the money I offered him, saying he would be at that same café that evening if I went there. I stood there with the tired old notes in my hand, thinking that either he takes the money now or I've hired him for the duration. We looked at each other for a long moment and then I put the money back in my pocket and he rode off grinning.

The rain clouds had moved away, and the sun was setting somewhere on the other side of the delta as I stood leaning out over the parapet of the balcony. Some teenagers were playing a game of volleyball on a paved parking area in front of one of the villas across the street. There was no one else around, and the voices of the players, two boys and two girls, were somehow muted. They were partly hidden by some old frangipani trees along the street whose white blossoms were catching the last rays of golden light, the same light that was playing on the tiled roofs. No breeze, no traffic. The concrete was warm under my arms, and I was very glad to be there. I had that retrospective sense you sometimes have when traveling that your seemingly random movements have actually been a trajectory designed to put you in this particular spot at this particular time.

In the evening I went back to the café and arranged with Tan to go sightseeing on his motorbike the next day. We had noodles and beer, and afterward I walked back along the esplanade. In bed that night I continued my rereading of *The Sea Wall*. In the novel we only ever know the French woman as Ma, so in a sense we only know her through her children's eyes. The building of the sea wall is Ma's attempt, however pathetic, to make her farm viable and profitable. For years, scraping a living in Saigon, she had observed her countrymen—the farmers, plantation owners, and property speculators—growing rich from the productivity of the colony's land and, needless to say, from the productivity of those native people who worked it. All she wanted was a share of that. In considering the culture of colonialism, Nicholas Thomas reminds us that many individual colonists were abject failures because they were "simply unable to imagine themselves, their situations and their prospects in the enabling, expansionist, supremacist fashion that colonial ideologies projected."[3] Ma's problem was not this; indeed, she spent years imagining the day when she would take her rightful place in the colonial project. Her problem was that the vision she had for her land was simply out of sync with the practicalities of rice farming and with the topographic possibilities of the farm she had bought.

The farm would never be viable unless she could grow rice on the lowlands, and she couldn't do this because the spring tides inundated them. In building the sea wall she was refusing to accept this. She took a stand against the sea, against nature, and she lost. But then the colony itself was a stand against nature and in the long term it failed too. A relative handful of colonists stood against the mass of the colonized, a tide that couldn't be held back indefinitely. As I reread the book in Vung Tau, it seemed to me that both the French and the American wars in Vietnam were analogous to the sea wall.

I woke in the middle of the night and lay for a while listening, wondering whether I could hear the sound of the waves on Bai Truoc Beach down at the end of the street or whether it was the sound of late-night traffic drifting up from the town. I picked up *The Sea Wall* from where it lay on the floor and read a few more pages. For the first time I was starting to see a link between Ma's attempt to control the sea and her effort to control the lives of her two children. The collapse of the sea wall made the breakup of her family inevitable. Her son and daughter were already looking outward, longingly, to the small local town and the more distant city, Saigon. With the failure of the farm there was no longer anything to keep them there. The family members were able to feed themselves only because the boy, Joseph, hunted wild waterbirds in the *rac* (estuarine wetlands) bordering the farm. When he wasn't hunting he was tinkering with their old Citroën B-12, which Duras uses as a metaphor for their penury: Its carburetor was "a sieve," and the doors were fastened on with wire. Their possession of that car marks their inferior status in the colonists' social order, especially in relation to the son of the local French plantation owner who is besotted with Ma's daughter, Suzanne, and who visits the farm in his gleaming Léon Bollée.[4]

Tan arrived right at 8:00 the next morning, and we had coffee and then rode out on the highway, up the peninsula past the military bases and gas stations. The traffic was heavy, and in places where the road was being rebuilt we bumped slowly along rough diversions in the company of trucks and minibuses and several generations of small Honda motorbikes, the oldest of them, skeletal by now, surely dating back to the war. Back from the road there were fields and fruit trees, and there was the faintest smell of the sea in the air, mixed with the dust and the traffic fumes.

There is a certain joy in being on the back of a motorbike, however small, on a warm morning in a foreign land. The passing scene unravels in an endless flow of detail, which, because you are a mere passenger, you have complete freedom to dwell on. Thirty-five years ago most of the Australian and New Zealand troops had entered the Vietnam War via this same road, riding in the back of army trucks from the Vung Tau airfield, down along the ten kilometers of this peninsula with their rifles loaded and cocked. Vung Tau, at the foot of the peninsula, was a relatively easily defended enclave—if you controlled the entry to the peninsula then you controlled Vung Tau. The Australian forces' field base at Nui Dat, in an area of rubber plantations, partly served that function of "defense." The troops rode into the war along this road and they rode back along it, whenever they were allowed, for a few days of R & R on the sand and in the bars and brothels of Vung Tau's Thuy Van Beach (Back Beach). In a way Vung Tau was outside the war, a liminal space between Vietnam and the West, between one reality and another, between danger and safety.

A few kilometers out of town, still on the peninsula, we turned off the highway and took a small road through some orchards and then down across swampy ground before rising into some low pine-covered hills. We passed through a cutting where the embankments were eroding, and I saw that the hills were dunes and that we must be close to the coast. On the highest of the bush-covered dunes, where the road turned and dropped down to the sea, a side track led to a guard post where there was a boom across the road, some low concrete structures further back, and, rising from the highest point through the trees, a badly rusted war-period radar dish. I guessed it must have been American. Taking the downhill road we arrived at a hollow behind the low foredune. Tan parked behind some trees, and we set off on foot along a path that led to a kiosk and an area of beach with umbrellas and beach chairs. Tan thought we should settle down under one of the umbrellas and listen to the Vietnamese pop music being piped through loudspeakers hitched to the top of bamboo poles.

I persuaded him to walk up the beach with me. We reached a group of bowl-shaped wicker boats, sealed with pitch, that had been pulled well up on the sand. There were clouds on the horizon, but overhead it was clear blue. In the withering heat we looked into the basket boats and saw nets and coils of rope. The beach stretched on ahead, away from Vung Tau, and the only source of shade I could see were the pines on the dunes. We plodded up through the soft sand toward them, then sat drinking water from a plastic bottle while he pointed out places further up the coast that were just discernible through the haze.

Away up there was Long Hai, a coastal town and resort, at a distance of perhaps ten kilometers. But between us and Long Hai was what seemed to be a deep embayment. I checked my copy of the military map: It turned out to be the estuary, or *rac*, of the Song Sai (Sai River). There were numerous subsidiary channels shown on the map and what appeared to be extensive bordering wetlands. Upriver from Long Hai, in the space between the solid land and the wetlands, the map showed an irregular grid of tiny rectangles. I stared at this for a while. There was a chance they were prawn farms but also, I thought, a good chance they were paddy fields. It looked like "sea wall" country. Tan was looking at the map, too, looking at the thing as a whole rather than any one part of it. I felt the vague uneasiness, not for the first time in my life, of being the stranger in possession of a more detailed representation of the landscape than any local person would be likely to have. Archaeologists are in this situation habitually and tend not to think about it too much. Topographic maps are just tools of the trade, like compasses and soil charts. But they allow us to stake some kind of claim to local terrain, to assert an authority over it that competes with the more intimate knowledge that local people have in their heads. I thought of the young missionary in Kiangan, in the Philippines, talking resentfully about the Japanese war tourists and how they came with their own maps.

I asked Tan how long it would take to get to Long Hai. He thought an hour or so, meaning we could easily have gone there that same day, but I was too hot and wanted to get back to Vung Tau. We decided to leave it till the following day. I had a dip in the sea and then we walked back up along the beach, retrieved the bike, and rode back up the highway.

The rain came late in the afternoon, about the same time as the day before. I was back on the balcony as the sky darkened, poring over my precious map. Previously the map had only meant the Vietnam War to me. Now intimations of *The Sea Wall* began to be revealed in it. The two were starting to come together. Strange, I thought, to be tracing a 1950s work of fiction, set in the 1930s, using a 1960s military map.

As I watched the rain move in I thought again about the similarities between *The Sea Wall* scenario and the war. Both projects had an aspect of recklessness about them, of throwing good money after bad, of beginning an engagement in something unsustainable and then hanging on for grim death. I went inside and squeezed the juice of one of the limes I'd bought on the way home into a glass of the duty-free vodka I'd been carrying around. By the time I got back to the veranda the rain was coming down solidly, moving in waves through the foliage in the gardens below. I moved the chair back from the parapet and sat watching it. I thought of a book by Paul Virilio, which I had in Bali, and visualized Virilio in the summer of 1958, looking out to sea from where he stood leaning against a Second World War German bunker on the Breton coast.[5] He'd been using the bunker as a cabana during his holiday. I suppose I thought of this because I'd been thinking about war and coastlines. Virilio's cabana-bunker was part of a line of seaward-facing fortifications known as the *Atlantikwall*. He began researching them, scouting out their locations, and photographing them.[6] I recalled that he had spoken about them in terms of their fragility.[7] The sheer physicality of the line of massive bunkers was seductive and therein lay its fragility: The Nazi state took comfort and a false sense of security from the *Atlantikwall* because of its vastness of scale. And, in the end, like Ma's sea wall, it proved to be next to useless.

The sun came out almost immediately when the rain stopped. Down on the street, yesterday's street scene was reenacted: the same kids (they seemed the same) playing volleyball in front of the villa; the same stillness in the air as the last of the sun tinted the trees and tiled roofs. Would it be like this every day through the wet season? I could imagine being here for weeks, months, in a life tinged with the scent of frangipanis and the smell of steam rising from the rain-soaked road.

After dark I walked down to the café and found Tan playing cards with a cyclo driver. Also at their table was an Australian, drinking coffee out of a glass and watching the passing traffic. His name was Harry. He was wiry and sun-tanned, and while he didn't strike me as talkative he did manage to convey a lot of information in intermittent, almost shy forays, delivered in a monotone. When he talked he looked out at the street, glancing at me from time to time. He told me he was having a relationship with a Vietnamese woman, and that the two of them were living on the hill in a bungalow rented from a friend of his, a Vietnamese official. He was a builder by trade and did repairs on the house to help pass the time. He'd known Vung Tau from the time he'd served as a volunteer with the Australian forces based at Nui Dat. I asked if he'd revisited Nui Dat or the other places he'd known. There was nothing left there, he said.

"And if you do go back there you have to pay fourteen dollars just to look around."

"Pay whom?" I asked, imagining there might be some kind of tourism facility.

"The local cop," he replied, following a passing cyclo with his eyes. "Hardly anybody goes there. Just the occasional vet who's come back to visit. And then there's nothing to see apart from a few concrete bunkers. It's all fields now or overgrown by bush. And they have to pay fourteen dollars for that."

I asked him how the local cop would know you were there if you just rode through on a motorbike.

"He'd know alright," he said, nodding slightly, as if in grudging admiration, and I wondered if this was how they might have spoken about the "Vietcong" (the PLAF) in the old days.[8] "You'd find he'd just come riding up behind you, out of nowhere, wanting his fourteen dollars."

He began explaining how, if the local officials wanted to, they could make a bit of money out of war tourism. Reerect a few of the buildings, recreate some of the sandbagged defenses around the bases. It wouldn't be difficult. They'd preserved the Vietcong tunnel system at Chu Chi, after all, and now it was a major attraction for foreign tourists day-tripping from Saigon.[9]

He asked if I'd been to Chu Chi. I said I hadn't. I said I didn't like tunnels, not that kind anyhow (I was more of a surface type).

I thought of my photocopied map in its brown envelope back at the hotel, a map of the area where he'd served, but some diffidence kept me from mentioning it. It probably wasn't very smart to be carrying a military map around with you in a place like Vietnam, not even one that was thirty years old.

"But they can't see that," he was saying. "Even to visit the concrete cross at Long Tan they want twelve dollars from you." The cross was erected in the middle of a field by Australians to commemorate a battle that technically they won but in which they suffered the largest number of casualties of any engagement in their part of the war.

There was a sense of injustice here, something that went deeper than the fourteen dollars. He seemed to regard the money as a way of telling him he'd never be anything more than a tourist in this place. I said that in the circumstances it was amazing that he was allowed back at all. He said he'd assumed that's what I would think and that it was true, in a way.

"But would you really want Long Tan and places like that turned into tourist attractions?" I asked him. "I'm sure you have your own memories of how it all was."

"Yeah, of course. It isn't that I can't remember. It's that other people—like yourself, for instance, or even Tan here —they come here and they see nothing that tells them there was a war here." He paused and took a sip of his coffee, looking more puzzled than angry.

"They see nothing."

None of us said anything for a while, and he looked across the road to the sea. Then he laughed and said, "Sometimes I wonder whether I didn't just imagine the bloody thing."

He wouldn't eat with us as he was going home for dinner. But he lingered on for another half-hour before setting off into the darkness along the ocean road, walking next to the sea wall along the base of which the waves were breaking. I stayed for another hour or so, half watching a soccer match on the wall-mounted TV that everyone in the café was glued to. The match was being played in Glasgow between a Spanish and a Scottish team. The Scots were playing badly, and in the café there was a general shaking of heads and muttering.

I set off back to the hotel, walking along the road next to the beach where the kiosks sold shell ornaments and lobster shells mounted in frames. A few of the cafés were still open. I guessed that most of these makeshift structures had only been there for the past ten years or so. They'd spread in a line along the sand next to the esplanade, pretty much blocking the view of the beach. I walked down between two of them and sat on the sand in the moonlight. Some men in T-shirts and baggy shorts were loading fishing nets into one of the boats that had been drawn up on the beach, getting it ready to take out. It was from this same beach, apparently, that in 1973 the last American combat troops were evacuated to ships waiting offshore. Several years after that a large part of Vung Tau's fishing fleet was converted for use as refugee boats for those fleeing the anticapitalist purges of the late 1970s. Harry had said the refugees, the boat people, often hid out in Vung Tau for weeks as they waited for the boats, waiting for the time of departure.

So it was on this beach that thousands of troops and refugees had parted contact with the landscape of Vietnam as they waded or swam out to the boats. The beach was now strewn with the usual bits of nylon rope, seaweed, and plastic. You could imagine the wet sand in the 1970s patterned with the imprint of boots, sandals, and bare feet as thousands of tangled personal trajectories all ultimately led to this beach. And with each tide the slate would be wiped clean.

Later, in bed, I dipped into *The Sea Wall* again and came upon something I'd missed, or hadn't properly assimilated earlier. In a very long sentence in which Duras is relating how the children of the region where the farm is located commonly died of hunger, she describes the region as being bordered on one side by the Pacific Ocean and on the other by a chain of mountains that ended as islands in the Gulf of Siam. The Gulf of Siam! How did the Gulf of Siam come into it? I got out of bed and fetched my 1:1,000,000 traveler's map of mainland Southeast Asia. There was indeed a chain of mountains running roughly north-south down through Cambodia, ending as islands in the Gulf of Thailand.[10] They went by the name of the Chuor Phnom Damrei, the Elephant Mountains. Could these have been the mountains Duras described as lying at the back of the plain on which the farm was situated? The fact that the mountains were in Cambodia wouldn't have been an issue: In the 1930s Cambodia was part of French Indochina.

I got up and had a shot of vodka to calm my nerves, then went back to the novel. What had initially convinced me that the farm was up the coast near Da Nang was her statement that it was eight hundred kilometers from the city, Saigon. I checked and found I hadn't been mistaken about that. If the farm had been somewhere near the Gulf of Thailand it would have been only about three hundred and fifty kilometers from Saigon. Perhaps Duras hadn't had a very highly developed grasp of distance or geography? This prompted me to think of my own grasp of geography. If my suspicions were now correct, then the fact that I wasn't in the right part of Vietnam to find the setting of *The Sea Wall* wasn't an issue: I wasn't even in the right country![11] I had a laugh about that then fell asleep again.

Tan picked me up mid-morning the next day, and we rode back along the peninsula out of Vung Tau. We continued north down the highway from where we'd turned off to the beach the previous day, and soon we were moving across a long causeway over mangrove flats. We reached the bridge that crossed the estuary I'd seen from a distance the day before and then rode for a few more kilometers over mangrove flats till we got to a road that veered right toward the town of Long Hai. The gridded pattern on the map, which I had taken to indicate either prawn farms or paddy fields, was along this road, on this side of Long Hai and close to the edge of the estuary. But examining the map now I saw that we could take an alternative road that ran inland and hit the coast at a town called Lang Phuoc Hai, well to the northeast of Long-Hai. If we went this way we could then come back in a circular, clockwise motion down the coast, through Long Hai and on toward where I thought the paddy fields were. It was a long diversion but it looked interesting, and we had plenty of time.

The first small town we came to was Ap Long, a nondescript collection of shop-houses and small buildings that we rode straight through, continuing on through an area of agricultural land with mountains on our right. We stopped when we reached the wooded country north of Lang Phuoc Hai, and I consulted the map again while Tan had a cigarette. It was difficult to ignore the overlay of military information that tended to jump off the map at you. According to the distribution of symbols, the greatest concentration of Vietcong minefields and "enemy sightings" in the whole area was along this very stretch of road.

Thirty-five years ago the countryside here was patterned with bamboo booby traps, underground tunnels, and the hundreds of country pathways along which Australian and New Zealand soldiers, whose sphere of operations it was, had tracked an enemy they rarely encountered in person. For them it was an unusually archaeological war in which they were constantly interrogating the physical traces their invisible enemy left behind: broken grass stalks where a Vietcong platoon had crossed a pathway, footprints, food remains, bird traps, even empty perfume bottles.[12] The Vietcong tracked the foreign troops via similarly subtle traces. In juxtaposition to the devastation wrought upon the landscape by the war (mainly, of course, by the foreigners through the aerial use of explosives and defoliants), both sides also required the intimate attention to landscape we generally associate with hunter-gatherers and horticulturalists. For tactical reasons, they needed a sensitivity to what Marina Roseman describes as the "palpability of the land" in her description of the Temiar people of the peninsula Malaysian rainforests, who, in their daily movements through the forests, "gather information from subtle signs: leaves in motion; sounds that penetrate through a densely foliated, visually opaque rainforest; traces of footprints, feces, cracked twigs, chopped logs."[13]

I passed the map to Tan. His eyes slid backward and forward over it a few times as he started telling me about the previous night, how he'd hung around the bars down on the esplanade until three in the morning hoping to find tourists who would want a ride back to their hotel. But the few who were there were all taking cyclos or walking. He shook his head, handing the map back to me. I said I'd heard there had been many Vietcong in this area during the war.

"Sure," he said in the drawn-out way he had of pronouncing that word. "Very bad," he added, nodding, without expanding on where or on which side the badness had been. So we both gazed out across the countryside, and I found myself nodding, too, somewhat inanely.

"But more tourists next year, I think," Tan said, breaking the silence. "People are saying that. What you think?"

"I don't know, Tan," I replied. "Probably. I hope so."

We proceeded on. Lang Phuoc Hai was another nondescript small town with street after street of shop-houses, food stalls, markets, bus stations, and vacant lots where the sand showed through the grass. It was situated right on the coast. The fact that it was built on low sand dunes perhaps added to the heat there. Just as we were leaving the outskirts of town to follow the coastline southwest toward Long Hai, we got a puncture in the back tire. Fortunately, there was a bike repair stall only fifty meters away where a tough-looking woman in her thirties took the tire off and plunged the tube into a basin of water to find the hole. She then scraped around the hole with an old hacksaw blade and applied a homemade patch. This took place under an awning almost on the footpath. There was a man dozing in a hammock at the back of the awning and two others standing around who were drunk on some local brew, sipping it from a plastic Schweppes bottle they passed between them. When they offered it to me, Tan shook his head vigorously. Some of the people walking past seemed surprised to see a Westerner at a tire repair stall in Lang Phuoc Hai and a few of them smiled at me if I smiled at them first.

A small boy of six or so who was carrying a school bag and wearing yellow shorts and a yellow shirt looked up as he stepped around me on the footpath. He stopped a few paces away and watched me, and I smiled in response to his interest, but his face remained set and his eyes steady. Then he extended his arm, and I saw that he was waiting to ferry a little girl past me. Safely past, she took his hand and they walked away up the long straight road, she perhaps a year younger than he was. Later I noticed them much further along and on the other side of the road, the little girl throwing stones into a big puddle, the boy standing motionless a little further along, waiting. Tan and I waited for the patch to set as the sky darkened.

The road stayed close to the sea on the way down the coast. Not a much-traveled route, as far as I could tell, it was built on sand and was one of those roads that are quite level with the terrain on either side. The gravelly tarmac looked like it had been rolled out across the surface of the land like a carpet. Grass and weeds growing on the sandy flats bordering the road encroached upon its edges, lapping over its sun-warmed surface. We passed a beach littered with great blocks of light gray rock, which had arranged themselves in squares and rectangles, their edges beautifully rounded. We stopped for a rest beside the road. In the midst of the rocks and leaning up against one pile of them was a rickety bamboo kiosk with a couple of canvas deck chairs outside and a wisp of smoke rising from an outdoor fireplace built into a rock crevice. There was nobody around.

The sun was still shining, but it disappeared shortly afterward behind the advancing clouds, and the rain itself caught up with us at Long Hai, so we parked the bike and sheltered in a thatch-roofed café on the beach. We ordered lunch there as the rain pounded on the sand outside, and the young waiters dashed about unfurling plastic sheets to keep the rain from blowing in through the open sides. The wind that had come with the rain and would depart with it pulled at the plastic so that the boys, now dripping wet, had to run out and find bigger rocks to weigh it down. They didn't seem to mind.

When the rain stopped we rode out of Long Hai and within a few minutes were at the edge of the delta, the main channel of which was here called the Raq Cua Lap, a few hundred meters over to our left but mostly out of sight. There were salt ponds between the road and the channel, and I thought it might have been these, rather than prawn farms or paddy fields, that the map had indicated as tiny rectangles. On our right there were paddy fields running to the edge of the hills. We rode on, and soon the salt ponds on our left also gave way to paddy fields. I asked Tan to stop. These paddies were extensive and the rice was quite high, perhaps just one or two months from harvest. Tan seemed bemused by this stopping and starting but was trying to be helpful, peering around as if to help me find whatever the hell it was I was looking for. Trucks and other motorbikes sped past. The sun came out again, and the road was already almost dry.

A little further on I spotted a road, really hardly more than a sand track, that ran toward the *rac* through the paddies. We stopped, and I told Tan I wanted to walk along this track and suggested that he could stay in the shade of some bushes beside the main road and mind the bike. He said we could take the bike along this track, no problem, but I said I wanted to walk. So he lit a cigarette and squatted down in the shade. I set off along the track, which soon narrowed to a footpath. Just beyond a clump of bushes beside the path I came to a small mound with two Chinese-style graves cut into it. This was unexpected, and I stood looking at the graves for a moment before following the path on to where it approached the edge of the water of the *rac*.

On one side was the rice, green and all of an even height, continuing as far as I could see. The rice came right up to the path, separated from it only by a narrow bund. No trees, except a few standing alone beside a thatched hut away in the distance across a stretch of water, and no people around. Where the path ended at the water's edge I squatted down and gazed around me. I could hear the muted drone of traffic on the distant road, but otherwise it was quiet.

The undeniable fact was that here, unlike in *The Sea Wall*, the rice at the edge of the *rac* was flourishing. Somehow, though, the farm in the novel did seem tangible here. I could easily imagine the house on stilts further up the *rac* with the canna lilies and the rusting Citroën B-12 outside it. And the sound of the record: "Ramona," playing on Joseph's old windup phonograph,

Figure 7.2.   Rice fields and estuary, near Long Hai, Vietnam, 1990s (Denis Byrne)

that "most disturbing record," which he played over and over and which he and his young sister thought was the most beautiful thing they had ever heard. It gave them hope that they'd not be stuck in that place forever. When they heard the song it revived their hope that "the cars that would carry them far away could not be much longer in coming."[14]

After the collapse of the sea wall, Ma's two children stopped believing in her. This had nothing to do with love, with a failure of love, it is just that her projects were no longer real for them, no longer credible. The productive rice fields that would be reclaimed from the *rac*, the viable farm that she had believed in and had persuaded them to believe in, turned out to be imaginary. Imaginary, like the Vietnam that had been dreamed in Washington and that the American and Allied troops were supposed to be trying to make real on the ground. But you can only sustain your presence in one of these imaginary landscapes as long as you are in thrall to the dream. Once you realize the project is an illusion, then you want to go home, home to the real world. You want those cars to come for you.

There wasn't a breath of air at the edge of the *rac*. I could have sat there longer, but Tan was waiting for me, so I got up and walked back along the path, turning around at one point to take a photo. When I got back to the road, Tan was standing next to his bike looking at me inquiringly. He asked what I had seen. I said there were only the paddy fields and the sea. He looked past me, back where I'd come from, as if there were something I was keeping from him. Earlier, over lunch in Long Hai, I'd tried to tell him about the novel and the sea wall, but we didn't have enough language between us for that.

NOTES

1. Arne Jacobsen (1902–1971) is the Danish architect whose chairs (bent plywood seats with tubular stainless steel legs) for Fritz Hansen, produced in the 1950s, are probably the best known and most copied of their type.

2. Duras 1985, 25.

3. Thomas 1994, 167.

4. Suzanne, incidentally, is a variation of the character of the girl in two of Duras's later novels, *The Lover* (1984) and *The North China Lover* (1991), all modeled on Duras's own girlhood experiences in Indochina in the late 1920s and early 1930s.

5. Virilio 1994.

6. By 1944 the *Atlantikwall* extended from Norway to the south of France, and on French shores alone comprised fifteen thousand individual concrete works (Virilio 1994). See also Dillier and Scofidio (1994).

7. Virilio (1994, 57) describes them as "symbols of the fragility of the Nazi state."

8. "Vietcong" was the name used during the war by American forces and the Western press for the People's Liberation Armed Forces.

9. See Schwenkel (2006, 11–17) for a discussion of the development of the Chu Chi tunnel complex as a key war tourism destination. After crawling through sections of the tunnels that have been especially widened to accommodate their wider bodies, Western visitors pay to shoot at targets with war-vintage AK-47s.

10. Siam was renamed Thailand in 1940 following the overthrow of the monarchy by a bloodless revolution in 1932.

11. For confirmation of this I had to wait for the publication of the English translation of Laure Adler's (2000) biography of Marguerite Duras. Adler, in addition to her archival research, traveled to Vietnam to interview people who had known the Donnadieu family (Duras's father's name). She describes how Marie Donnadieu, while headmistress of a school in the town of Sa Dec, 160 kilometers east of Saigon, had been granted a farming concession at Prey Nop, which is 170 kilometers southeast of Phnom Penh on the highway between there and the coastal town of Sihanoukville on the Gulf of Thailand (2000, 39–48). Colonial documents in Saigon revealed that Marie Donnadieu and dozens of other French would-be farmers, all of whom had been granted land that, unknown to them, was seasonally subject to inundation by the sea, paid the peasants to build mud and log sea walls to hold back the tides (Adler 2000, 45). Using up her savings as a civil servant, Marie Donnadieu actually built two sea walls in succession, both of which collapsed. Marguerite Duras records that her mother "brought in several hundred workers" to build the walls (Adler 2000, 47, quoting an unpublished piece by Duras).

12. In his memoir of the war in the Australian zone of operations, Barry Petersen describes how his platoon tracked a group of Vietcong, concluding they had women soldiers with them from "a few small scent bottles" they had left behind (1988, 186).

13. Roseman 2003, 119–20.

14. Duras 1985, 55.

• 8 •

The Divine Underground

$\mathscr{I}$ went to Fang in December 1989 because of Carl Bock. He was a Norwegian naturalist who had spent time at Fang in 1882 and who had made a collection of the bronze statues of the Buddha that he found in the ruined temples there. Bock's activities in Fang were known to me from his own popular account of his journey, *Temples and Elephants*, published in London in 1884.[1] The book provided a rare insight into the mentality of an antiquities collector in the pre-twentieth-century Southeast Asian context. It was particularly interesting to me since one of my heritage interests in the region was the present-day widespread "looting" of ancient sites to supply the burgeoning antiquities trade.[2]

Fang is a very small town in northern Thailand, close to the Burmese border, 190 kilometers by road from Chiang Mai. I arrived at Fang by bus on a fine December afternoon and found it to be little more than a large village surrounded by fields and orchards. I walked slowly up the main street looking at the old teak shop-houses that were open to the street. Toyota pickup trucks and small motorbikes seemed to be the vehicles of choice here, but there were also *samlors* (bicycle rickshaws), several of which were parked in the shade of shop awnings, their weather-beaten drivers asleep on the passenger seats with their bare legs hanging over the side. A hundred meters or so along the main street you got the feeling you'd already passed the center of town. It was a prosperous place, in a ramshackle sort of way, but it seemed to me that it had barely the faintest resemblance to the place Carl Bock encountered on this spot a little more than a century earlier.

Bock entered the valley of the Fang River on 9 February 1882. The area was at that time one of the more thinly populated parts of Laos. It was destined, a few years later, to be absorbed into Siam, which, under King

147

Chulalongkorn (r. 1868–1910), was busily reorganizing itself as a modern nation-state. Bock and his party, which included native hunters, porters, and nine elephants, moved through the wooded country at the head of the valley, and the following day they emerged from the forest into the tall grass that covered the greater part of the wide valley floor. As they filed down through the warm grass, the ranges of hills in the east and the west would have looked like low walls, shimmering in the distance through the haze that engulfs the region at that time of year.

The previous year Bock had published a thick volume on his 1878–1879 travels in Sumatra and southeast Borneo.[3] At this stage of his life he was financing his travels by selling the natural history collections he shipped back to Europe and by seeking funding from private and government sponsors. The present expedition was supported financially and in other ways by King Chulalongkorn. He began his present journey early in November the previous year, traveling up from Bangkok by boat along the Chao Phraya and Ping rivers and then overland by elephant through the tributary Lao states to the walled town of Chiang Mai. Nearly a month was spent in Chiang Mai seeking advice from the American Presbyterian missionaries there and pleading with the local ruler and his functionaries for letters of authority to travel further. He was also kept busy trying to find the elephants and the twenty bearers needed for his luggage and supplies. Now he was almost within sight of Fang, the place he had decided would be the base for his collecting activities in the surrounding countryside.

On the afternoon of 8 February Bock and his party passed through the ruined gates of Muang Fang. According to an early Thai chronicle, a city named Wiang Chaiprokan had been founded in the tenth century on that spot by a Lao ruler, Prince Phrom.[4] In 1017 the area was invaded by a Mon king from Thaton, in Lower Burma, and Wiang Chaiprokan was abandoned by its population.[5] It was subsequently resettled but was sacked and all but destroyed by a Burmese army in the early nineteenth century and was abandoned again. Ancient settlements like Fang often tend to be spoken of as "cities," but really they were religious and administrative centers rather than great centers of population. In this part of mainland Southeast Asia each valley had a *muang* settlement based on the rice-growing potential of the valley floor. The *muang* housed the prince, his family and retainers, and the Buddhist monks whose presence—along with the temples, the stupas with relics encased in them, and the precious bronze Buddha images—gave legitimacy to the prince. The economic base of the *muang* lay in the villages of farmers that it contained and, indeed, it because of this that Muang Fang had come to be deserted throughout most of the nineteenth century. Because people equaled wealth, one scholar explains, "wars were fought for population," and

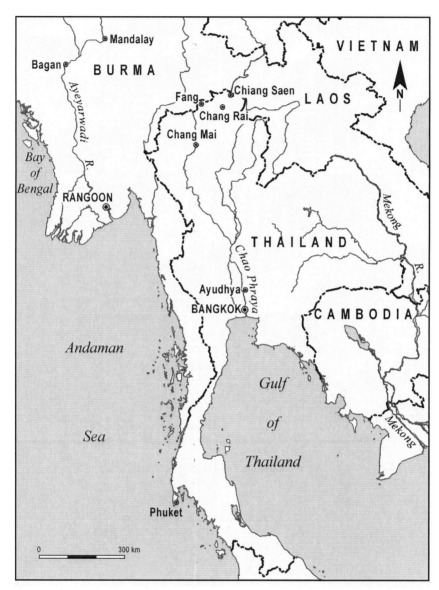

Figure 8.1. Map of Thailand and Burma

whole *muang* populations were captured and taken off to settle underpopulated areas in the victor's realm.[6]

To enter through the ruined walls of Fang as Bock did on that February afternoon in 1882, with the four o'clock sun in his eyes, was not a jaw-dropping experience. The ancient town was by that time a jungle-infested wasteland. He found there was precious little to see:

> [A]ll that now remains are fragments of the city walls, with here and there the ruins of temples and phrachedees [stupas]. All the rest is buried beneath a dense growth of grass, jungle, and thin forest, which the present inhabitants, who, at the time of my visit, had only been settled there a twelvemonth, were busily engaged—men, women, and children—in clearing. There were no houses, merely a few temporary huts and sheds, and no paths or roads whatever.[7]

This was not Angkor as it was encountered in the jungle by Henri Mouhot in 1860. There were no monumental stone structures here. The more permanent buildings, like the stupas, were of brick and stucco, and the wooden structures that would have predominated in old Fang were long gone.

Bock busied himself with the preliminary tasks of a naturalist establishing a field base. He met with the headman, found a hut to rent, and had its thatch roof repaired. He informed the local men of the birds, insects, reptiles, and mammals he wanted them to hunt for him in the surrounding countryside. In the days that followed they brought him flying squirrels, hornbills, and monkeys. But then, to his irritation, the locals went back to the job of clearing the jungle, and the flow of specimens dried up. In the meantime he discovered he only had a fraction of the volume of rice needed to support his party in Fang and he had to send his men and elephants to Muang Pau (present day Phrao), three or four days away, for more supplies.

While waiting for them to return, Bock developed a fever. He had first contracted malaria while traveling in Sumatra, and as the present bout progressed over a period of days he became very weak. He was barely eating. When he began to recover, and while still biding his time waiting for his men to return from Muang Pau, he started exploring the ruins of old Fang.

> I wandered about in the forest, stumbling, at almost every step, over ruins, from beneath which here and there peeped the head or arm of an ancient figure of the Buddha. The ground in some places, particularly where the *débris* of brickwork and masonry indicated the site of a former tope or temple, was thickly strewn with these discarded and almost forgotten relics of former grandeur and religious fervour. Seeing that the natives paid no heed to the presence of these once sacred figures, I determined to make a selec-

tion of a few of the finest, and spent several days in examining the ground, and partially excavating some of the heaps of ruins, and was fortunate to find some very fine specimens of ancient workmanship.[8]

The seemingly effortless way that Bock veered from the collection of natural history specimens to the collection of bronze Buddha images was something I noticed early on.[9] In Sumatra and Borneo he had collected the material culture of local people as a sideline to the collecting of plant and animal specimens, buying them for cash or swapping them for food or useful items such as steel parangs.[10] But whereas in those places the artifacts were always encountered in the hands of locals or in their canoes or their houses, in the case of the Buddha images at Fang, his narrative makes a point of situating them in nature—they peep at him from the tangled vegetation—rather than in the context of contemporary culture. It seemed to me that in doing this, he was preparing a justification for his acquisition and removal of the images against the explicit wishes of the local people.

Having recovered from his fever, Bock went "Buddha hunting" in earnest:

[I] extended the range of my search . . . and crawled up the crumbling sides of a couple of large phrachedees [stupas]. The ruined brickwork was overgrown with trees and other vegetation, which afforded a slight foothold; but as I made my way up, now clinging to the branch or root of a tree, now by the help of a projecting brick or stone, masses of rubbish would roll down, half smothering me in dust, and often nearly carrying me down with them, much to the amusement of the group of natives who always followed me about to spy on my movements. At last I reached the recesses of what remained of the spire, and was rewarded by finding some very fine figures, two of them choice Buddhas bearing an inscription.[11]

It wasn't apparent at the outset that there was going to be trouble. When one day he came upon a "heap" of cast bronze Buddha images in the ruins, he persuaded some local men to carry two of moderate size back to his hut and to place them on the ground in front of it. It took four of them to lift each one. His activities, he tells us, at first attracted mere curiosity, and the statues in front of his hut were admired by all who passed by. But as the days and weeks passed and he continued to scavenge the ruins and collect more bronze images, he found himself being "more and more closely watched." Then one day two monks came to tell him they were going to build a new temple in Fang where they would house the images presently scattered through the ruins.[12]

At this point Bock announces to the locals that the princes in Chiang Mai had told him about Fang's temple ruins, suggesting he might find Buddha images there, "which were not within the sanctuary of a temple."[13] We have no way of knowing what precisely the princes had told him, but certainly the idea that the Buddha images were no longer on sacred ground or were no longer sacred objects was a misunderstanding, surely on Bock's part. Unlike Christian churches and church grounds, which can be ritually deconsecrated, the ground upon which Theravada temples like those at Fang were situated remained sacred in perpetuity.

Whereas in Theravada doctrine the being of the Buddha was totally extinguished when he died and attained *nibbana*, ceasing to exist even as a divine entity, in popular belief the Buddha was and is believed to be present in his relics and in consecrated images of him.[14] Just as the radiant power of a relic will infuse the physical fabric of the stupa that encases it with power, so the divine power of the sacred structures and objects at a temple will be sedimented into the site of the temple. While this power might weaken over time, its embeddedness in a place is such that it cannot be ritually removed. It becomes the place. There are no Theravada rites for the deconsecration of temples.

The same applies to Buddha images. The fact that an image might be found "abandoned" in the jungle is irrelevant to the nature and relative extent of its power. There have been numerous cases where images discovered in the wilderness, or uncovered by farmers in their fields, have announced their powers by performing miracles. They might cause displays of light to occur around them, they might fly through the air or effect miraculous cures for those who appeal to them. The wars fought for the possession of particular Buddha images in the past in Southeast Asia were inspired not by their aesthetic charm but by their renown as miraculous objects.[15]

I planned to stay in Fang only a day or two. I would try to find remnants of the old town wall and visit the town's temples, some of which were very likely located in the same places where Bock had climbed through the vegetation, hunting for Buddha images.

A cardboard guesthouse sign tacked to a telegraph pole pointed me down a lane to a grassy compound surrounded by a dozen or so small bungalows. The place seemed deserted, but I found a woman reading a magazine in a little office. The bungalow she showed me had two small beds with flowery quilt covers and a veranda just wide enough for a cane chair and table. I dropped my bag and went off to explore Fang.

On the north side of town were three temples, quite close together, each surrounded by a whitewashed wall. The buildings were small in scale, also washed in white, and had the minimal decoration typical of village temples (*wat* in Thai). The stupas at these *wat* were small, white, and equally plain—

nothing ostentatious and nothing more than about fifty years old. There were many old wooden houses in Fang, with wooden or bamboo fences around them, and there were some newer houses of pastel painted concrete. There were dusty laneways along which vendors of noodles and fruit and Shanghai ice slowly pushed their carts. There were trees with dusty foliage to provide shade, and there were people strolling to and from the shops or coming in from the fields, all wearing the loose, comfortable clothes of the countryside and with plastic thongs on their feet. Girls and boys in white shirts were coming home from school on bicycles, holding hands as they rode slowly along.

Back in the guesthouse compound a small boy was teaching himself to ride an old bicycle that was much too big for him. He wobbled his way slowly round and round on the hard, thinly grassed ground. Sometimes he lost balance and the heavy bike toppled over, but he always managed to get his leg over the bar and land on his small bare feet before his leg was crushed. It was nerve-wracking to watch.

I sat on the veranda reading until the light faded. The sun would be going down over the eastern edge of the valley, over the Burmese border, and then going down over Burma itself. A man came from behind the old teak house next to the hotel office and walked over to where the boy was mounting the bike once more. He took hold of the bike in one hand and took the boy's hand in his other and together they walked back to the house. Somewhere a radio started playing Thai country music.

The following day I found some remnants of the old town wall and then visited a temple close to the center of town, its white wall fronting the main street. Most of the buildings seemed only a few decades old, though the stupa was probably a bit older than that. Lessons had finished for the day at the monastery school, and a scattering of young novices and lay students were talking to each other under the trees or clustered around the noodle and fruit barrows. Along one side of the compound the footings for a new building were being dug. Looking down into the trenches, I could see traces of the brickwork of a previous structure, but even these bricks seemed relatively recent, perhaps belonging to an earlier twentieth-century building.

At about this point a middle-aged monk came over and introduced himself as the abbot. When he discovered that I didn't speak Thai he waved over a young monk who, he indicated with some pride, had learned English. I asked the young monk about the *chedi* (stupa). He said it was a hundred years old, but the abbot, who had been listening carefully and must have understood something of what was being said, interjected in Thai. The young monk listened to him, then turned to me and said, "Oh, he say three hundred years old." By now we were, all three, gazing at the *chedi*, the nice crisply stuccoed *chedi*, which looked to me like it might have been pushing twenty years old.

But either of them could have been right. The question was this: What was inside the outmost layer? In the late 1980s I had tagged along with a team from the archaeology division of the Thai government's Fine Arts Department who were surveying for archaeological sites in the countryside south of Chiang Mai. On at least three occasions we had come upon ruined *chedi* that had crumbled or split open to reveal a series of older, smaller *chedi*. These smaller structures had been consumed by "restorations" of the *chedi* that had encased them, like Russian dolls, in new layers of brick and stucco. There was every chance that the circa-1980 *chedi* the three of us were looking at now was a shell encasing a dilapidated one-hundred-year-old *chedi*. And that this latter had been constructed around the ruins of one of those *chedi* that Carl Bock had rifled, a *chedi* that had been standing on the spot when the town fell to the Burmese in the early nineteenth century.

That night I had dinner at a place on the other side of town, and when the time came to return to the guesthouse a fine misty rain was falling so I caught a *samlor*. But as we were going down the main street it began to rain heavily, and I called to the driver to stop. He pedaled under the awning of a closed food stall, and we both got down, shaking our heads and laughing. He was already almost saturated. When he pulled off his T-shirt to wring it out, I saw he had a leaping tiger tattooed across the full width of his chest. He looked up and saw me staring and then looked down at the tiger, shrugging and saying a word he repeated a couple of times. The tattoo was an invulnerability charm and not uncommon in Thailand, but I'd never seen one up close before. There was surely a kind of justice in the fact that no amount of money or finesse could produce a tattoo on a Western body that would look even remotely as good as this tiger did on the chest of a young man from upcountry Thailand trying his luck as a *samlor* driver in Fang.

It is well documented that tattoos in this part of mainland Southeast Asia are designed to protect people against spiritual and physical assault.[16] They are often executed in monasteries by monks who recite incantations in *khom* (ancient Khmer) in order to activate the motifs. So efficacious are these tattoos believed to be that patients in hospitals have been known to require the spells be ritually lifted in order to make it possible for hypodermic injections to be administered.[17]

When the rain eased off, the *samlor* driver put his T-shirt back on, and we continued back to the guesthouse, where I sat on the veranda with my copy of *Temples and Elephants*. Bock's problems with the local people of Fang had begun in earnest when, in a series of night attacks, tigers killed a number of their buffalo. They attributed this misfortune to his pillaging of the temple ruins and sent a deputation to beg him to return at least the largest Buddha image, the one still on display in front of his hut. Predictably, he told them that the appetite of the tigers had nothing to do with his collecting activities and he helpfully offered to shoot the tigers for them. They were not placated. If the perceived cause of their misfortune was the desecration of the temple sites, then the removal of the tigers wouldn't prevent misfortune being visited upon them in some other guise.

After this he tried recruiting local people to dig for relics around the edges of the stupa ruins, "but no bribe would induce them to help me."[18] The local farmers, officials, and monks made further protests against him for disturbing their peace and angering the spirits with his fossicking. They also complained about his excavations. The spirits (*phi*) principally at issue here are likely to have been the guardian spirits of the stupas and temple sites. In the 1980s the tutelary spirits of four villages in the Chiang Mai area were found to be situated in ruined monasteries, and when previously unknown ruins were discovered, the locals would seek to identify the resident spirits by bringing in a medium to channel them.[19]

In his book, Bock relates how he began to turn his mind to the problem of getting himself and his collection out of Fang in one piece. While pondering this he made a few side trips from Fang, including one to the ancient town of Chiang Saen, on the Mekong. Eventually, after several weeks and with the help of bribes, he managed to get his "archaeological booty" loaded on the elephants and back on the trail to Chiang Mai. He leaves us with an assessment of the natives' moral character: "They are mean to a degree; liberality and generosity are words they do not understand; they are devoid of ordinary human sympathy. . . . Their highest earthly ambition is to hoard up money, vessels and ornaments of gold and silver, and anything else of value; as to the means for obtaining which they are not over scrupulous."[20]

This was a man with an undeveloped sense of irony. I looked at the engraved portrait of him at the opening of his book. His face seems completely without humor. Beneath a full beard his lips are turned down at the corners into what amounts almost to a pout. High forehead, rimless spectacles, cravat wrapped around a thick neck, the top button of his topcoat straining against his bulk. Hardly an objective reading, of course.

In many ways, things haven't changed much since the 1880s. Even by the 1970s it was estimated that as many as 90 percent of Khmer-style sanctuaries in the southern provinces of northeast Thailand had been "severely damaged" by looters.[21] In 1988, for instance, two Bangkok antique dealers, who had been charged with the theft of the heads from two Buddha images from a city temple, were found to be running a looting syndicate that maintained catalogs of potentially obtainable items customers could order, leaving the rest to the "cutting teams."[22]

At the time I went to Fang I was beginning to realize that the looting phenomenon was more complicated than I'd originally thought. To begin with, it seemed clear that at least a sizable portion of the Thai population was not averse to the idea of looting archaeological sites, even if one allowed that this would be thought of as looting or, indeed, that the sites be thought of as archaeological. While the actual market for antiquities was situated in the cities and abroad rather than in the villages, the "spadework" of looting was mostly done by locals. And it was too easy to blame the phenomenon on avaricious foreign collectors, ignoring the role of collectors from the rapidly expanding Thai middle class.[23] It was also too easy to ignore the role of heritage discourse itself in bolstering the potential of antiquities to function as cultural capital.[24]

Then there was the matter of the magical supernatural. Reading between the lines of Bock's account, it occurred to me that the Fang locals turned against Bock only when they realized that he had no belief in the supernatural power of the bronze statues he was collecting. At a practical level, there seems to be no absolute embargo in Thai popular religion on the removal of sacred objects from sacred places. But *any* kind of interaction with sacred objects is potentially fraught at a spiritual level, and what counts in this is the state or strength of one's personal merit (*bun* in Thai) and the ritual acts that hedge such interactions.[25] At Fang in 1882 it may not have occurred to the locals until quite late in the piece that Carl Bock was oblivious to all this and thus posed a danger to all concerned.

He was more than just oblivious, of course. As a rationalist and a scientist, Bock was predisposed to ridicule the idea that the statues were magically empowered. This idea remains a key tenet of popular religious culture in this part of mainland Southeast Asia,[26] and it extends not just to Buddha images and other religious artifacts but to almost any category of ancient object, including ceramics and prehistoric stone tools.[27]

Back in Fang, after breakfast the next morning I visited on the north side of town a temple that stood on a low hill and was reached by a long *naga* staircase.[28] The sounds of the town gradually dropped away as I climbed the steps, and at the top I found the temple sequestered in a haze of aromatic smoke that appeared to come from a pile of smoldered leaves. I spoke to a novice monk who had been watering a bed of gerberas along the wall of the monastery's compound. He said there were three monks there and four novices, including himself. He was twenty and would be ordained in March. "A happy time for you?" I asked.

"I don't know," he replied with a calm countenance. "What do you think?"

I said it seemed like a peaceful life up there compared to the troubles that plagued those of us living down there—I gestured down to the town.

After he had gone I sat for a while at the top of the staircase. I could see the guesthouse and could make out the location of other temples. I was already thinking about packing my bag and catching the bus back to Chiang Mai, but I forced myself to sit there a bit longer looking down on Fang. I thought of Carl Bock down there somewhere a century ago when it was still mostly jungle, sitting in his bamboo hut fuming about the natives and their superstitions. The large bronze Buddha image that was outside his hut is now displayed like a dead thing in some Norwegian museum. Who in the cool, disenchanted landscape of northern European Protestantism would believe in the statue's radiant supernatural power? In Norway, the miraculous efficacy of objects was an idea that the Protestant Reformation had consigned to history. Might that sense that they belonged to history, indeed, have been what motivated Bock in lugging these bronze images all the way back to Europe?

While I was in Fang I was conscious of the presence of Burma just over the range of hills in the east. Burma, that isolated, long-suffering land that had the misfortune to be ruled by the last surviving military dictatorship in Southeast Asia. No longer did Burmese armies cross the ranges to pillage the towns of Laos and Siam; these days they were too busy stifling any sign of dissent in their own population. For a long time I'd wanted to go to there but was waiting for the political situation to improve. In the end, in July 2005, I went anyway, taking the flight from Bangkok to Rangoon.

A few days after arriving I was on one of the riverboats that make the seven-hour trip down the Ayeyarwadi (Irrawaddy) River from Mandalay to Pagan, the urban-religious center that had dominated Upper Burma between the eleventh and thirteenth centuries. The boat, a large two-decker, catered mainly to foreign tourists but wasn't at all luxurious. The toilets, for instance, were blocked up and the coach-style seats in the main cabin were liable to collapse when the lever to adjust the back support was pulled.

There were only a few dozen passengers in a vessel that could comfortably hold ten times that many, and it was easy, if you wanted, to find somewhere to be alone with the river. Some passengers rented deck chairs on the topside afterdeck, others stood alone or in twos and threes along the rail, and a few even sat at the small round tables in the dining cabin, which was where most of the crew spent the trip either playing cards or watching video movies. One of these was a Burmese B-grade thriller, which, interestingly, was set on a riverboat much like ours. People were stalking each other along companionways with machetes; bodies were dropping overboard. The waiters were too involved in their card game and video to attend to the passengers whom they seemed to regard as a mildly interesting diversion to life on board.

The effect of watching the surprisingly arid country slip by was almost hypnotic. The temperature climbed toward forty degrees Celsius in the course of the morning, and there was no breeze apart from that created by the boat's own movement through the stillness. We were moving downstream with the river's current. If you kept your eyes on the water it seemed we were going quite slowly, but you realized this was an illusion when you looked up and saw the land slipping by at a greater rate. The country on either side was flat and drought-stricken. In Mandalay the monks had been praying for rain; their chanting, amplified by loudspeakers in the trees around the monasteries, hung in the air of the dusty streets.

The river was about a kilometer wide, narrower in places, and was the color of milky coffee. There were eddies and minor whirlpools. A fisherman casting a net from a canoe, people bathing at the water's edge, a boy leading a water buffalo across a field: The things to notice seemed evenly spaced out with small intervals in between. A few two-deck riverboats passed in the opposite direction, the captains exchanging long hoots and the passengers waving to each other. These other boats seemed much more run-down than ours and far more crowded. Under normal circumstances we kept mainly to the middle of the river. I was a novice when it came to river travel, and one of the things I was only now appreciating was the fact that two landscapes were unfurling themselves simultaneously, one on either side of the boat. If you tired of the scenery on one side, you simply stepped across the six meters of deck to the other rail and saw something different. It seems an ideal way to travel.

But the major surprise for me were the stupas (*zedis*). I hadn't realized the cruise would be a kind of safari tour for observing these in their natural habitat. Shortly after leaving Mandalay, the former royal capital of Amarapura came into view on the right bank. This had been the Burmese royal capital for the periods from 1783 to 1823 and from 1841 to 1860, after which the court moved to Mandalay, only eleven kilometers upriver. It wasn't a large place. There were several temples in white-walled compounds and other buildings scattered over a wooded hillside and along the riverfront. The white *zedis* sparkled in the oblique morning sunshine, looking like sharpened, gold-tipped teeth. Smaller *zedis* clustered around the larger, monumental ones, all of them bell-shaped and tapering to elegant golden spires.

The only dwellings I could see were a few villas on the hill and along the stone-walled embankment. The older villas, with their ochre-washed walls and shuttered windows, surely dated from Amarapura's nineteenth-century heyday. I strained to see more than three or four figures moving around onshore. The overriding impression was of tranquility, the peace that comes with abandonment.

Amarapura slipped astern, and we were moving through the plain once more. There were stupas everywhere now. I don't mean they were thick on the

Figure 8.2. Buddhist stupas and temples at Amarapura, central Burma, 2005 (Denis Byrne)

ground but rather that in every direction you looked there would be one in view, either in the near or middle distance, or as a barely discernible fleck of white and gold far off. They seemed endemic to the plain, as if they had sprouted out of its soil. Some of them were attached to the temples in the impoverished-looking villages we passed—temples so small it was hard to imagine they had resident monks—but many of them stood in isolation among the fields or on the top of low prominences.

Each of these stupas contained a fragment of a single historical personage, the Sakyamuni Buddha (the historical Buddha).[29] Relics from his cremation came to be distributed throughout the area across which the faith had spread and stupas were erected over them. These relics are attributed with the power to magically replicate themselves, which explains how thousands of stupas in mainland Southeast Asia are now believed to contain such fragments. The radiant power of a relic transmits itself to the physical fabric of the stupa encasing it. It is not uncommon, when a stupa deteriorates and crumbles, for fragments of it to be taken away to be encased within new stupas, the empowered fabric of the old stupas thus seeding new ones. On the plains of central Burma, with stupas dispersed across hundreds of square kilometers of terrain as far as the eye could see, you could begin to get a sense of the immense web of connectivity they represented.

I'd come to Burma directly from a queer studies conference in Bangkok, and my traveling companion in Burma was Aung Aung, who worked in Rangoon for a French NGO promoting safe sex. While I was *zedi*-spotting he was standing at the rail looking at the passing dwellings. He said he liked imagining living in different types of houses (he was an avid reader of the Burmese equivalent of *Vogue Living*). Most of the places we passed were mere shacks, but there were also a few larger, unpainted teak weatherboard structures with louvered shutters and verandas. Some even had flowering shrubs around them. To pass the time we took turns at "owning" the successive riverside dwellings that came into view alongside the boat. Once you'd embarked on this little game you had no choice but to accept whatever the riverbank had in store for you. Aung Aung had a peculiar knack for it: Time after time I was left to live in something little better than a grass hut, a total dump compared to the charming little villa just downstream that fell to him. He seemed to derive a righteous satisfaction from this, as if it entailed a postcolonial rebalancing of power relations.

I went down to the lower deck and sat on a bench outside the engine room, the throbbing of the twin engines communicating itself to my back through the metal panels. Much of the passing countryside was brown open plain. An old teak house on stilts came into view, and I watched a young girl in a light-blue dress walk through its door and down the stairs, then begin running toward the water's edge where some women were washing clothes. By the time she reached them she had almost passed out of sight astern. At times it felt as though the landscape were moving rather than us, that Burma was being unreeled in front of our eyes.

I got up and peered down through the open doorway into the engine room. The two green-painted diesel motors lay embedded in the gray-painted steel floor, heat and the smell of hot oil rising off them. The willowy engineer, who had the red lips of a betel chewer, moved around the motors, wiping them with a rag, keeping the whole place looking immaculate. There were the usual levers and dials in polished brass and a big white-faced clock with a damaged second hand on the stern bulkhead. On a shelf on the forward bulkhead, above the bank of generators, was a gold Buddha image resting on a white dinner plate, surrounded by fresh frangipani blossoms. It faced forward, downriver through the steel bulkhead, which, only centimeters from its face, provided no obstacle to its transcendental gaze. Next to it was a plate of rice with a fried egg on top, and above it, hanging from a bolt, some garlands of cloth flowers and a string of wooden beads. Having finished checking the dials, the engineer climbed up the ladder to the doorway and stepped out onto the deck, spitting a stream of red betel juice into the brown all-accepting waters of the Ayeyarwadi. When not checking his engines, he was, I noticed, sprawled full length on a row of seats in the near-empty lower-deck cabin, reading what looked to be a well-worn Burmese martial arts paperback.

Midday came and went. I had fried rice with Aung Aung, and we sliced up some of the mangoes that we'd bought off a barrow in Mandalay the previous evening. I walked along the companionway to ask for tea. The gray-haired cook was sitting on a plastic stool next to his great cutting board just inside the galley door, smoking a cheroot and staring into space. He was wearing a blue *longyi* (sarong) and had one leg drawn up under him, the green plastic thong on the other foot jiggling to the throb of the engine. I didn't like to disturb him, but he jumped up and poured steaming water for the tea out of an immense blackened kettle.

Aung Aung grew up on a farm a couple of hours out of Rangoon. It was an area with a great many poisonous snakes, so his father had a pattern of blue dots tattooed onto Aung Aung's arm when he was a young boy as protection against them. To ensure the tattoo's efficacy Aung Aung was expected to make a lifelong sacrifice, and it was decided he'd abstain from eating pork. He related this to me one morning in Rangoon while we were breakfasting on Chinese steamed pork buns. When asked if this was problematic, he said pork buns didn't count because you couldn't actually see the meat.

It was only toward the end of the riverboat trip that I noticed something was missing from the landscape we'd passed through. I hadn't seen a single soldier. From what I knew, though, this didn't mean the dictatorship's reach didn't penetrate into the countryside. There were frequent roadblocks in rural areas—we'd encountered one coming into Mandalay—where the military checked the papers of travelers, making it difficult for people to gather anywhere for clandestine political meetings. The regime was known for its ability to field informers in all of the thousands of villages as well as in every nook and cranny of the cities. Arguably, the military's underground presence loomed larger than its visible presence on the surface—I actually saw more *nats* (spirit beings) in Burma than I did soldiers.

George Orwell served in the Indian Imperial Police in Burma from 1922 to 1927, and it is his novel *Burmese Days* (1934) that we associate with this experience. Yet, as Emma Larkin discovered when she went looking for traces of Orwell in Burma, the novel *Nineteen Eighty-Four* (1949) is far better known there; and Burmese "teahouse intellectuals," some of whom refer to Orwell as the Prophet, are convinced it was written as a vision of what Burma would become.[30] The government takes the same view: *Nineteen Eighty-Four* is banned in Burma.

The boat was running ahead of schedule, and we came upon Pagan unexpectedly. A small orange-brick *zedi*, partly in ruins, was seen at the top of a high bank on the left side of the boat. Then, in the distance, the tops of some similar structures, more monumental in size, made an appearance. Those closest to the eroding bank of the river were clearly in danger of toppling down into it. Mentally unprepared for Pagan, the first thing that came to mind was *The Sea Wall* and the spectral coastline on the north side of Bali.

Between the eleventh and thirteenth centuries Pagan had been the capital of a succession of Burmese kings, beginning with the still-revered King Anawratha, who came to the throne in 1044. Today the remains of that capital lie inside a large bend in the Ayeyarwadi, covering an area of some fifty square kilometers. Most of Pagan's ancient architecture would have consisted of wooden structures: houses, granaries, administrative buildings. These have melted away, leaving only the religious structures of brick and stone, which survive in varying states of decay, distributed across the plain often a kilometer or more apart. At Pagan you feel not so much that you are at an ancient site as in an ancient country.

Virtually all of the more than two thousand monuments at Pagan are stupas. In addition to *zedis*, which are present in a great range of sizes, there are *pathos*, stupas that rather than being solid have interior galleries and chambers housing statues of the Buddha. All of these structures were originally covered in decorative stucco or ceramic tiles, but most of this is long gone and what you see instead is the underlying orange-brown brick that is virtually the same color as the ground. In the dry season the ground surface below the tough acacia scrub is either completely exposed or at least visible through only the thinnest cover of dry grass. If you walk around during the heat of the day, which means anytime between about eight in the morning and six in the evening, the sun beats on your body and radiant heat rises beneath you from the ground and toward you from any monument you happen to be standing near. After the sun has gone down the monuments continue to give off heat. This is what you sense, as a tourist, a rationalist, and a nonbeliever. Whatever divine radiant energy emanates from the relics and Buddha images contained in the stupas and from the fabric of the stupas themselves is not sensed by us, but presumably it flows over us anyway.

At seven in the morning, two days after we arrived, Aung Aung and I were in a horse cart joggling down the narrow sealed road that led through the remains of Old Pagan's west gate toward the village of Nyaung U, there to catch a pickup truck to Mount Popa. Mount Popa is the home of Burma's thirty-seven most powerful *nats*, those spirit beings who are descended from known historical people and are represented in human form in their shrines.[31] The presence of Thagyamin—a Hindu deity who is considered the king of *nats* but who is also a Buddhist *deva* (a benevolent deity)—among the pantheon of Mount Popa *nats* illustrates the entanglement of animist *nat* worship and Buddhism in Burma.[32] Not surprisingly, Mount Popa is one of Burma's major pilgrimage sites. It would be more authentic and interesting to go there by "local transport," I'd thought, rather than by the hotel's taxi service.

The small horse with its cracked leather harness was as compact and tough looking as our driver. Every time the latter flicked the horse's flank with his whip, I flinched, to the amusement of Aung Aung who mimicked me with exaggerated flinches of his own. Bouncing along in the cart I thought we were moving at quite a decent pace until a youth overtook us effortlessly on a bicycle. His green checked *longyi* was gathered up over his knees and the message on the back of his white T-shirt read, "Too fast to live, too young to die." Like me, Aung Aung was going to Mount Popa for the first time and had put on his best shirt for the occasion.

We caught the pickup truck for the fifty-kilometer ride to Mount Popa after waiting around the Nyaung U bus station for an hour or so. I hadn't bargained on the fact that it would stop along the way to pick up people who waited for the truck in whatever shade they could find alongside the mostly straight road. Many of these passengers were going only short distances, so if we weren't stopping to pick someone up we were stopping to let someone off. Aung Aung and I were sitting in the front with the driver, one look at the wooden bench in the back having decided for me that whatever premium I had to pay for a front seat would be worth it. As it was, the ancient vehicle's suspension was but a distant memory, gone the way of its door handles and interior upholstery. Increasingly hot air blasted in through the window along with the dust. I tried to maintain an increasingly frozen "interested and amused" expression on my face as a counter to Aung Aung's "I told you we should have taken the taxi" expression.

On the narrow road winding up through the hills that surround Mount Popa the pickup truck slowed down, crawling in second gear up the steeper slopes. The village at the base of the Mount Popa pinnacle seemed to be supported entirely by the pilgrim trade. Its two or three streets were lined with open-fronted cafés and stalls selling fruit, drinks, flowers, talismans, and souvenirs. We bought bottles of water, passed between the two stucco white elephants guarding the pinnacle's entrance and began climbing the concrete stairway that curved steeply up around the scrub-covered slopes. On the steepest sections it gave way to steel ladder-like stairs attached directly to the rock face of what was actually the relict plug of an extinct volcano. Climbing the first one of these it crossed my mind that we were climbing a beanstalk into the sky. Aung Aung had a following of women and kids wanting to sell him bunches of flowers for the thirty-seven *nats* and peanuts for the monkeys that clung to the rocks and the balustrades. On small, level shelves at even stages up the pinnacle there were chapels to various of the *nats*, each of whom the pilgrims honored with a prayer and a propitiatory offering of flowers or money, but preferably both.

"This is what they like," Aung Aung said as he inserted a folded bank-note into the headdress of one of the *nats*: "flowers and money." To miss one of the *nats* would be to incur its displeasure and defeat the whole purpose of making the pilgrimage. As he dug into his pocket to buy another handful of peanut cones he explained that the monkeys were the friends of the *nats*, so you really needed to keep them on your side as well. He was rapidly going through his cash.

The shrines and statuary were rustic and unrefined, which didn't seem to bother anyone. The interiors of the shrines, like many of the Buddhist pago-das in Burma, were covered with mirror mosaics, and the glitter effect was en-hanced by an extravagant use of multicolored blinking fairy lights imported from China.

Most of the time that Aung Aung spent propitiating the *nats* I spent standing at the edge of the stairway looking out over the countryside. Stupas stood on every prominence around the pinnacle and had colonized the pinna-cle itself, clinging to its rock face and perching on top of boulders. Buddhism and the *nats* seemed to be jostling for position here. But you had to remember that the propitiation of *nats* predated the introduction of Buddhism to Burma and so, in that respect, the *nats* had the prior claim. It would be wrong, though, to think of there being some kind of standoff between animism and Bud-dhism; they'd learned to accommodate each other long ago. The stupas you saw on so many of the country's hilltops were evidence of Buddhism's mission to encompass the prior "cadastral cult," not to displace it.[33]

After climbing back down to the base of the pinnacle, we headed for the nearest café and ordered cold drinks, which, when they arrived, turned out to be hardly less warm that the air around us. Aung Aung sang snatches of Burmese pop songs in his unselfconscious way. I was thinking how, in the West, after having made such an industry of music recording and reproduc-tion, it was now almost socially unacceptable to sing aloud in public. I was looking at the coming and going of people in the street below. He was look-ing at the space above my head.

"Do they have *nats* in America?" he asked, a note of surprise in his voice.

Turning around, I saw on the wall above me a picture of Mount Rush-more on a poster advertising Salem cigarettes. I said the stone colossi were ac-tually former US presidents, not *nats*, but how did one explain Mount Rush-more to a Burmese in purely secular-rational terms?[34] He continued singing, and I sat there smirking to myself over the idea of George W. Bush turning into a *nat*.[35] Would there be first lady *nats* as well and would people propiti-

Figure 8.3.   Buddhist stupas on Mount Popa, central Burma, 2005 (Denis Byrne)

ate them with flowers and banknotes (that's what they like)? You had to wonder at the coincidence of *that* poster occurring in *this* place.

Standing in the street at the foot of the pinnacle while Aung Aung was
negotiating with a driver, I noticed Mount Fuji's sublime snow-covered volcanic cone displayed on a Fuji Film billboard above a shop on the other side
of the road. Preoccupied though I was with the heat and the impending long
ride back to Nyaung U, Fuji, looking cool in every sense of the word, nevertheless held my attention. Was it a little on the short side considering its great
width? I didn't think so. It looked impeccable, but then I didn't have to look
at it every day.

Aung Aung was calling me from along the street. In the hurry to get into
the front of the pickup truck taxi and to check that we had enough water, it
wasn't till we were moving off that I glanced back at the billboard and
thought, "Oh, Fuji. Of course it would be here." Popa, Rushmore, and the
Honorable Fuji as well.

We'd gone no more than a kilometer down the winding road when the
engine started coughing. The truck kept moving in fits and starts, but then
the engine died altogether. The fare collector, a young man in his twenties
with dark skin and buzz-cut hair, climbed out of the back and lifted the hood.
He bent over the engine and started sucking gasoline out of a rubber line that

looked like it fed into the fuel pump. Raising his head he then spat a mouth-ful of gas into the top of the open carburetor in a steady narrow stream with the deadly aim of a betel chewer. The engine started and we continued on, in-termittently stopping to pick up passengers waiting by the roadside and to let off others.

The engine coughed sporadically and died again before we reached the plain. The fare collector hopped down and repeated the same routine with the fuel line, and then repeated it on each of the eight occasions the engine died again over the next hour and a half. The heat in the cab was fantastic. At one point I looked down and realized the sun had been shining directly on my camera; when I picked it up off the seat beside me it was almost too hot to hold. Aung Aung and the driver exchanged the odd word, but mostly the three of us were silent, listening attentively to the engine, waiting for it to cough.

Somewhere on the long, straight road through the desolate country be-tween the town of Kyaupadaung and Nyaung U village, the engine died for the last time, and no amount of sucking and spitting would fix it. So instead they filled a ten-liter plastic jerry can with gasoline siphoned out of the main tank, hoisted this onto the roof, lashed it in place with a nylon rope, and ran a clear plastic tube from it directly down into the carburetor. Sitting in the front seat, covered in dust and almost comatose in the heat, I watched this operation with a mixture of disbelief and resignation. Incredibly, the engine started. The fare collector allowed himself a brief smile of satisfaction, and we moved off again. A little later we pulled up outside a roadside food stall, and the fare collector strolled over and leaned against its counter while the rest of us sat baking in the truck. Aung Aung said the man was drinking water because he'd been sucking gasoline for the last two hours. It hadn't occurred to me that all this time there'd been no water in the back of the van for him to wash his mouth out with. Myself, I'd been dreaming of bottles of Myanmar beer, cold as the snows of Mount Fuji, waiting for us back at the Thande Hotel.

The Thande was perhaps the oldest hotel in Pagan. It comprised a collection of small bungalows set in a carefully tended garden that featured several huge casuarinas and reached down to the very edge of the Ayeyarwadi. There was a newish swimming pool surrounded by brick paving and flower beds, the bricks looking identical to those used in the restoration of Pagan's ancient stu-pas. On the far side of the pool, just beyond a garden wall, was a *zedi* about ten meters high that seemed newly constructed, and just beyond it stood a larger one that was clearly old. Just before dusk on the day of our trip to Mount Popa, I was sitting with Aung Aung on the wooden steps to our bun-galow, looking across the lawn to the swimming pool and the two orange brick *zedis* whose reflections were visible on the rippled aqua-blue surface of the pool. Completing this picture were the palm frond–thatched sun umbrellas on the terrace between the pool and the stupas.

Aung Aung asked, with obvious pride, whether I had seen anything like this elsewhere in the world, and I said I hadn't. Whatever qualms I had about the stupa-reflecting pool and the hotel intruding their presence into the middle of an archaeological conservation zone and a World Heritage Site had to be balanced against the undeniable pleasure of being there. Initially, the afternoon we arrived from Mandalay, I'd assumed the new-looking *zedi* had been erected, like a piece of stage scenery, to lend a touch of authenticity to the garden. Later I discovered that while most of it was new, it had been constructed on top of an old brick base, presumably belonging to a former stupa that had stood there. Fresh offerings of incense and flowers had been placed in a niche in front of the structure.

A total of 2,237 religious structures had been recorded at Pagan.[36] The stupas there had been decaying and disintegrating for the past seven hundred years or so, and occasionally, in the event of earthquakes, disintegration was catastrophic. But the restoration of stupas is a principal means of building merit for a better reincarnation, and so the relentlessness of decay and disintegration has been countered by the enthusiasm of successive generations of Burmese Buddhists for restoring them. "Renewal" might be a better word than "restoration" in this context: People seek to reinstate the complete form of the structure, not to stabilize it in its ruined state. It is no surprise, then, to find so many ostensibly "new" monuments standing alongside the "old" on the plain at Pagan.[37] Like the one near the swimming pool, these represent meritorious acts of rebuilding, but they elicit murmurs of disquiet from Western tourists who have come all this way to see *ancient* monuments, not new ones.

And, for the most part, the major monuments are managed in a way that does keep them looking ancient. The Burmese authorities, with the help and persuasion of UNESCO, see to that. This is an intervention in local practice that began with the British: While George Orwell was tracking down criminals in Mandalay, other colonial officials were preventing the Burmese from making merit by rebuilding stupas at Pagan. The Superintendent of the Archaeological Survey of Burma, for instance, reported on the precise instructions given in the years 1923 and 1924 to local people at Pagan as to how far they were allowed to go in restoring the Bupaya stupa there. Consent was given for whitewashing and regilding only; they were allowed to make no "repairs or alterations to the building whatsoever."[38] Despite appearances, this should not be taken as evidence of an active contempt for local religious practice on the part of the British; it was simply an effort to remove archaeological sites from the context of that practice. The divine becomes a kind of underground in the landscape of heritage.

One of the largest of the Pagan stupas is the fifty-five-meter-high Gaw-dawpalin Pahto. After sundown, the food stalls and vendors of postcards and souvenirs still cluster around the gateway to the stupa, catering to Burmese pilgrims. If you look past the stalls and down the pathway to the entrance to the stupa's interior, you see the twinkling of lights from inside the main chamber. Closer inspection reveals that colored fairy lights have been arranged to represent rays of radiating light emanating from the heads of the small Buddha images situated at the base of the monumental statue of the Buddha that fills the chamber. Long after we tourists have gone back to our hotels, the electric aureoles inside this and other stupas on the nighttime plain of Pagan continue pulsing.

NOTES

1. Bock 1986.
2. Byrne 1999.
3. Bock 1985.
4. Wyatt 1982, 31.
5. Ibid., 33.
6. Wijeyewardene 1987, 35.
7. Bock 1986, 270.
8. Ibid., 276.
9. The convention in art historical discourse is to refer to statues of the Buddha as "Buddha images."
10. See Bock 1985.
11. Bock 1986, 277–78.
12. Ibid., 277.
13. Ibid.
14. Tambiah 1984.
15. See Reynolds (1978) for an account of the career of the Emerald Buddha jewel (Pra Kaeo Morakot), captured in Vientiane by a Thai general in 1778 and taken to Thonburi where it remained until Rama I (r. 1782–1809) placed it in the Royal Chapel of the Grand Palace in Bangkok where it resides today. The Emerald Buddha is the palladium of the Thai state and of the Chakri dynasty.
16. In the Western knowledge system, invulnerability tattoos come under the category of contagious or homeopathic magic (Frazer 1911, 9). Contagion, in this respect, means that physical contact is required for the transference of magical efficacy from the source (e.g., the empowered tattooist) to the body. Transference can also be effected by ingesting magical objects or texts. In northern China in the summer of 1900, the Boxers (or Spirit Boxers), young anti-Western rebels, swallowed pieces of paper inscribed with magic texts, believing these would deflect the bullets and swords of their enemies (Cohen 1997, 132).
17. Turton 1991, 162.

18. Bock 1986, 287–88.
19. Wijeyewardene 1986, 147–48, and personal communication 1990.
20. Bock 1986, 315.
21. Woodward 1978, 92.
22. *Bangkok Post*, 27 October 1988.
23. The 1980s campaign surrounding the ultimately successful effort to have an ancient Khmer carved stone lintel returned to Thailand from the collection of an American museum exemplifies the popular tendency to portray the looting of the country's antiquities as being primarily driven by foreign collectors (see Keyes 1991).
24. Byrne 1993.
25. Ibid.
26. The category of Thai-Buddhist popular religion encompasses those canonical and noncanonical beliefs and practices that permeate everyday life and tend to be concerned with obtaining assistance with such mundane concerns as health, fertility, weather, money, and love. There is an emphasis on the magical supernatural. See, for instance, Jackson 1999; Kitiarsa 2005.
27. Byrne 1993.
28. A staircase whose masonry balustrades take the form of the undulating body of a *naga* (a mythical water snake or dragon).
29. Theravada scripture assigns a birth date of 624 BC to Siddhattha Gotama and maintains that he died at the age of eighty.
30. Larkin 2004.
31. The thirty-seven *nat* pantheon was instituted by King Anawratha (r. 1044–1077), who had figures of each of them placed at the bottom of the Shwezigon Paya stupa at Pagan.
32. Spiro 1967, 248.
33. See Paul Mus (1975) on the "cadastral cult" in Southeast Asia. Mus (1975, 11) maintained that it was not so much a case of there being a "god of locality" as that "the locality itself is a god." Spiro (1967, 250) assumed that the "juxtaposition of the two systems . . . served to Buddha-ize the nats . . . [and] to remind the nat devotee that his primary loyalty was—and is—to Buddhism." Mandy Sadan (2005, 98) was told by a trustee of the Sule pagoda in Rangoon that the spirits (*nats*) of hills are as old as the hills, and that when a pagoda (stupa) is built on a hill it is the spirit's duty to guard it. In Sadan's view, "this is protection by an animist spirit over a territory in which it already resides, rather than the descent into a territory of a spirit from a higher plane" (2005, 98).
34. I was unaware at the time that for Native Americans the mountain is a sacred site, its religious significance preceding the 1927–1941 sculpting of the former presidents' faces.
35. The idea of American presidents as *nats* is not as far-fetched as it may seem. Gustaaf Houtman (2005, 140) records that some Burmese believe Aung San Suu Kyi to be a *nat*.
36. Gutman and Hudson 2004, 165.
37. These include the hundreds of monuments reconstructed since 1998 in a program sponsored by the military junta (Hudson 2000).
38. Superintendent, Archaeological Survey, Burma, 1924, 7–8.

References

Adas, Michael. 1989. *Machines as the Measure of Men.* Ithaca, NY: Cornell University Press.

Adler, Laure. 2000. *Marguerite Duras: A Life.* London: Phoenix.

Anderson, Benedict R. 1990. *Knowledge and Power.* Ithaca, NY: Cornell University Press.

Anderson, Benedict R., and Ruth T. McVey. 1971. *A Preliminary Analysis of the October 1, 1965, Coup in Indonesia.* Ithaca, NY: Cornell Modern Indonesia Project.

Ardika, I. Wayan. 1991. The Beginnings of Bronze Metallurgy in Bali. Paper presented at the High Bronze Age of Southeast Asia and South China Conference, January.

Barrett, John C. 1994. *Fragments from Antiquity: An Archaeology of Social Life in Britain, 2900–1200 BC.* Oxford: Blackwell.

Barton, R. F. 1930. *The Half-Way Sun.* New York: Brewer & Warren.

Bock, Carl. 1985. *The Head-Hunters of Borneo.* Originally published in Dutch, 1881. Singapore: Oxford University Press.

———. 1986. *Temples and Elephants: Travels in Siam in 1881–1882.* First published 1884. Singapore: Oxford University Press.

Bonner, Raymond. 1987. *Waltzing with a Dictator.* London: Macmillan.

Boon, James A. 1977. *The Anthropological Romance of Bali 1597–1972.* Cambridge: Cambridge University Press.

———. 1979. Balinese Temple Politics and the Religious Revitalisation of Caste Ideals. In *The Imagination of Reality,* ed. A. Becker and A. Yengoyan. Norwood, NJ: Ablex.

Booth, Windsor P. 1963. Disaster in Paradise. *National Geographic* 123(3): 436–47.

Bosco, Fernando J. 2004. Human Rights Politics and Scaled Performances of Memory: Conflicts among the *Madres de Plaza de Mayo* in Argentina. *Social and Cultural Geography* 5(3): 381–402.

Boutsavath, Vongsavath, and Georges Chapelier. 1973. Lao Popular Buddhism and Community Development. *Journal of the Siam Society* 61(2): 1–38.

Breckenridge, Carol A. 1989. The Aesthetics and Politics of Colonial Collecting: India at World Fairs. *Comparative Studies in Sociology and History* 31: 195–215.

Brooks, Karen. 1995. The Rustle of Ghosts: Bung Karno in the New Order. *Indonesia* 60: 61–99.

Buchli, Victor, and Gavin Lucas, eds. 2001a. *Archaeologies of the Contemporary Past.* London: Routledge.

———. 2001b. Bodies of Evidence. In *Archaeologies of the Contemporary Past*, ed. V. Buchli and G. Lucas. London: Routledge.

Buenafe, Manuel E. 1950. *Wartime Philippines.* Manila: Philippine Education Foundation.

Byrne, Denis. 1993. The Past of Others: Archaeological Heritage Management in Thailand and Australia. PhD thesis, Australian National University, Canberra.

———. 1995. Buddhist Stupa and Thai Social Practice. *World Archaeology* 27(2): 266–81.

———. 1999. The Nation, the Elite, and the Southeast Asian Antiquities Trade with Special Reference to Thailand. *Conservation and Management of Archaeological Sites* 3: 145–53.

———. 2003. Nervous Landscapes: Race and Space in Australia. *Journal of Social Archaeology* 3(2): 169–93.

———. 2005. Messages to Manila. In *Many Exchanges: Archaeology, History, Community and the Work of Isabel McBryde*, ed. A. Macfarlane. Canberra: Aboriginal History.

Caldwell, Malcolm, ed. 1975. *Ten Years of Military Terror in Indonesia.* Nottingham: Spokesman Books.

Calkin, Robert R., and J. Stephen Jellinek. 1994. *Perfumery: Practice and Principles.* New York: John Wiley & Sons.

Clifford, James. 1997. *Routes: Travels and Translation in the Late Twentieth Century.* Cambridge: Harvard University Press.

Clunas, Craig. 1997. *Art in China.* Oxford: Oxford University Press.

Cohen, Paul A. 1997. *History in Three Keys.* New York: Columbia University Press.

Conkey, Margaret W. 2005. Dwelling at the Margins, Action at the Intersection? Feminist and Indigenous Archaeologies. *Archaeologies* 1(1): 9–59.

Conklin, Harold C. 1980. *Ethnographic Atlas of Ifugao.* New Haven: Yale University Press.

Connery, Christopher L. 1995. Pacific Rim Discourse: The U.S. Global Imaginary in the Late Cold War Years. In *Asia/Pacific as a Space of Cultural Production*, ed. Rob Wilson and Arif Dirlik. Durham: Duke University Press.

Cribb, Robert, ed. 1990. *The Indonesian Killings 1965–1966.* Melbourne: Centre of Southeast Asian Studies, Monash University.

Crossland, Zoë. 2002. Violent Spaces: Conflict over the Reappearance of Argentina's Disappeared. In *Matériel Culture: The Archaeology of Twentieth Century Conflict*, ed. John Schofield, William Gray Johnson, and Colleen M. Beck. London: Routledge.

Crouch, Harold. 1973. Another Look at the Indonesian "Coup." *Indonesia* 15: 1–20.

Da Silva, Carlos E. 1961. Discovery of Rizal's Improvised Chapel-Cell at Fort Santiago. *Journal of the Philippine National Historical Society* 9(2 & 3): 221–26.

Dazai, Osamu. 1991. *Self Portraits.* Trans. from the Japanese by Ralph F. McCarthy. Tokyo: Kodansha.

De Certeau, Michel. 1984. *The Practice of Everyday Life.* Trans. from the French by Steven F. Rendall. Berkeley: University of California Press.

De la Costa, Horatio S. J. 1975. The Walls of Intramura. *Archipelago* 5: 8–13.

Dillier, Elizabeth, and Ricardo Scofidio, eds. 1994. *Back to the Front: Tourisms of War.* New York: F.R.A.C. Basse-Normandie and Princeton Architectural Press.

Dobres, Marcia-Anne. 2000. *Technology and Social Agency.* Oxford: Blackwell.

Duras, Marguerite. 1985. *The Sea Wall.* Trans. from the French by Herma Briffault. First published 1950. New York: Farrar, Straus & Giroux.

Eiseman, Fred B. 1990. *Bali: Sekala and Niskala.* Vol. 1. Hong Kong: Periplus.

Foucault, Michel. 1973. *The Order of Things.* Trans. from the French by A. Sheridan-Smith. First published 1966. New York: Vintage.

Frazer, James. 1911. *The Golden Bough: A Study in Magic and Religion.* Vol. 1. London: Macmillan.

Friend, Donald. 2006. *The Diaries of Donald Friend.* Vol. 4. Canberra: National Library of Australia.

Fry, Howard T. 1983. *A History of the Mountain Province.* Quezon City, Philippines: New Day.

Gell, Alfred. 1998. *Art and Society: An Anthropological Theory.* Oxford: Clarendon Press.

Ghosh, Amitav. 1992. *In an Antique Land.* London: Granta.

Gie, Soe Hok. 1990. The Mass Killings in Bali. In *The Indonesian Killings 1965–1966,* ed. Robert Cribb. Melbourne: Centre of Southeast Asian Studies, Monash University.

Greene, Graham. 1974. *The Quiet American.* First published 1955. London: Penguin.

Gutman, Pamela, and Bob Hudson. 2004. The Archaeology of Burma (Myanmar) from the Neolithic to Pagan. In *Southeast Asia from Prehistory to History,* ed. Ian Glover and Peter Bellwood. Abingdon, UK: RoutledgeCurzon.

Hamilton, Paula. 1994. The Knife Edge: Debates about Memory and History. In *Memory and History,* ed. Kate Darian-Smith and Paula Hamilton. Melbourne: Oxford University Press.

Hanna, Willard A. 1990. *Bali Profile: People, Events, Circumstances 1001–1976.* First published 1976. Banda Naira, Moluccas: Rumah Budaya.

Hodder, Ian. 2004. The "Social" in Archaeological Theory: An Historical and Contemporary Perspective. In *A Companion to Social Archaeology,* ed. Lynn Meskell and Robert W. Preucel. Oxford: Blackwell.

Houtman, Gustaaf. 2005. Sacralizing or Demonizing Democracy: Aung San Suu Kyi's Personality Cult. In *Burma at the Turn of the 21st Century,* ed. Monique Skidmore. Honolulu: University of Hawai'i Press.

Hudson, Bob. 2000. The Merits of Rebuilding Bagan. *Orientations* 31(5): 85–86.

Hughes, John. 1968. *The End of Sukarno.* Sydney: Angus & Robertson.

Hutterer, Karl L. 1978. Dean C. Worcester and Philippine Anthropology. *Philippine Quarterly of Culture and Society* 6: 125–56.

Iskander, Maskun. 1990. Purwodadi: Area of Death. Originally published in *Indonesia Raya,* March 1969. Trans. from the Indonesian by Robert Cribb. In *The Indonesian Killings 1965–1966,* ed. Robert Cribb. Melbourne: Centre of Southeast Asian Studies, Monash University.

Ivy, Marilyn. 1995. *Discourses of the Vanishing: Modernity, Phantasm, Japan.* Chicago: University of Chicago Press.

Jackson, Peter. 1999. Royal Spirits, Chinese Gods, and Magic Monks: Thailand's Boom-Time Religions of Prosperity. *South East Asian Research* 7(3): 245–320.

James, D. Clayton. 1975. *The Years of MacArthur.* Vol. 11. Boston: Houghton Mifflin.

Jenks, Albert Ernest. 1905. *The Bontoc Igorot.* Manila: Bureau of Public Printing.

Jordan, Glenn, and Chris Weedon. 1995. *Cultural Politics: Class, Gender, Race, and the Postmodern World.* Oxford: Blackwell.

Juanico, Meliton B. 1983. *Metro Manila: A Travel and Historical Guide.* Quezon City, Philippines: M. J. Editorial Consultants.

Keesing, Felix M. 1962. *The Ethnohistory of Northern Luzon.* Stanford: Stanford University Press.

Keyes, Charles F. 1991. The Case of the Purloined Lintel: The Politics of a Khmer Shrine as a Thai National Treasure. In *National Identity and Its Defenders: Thailand, 1939–1989,* ed. Craig Reynolds. Monash Papers on Southeast Asia No. 25. Melbourne: Centre of Southeast Asian Studies, Monash University.

Kitiarsa, Pattana. 2005. Beyond Syncretism: Hybridization of Popular Religion in Contemporary Thailand. *Journal of Southeast Asian Studies* 36: 461–87.

Labrousse, Pierre. 1994. The Second Life of Bung Karno: Analysis of the Myth (1978–1981). *Indonesia* 57: 175–96.

Larkin, Emma. 2004. *Secret Histories: Finding George Orwell in a Burmese Teashop.* London: John Murray.

Lewis, Norman. 1995. *An Empire of the East.* London: Picador.

Lucero, Cesar T. 1975. City Planning and Administration in the Confines of Intramuros. In *Intramuros and Beyond.* Manila: Letran College.

MacArthur, Douglas. 1964. *Reminiscences.* London: Heinemann.

Maclaren, Fergus T., and Agusto Villalón. 2002. Manila's Intramuros: Storming the Walls. In *The Disappearing "Asian" City,* ed. William Logan. Oxford: Oxford University Press.

Manchester, William. 1978. *American Caesar: Douglas MacArthur.* Melbourne: Hutchinson.

Mathews, Samuel W. 1963. Devastated Land and Homeless People. *National Geographic* 123(3): 447–58.

McElwee, Pam. 2001. Parks or People: Exploring Alternative Explanations for Protected Areas Development in Viet Nam. *Conservation and Sustainable Development—Comparative Perspectives.* Yale Center for Comparative Research 2: 1–24. http://research.yale.edu/CCR/environment/EnvironmentWorkshop2001.htm (accessed February 2006).

McKie, Ronald. 1969. *Bali.* Sydney: Angus & Robertson.

Meech, Julia. 1995. The Spaulding Brothers and Frank Lloyd Wright: Opportunity of a Lifetime. *Orientations* 26(3): 36–49.

Merridale, Catherine. 1996. Death and Memory in Modern Russia. *History Workshop Journal* 42: 1–18.

Meskell, Lynn. 2004. *Object Worlds in Ancient Egypt.* Oxford: Berg.

Meskell, Lynn, and Robert Preucel, eds. 2004. *A Companion to Social Archaeology.* Oxford: Blackwell.

Mikesh, Robert C. 1981. *Zero Fighter.* London: Jane's Publishing.

Mirsky, Jonathan. 2000. The Never-Ending War. *New York Review,* 25 May.

Miyoshi, Masao. 1991. *Off Center: Power and Culture Relations between Japan and the United States.* Cambridge: Harvard University Press.

Moore, T. Inglis. 1931. Stairways of the Gods. *Travel* 56(4): 7–11, 48, 50.

Mueggler, Erik. 1998. A Carceral Regime: Violence and Social Memory in Southwest China. *Cultural Anthropology* 13(2): 167–92.

Mus, Paul. 1975. *India Seen from the East: Indian and Indigenous Cults in Champa.* Trans. from the French by Ian Mabbett. First published 1933. Melbourne: Monash Papers on Southeast Asia 3, Centre of Southeast Asian Studies, Monash University.

Nakpil, Carmen Guerrero. 1967. Consensus of One. *Sunday Times Magazine,* 23 April.

Ninh, Bao. 1993. *The Sorrow of War.* English version by Frank Palmos. Trans. from the Vietnamese by Vo Bang Thanh and Phan Thanh Hao with Katerina Pierce. London: Secker and Warburg.

O'Connor, Richard. 1978. Urbanism and Religion: Community, Hierarchy, and Sanctity in Urban Thai Buddhist Temples. PhD dissertation, Cornell University, Ithaca, NY.

Ogawa, Tetsuro. 1972. *Terraced Hell: A Japanese Memoir of Defeat and Death in Northern Luzon, Philippines.* Tokyo: Tuttle.

Petersen, Barry. 1988. *Tiger Men: An Australian Soldier's Secret War in Vietnam.* Melbourne: Macmillan.

Petillo, Carl Morris. 1981. *Douglas MacArthur, the Philippine Years.* Bloomington: Indiana University Press.

Rabinow, Paul. 1977. *Reflections on Fieldwork in Morocco.* Berkeley: University of California Press.

Read, Peter. 1996. *Returning to Nothing: The Meaning of Lost Places.* Cambridge: Cambridge University Press.

Reynolds, Frank E. 1978. The Holy Emerald Jewel: Some Aspects of Buddhist Symbolism and Political Legitimation in Thailand and Laos. In *Religion and Legitimation of Power in Thailand, Laos, and Burma,* ed. B. Smith. Chambersburg, PA: Anima.

Robinson, Geoffrey. 1995. *The Dark Side of Paradise: Political Violence in Bali.* Ithaca, NY: Cornell University Press.

Rogers, Paul P. 1991. *The Bitter Years: MacArthur and Sutherland.* New York: Praeger.

Romulo, Carlos P. 1946. *I See the Philippines Rise.* New York: Doubleday.

Roseman, Marina. 2003. Singers of the Landscape: Song, History, and Property Rights in the Malaysian Rainforest. In *Culture and the Question of Rights,* ed. Charles Zerner. Durham: Duke University Press.

Sadan, Mandy. 2005. Respected Grandfather, Bless this Nissan: Benevolent and Politically Neutral Bo Bo Gyi. In *Burma at the Turn of the 21st Century*, ed. Monique Skidmore. Honolulu: University of Hawai'i Press.

Said, Edward. 1985. *Orientalism*. First published 1978. Harmondsworth, UK: Peregrine.

Savage-Landor, A. Henry. 1904. *The Gems of the East*. New York: Harper.

Schaller, Michael. 1989. *Douglas MacArthur: The Far Eastern War*. New York: Oxford University Press.

Schwenkel, Christina. 2006. Recombinant History: Transnational Practices of Memory and Knowledge Production in Contemporary Vietnam. *Cultural Anthropology* 21(1): 3–30.

Scott, William H. 1975. *History on the Cordillera*. Baguio, Philippines: Baguio Printing & Publishing.

———. 1977. *The Discovery of the Igorots*. Revised edition. Quezon City, Philippines: New Day Publishers.

Sharp, Lauriston, and Lucien M. Hanks. 1978. *Bang Chan*. Ithaca, NY: Cornell University Press.

Spiro, Melford E. 1967. *Burmese Supernaturalism*. Philadelphia: Institute for the Study of Human Issues.

Spurr, David. 1993. *The Rhetoric of Empire*. Durham: Duke University Press.

Superintendent, Archaeological Survey, Burma. 1924. *Report of the Superintendent, Archaeological Survey, Burma for the Year ending 31st March 1924*. Rangoon: Superintendent, Government Printing, Burma.

Tambiah, Stanley J. 1984. *The Buddhist Saints of the Forest and the Cult of Amulets*. Cambridge: Cambridge University Press.

Tanudirdjo, Daud Aris. 2006. Heritage for All: Changing Perspectives of Heritage Management in Indonesia. Paper presented at the Conference on Rethinking Cultural Resource Management in Southeast Asia. Singapore, National University of Singapore.

Thomas, Julian. 2004. *Archaeology and Modernity*. London: Routledge.

Thomas, Nicholas. 1994. *Colonialism's Culture*. Melbourne: Melbourne University Press.

Tóibín, Colm. 1992. *The Blazing Heather*. London: Picador.

———. 1999. *The Blackwater Lightship*. London: Picador.

Tsing, Anna Lowenhaupt. 1993. *In the Realm of the Diamond Queen*. Princeton: Princeton University Press.

Tumarkin, Maria. 2005. *Traumascapes*. Melbourne: Melbourne University Press.

Turton, Andrew. 1991. Invulnerability and Local Knowledge. In *Thai Constructions of Knowledge*, ed. M. Chitakasem and A. Turton. London: School of Oriental and African Studies, University of London.

Van der Kroef, Justus. 1972. Origin of the 1965 Coup in Indonesia: Probabilities and Alternatives. *Journal of Southeast Asian Studies* 3: 277–98.

Vickers, Adrian. 1989. *Bali, a Paradise Created*. Ringwood, Victoria, Australia: Penguin.

Villalón, Agusto. 2005. World Heritage Inscription and Challenges to the Survival of Community Life in Philippine Cultural Landscapes. In *The Protected Landscape Approach: Linking Nature, Culture, and Community*, ed. J. Brown, N. Mitchell, and M. Beresford. Gland, Switzerland: IUCN.

Virilio, Paul. 1986. *Speed and Politics*. Trans. from the French by Mark Polizzotti. New York: Semiotext[e].

———. 1994. *Bunker Archaeology*. Trans. from the French by George Collins. First published 1975. New York: Princeton Architectural Press.

Waterson, Roxana. 1990. *The Living House*. Singapore: Oxford University Press.

Wijeyewardene, Gehan. 1986. *Place and Emotion*. Bangkok: Pandora.

———. 1987. The Theravada Compact and the Karen. *Sojourn* 2: 31–54.

Woodward, Hiram W. 1978. History of Art: Accomplishments and Opportunities, Hopes and Fears. In *The Study of Thailand*, ed. E. Ayal. Ohio University Center for International Studies, Southeast Asia Series No. 54.

Woolf, Virginia. 1992. *The Waves*. First published 1931. London: Penguin.

Worcester, Dean C. 1906. The Non-Christian Tribes of Northern Luzon. *Philippine Journal of Science* 1(8): 791–876.

Wright, Hamilton M. 1990. *A Handbook of the Philippines*. Chicago: A. C. McClury.

Wyatt, David. 1982. *Thailand: A Short History*. New Haven: Yale University Press.

Yoneyama, Lisa. 1999. *Hiroshima Traces: Time, Space, and the Dialectics of Memory*. Berkeley: University of California Press.

Index

Note: Page numbers in italics indicate illustrations.

About the Author

Denis Byrne is manager of the cultural heritage research program at the Department of Environment and Conservation NSW in Sydney. He is also adjunct professor at the Trans/forming Cultures Centre, University of Technology, Sydney.